Recent volumes include:

Key Concepts in Youth Studies
Mark Cieslik and Donald
Simpson

**Key Concepts in Hospitality
Management**
Edited by Roy C. Wood

Key Concepts in Sociology
Peter Braham

Key Concepts in Tourism Research
David Botterill and Vincent
Platenkamp

**Key Concepts in Sport and Exercise
Research Methods**
Michael Atkinson

**Key Concepts in Media and
Communications**
Paul Jones and David Holmes

Key Concepts in Sport Psychology
John M. D. Kremer, Aidan Moran,
Graham Walker and Cathy Craig

Fifty Key Concepts in Gender Studies
Jane Pilcher and Imelda Whelehan

The SAGE Key Concepts series provides students with accessible and authoritative knowledge of the essential topics in a variety of disciplines. Cross-referenced
throughout, the format encourages critical evaluation through understanding.
Written by experienced and respected academics, the books are indispensable
study aids and guides to comprehension.

SECOND EDITION

Key Concepts in
Medical Sociology

Edited by
JONATHAN GABE AND LEE F. MONAGHAN

Los Angeles | London | New Delhi
Singapore | Washington DC

SAGE

Los Angeles | London | New Delhi
Singapore | Washington DC

SAGE Publications Ltd
1 Oliver's Yard
55 City Road
London EC1Y 1SP

SAGE Publications Inc.
2455 Teller Road
Thousand Oaks, California 91320

SAGE Publications India Pvt Ltd
B 1/I 1 Mohan Cooperative Industrial Area
Mathura Road
New Delhi 110 044

SAGE Publications Asia-Pacific Pte Ltd
3 Church Street
#10-04 Samsung Hub
Singapore 049483

Editor: Chris Rojek
Editorial assistant: Martine Jonsrud
Production editor: Katherine Haw
Project manager/Proofreader: Sharon Cawood
Copyeditor: Audrey Scriven
Marketing manager: Michael Ainsley
Cover designer: Wendy Scott
Typeset by: C&M Digitals (P) Ltd, Chennai, India
Printed by: CPI Group (UK) Ltd, Croydon, CR0 4YY

All Editorial Matters and
  Introduction © Jonathan Gabe
  and Lee F. Monaghan 2013
Chapter 1 © Graham Scambler
Chapter 2 © Ellen Annandale
Chapter 3 © James Y. Nazroo
Chapter 4 © Sally Macintyre and
  Anne Ellaway
Chapter 5 © Graham Scambler
Chapter 6 © Antonia Bifulco
Chapter 7 © Antonia Bifulco
Chapter 8 © Roberto De Vogli, Ted
  Schrecker and Ronald Labonté
Chapter 9 © Tarani Chandola
Chapter 10 © Orla McDonnell
Chapter 11 © Jonathan Gabe
Chapter 12 © Lee F. Monaghan
Chapter 13 © Lee F. Monaghan
  and Simon J. Williams
Chapter 14 © Simon J. Williams
  and Lee F. Monaghan
Chapter 15 © Gillian Bendelow
Chapter 16 © Mike Bury and Lee
  F. Monaghan
Chapter 17 © Nicholas Watson
Chapter 18 © Mike Bury and Lee
  F. Monaghan
Chapter 19 © Jonathan Gabe
Chapter 20 © Mike Bury and Lee
  F. Monaghan
Chapter 21 © Alison Pilnick

Chapter 22 © Mary Boulton
Chapter 23 © Lee F. Monaghan
Chapter 24 © Mike Bury
Chapter 25 © Orla McDonnell
Chapter 26 © Gareth H. Williams
Chapter 27 © Jane Sandall
Chapter 28 © Alex Faulkner
Chapter 29 © Michael Hardey
Chapter 30 © Rebecca Dimond
  and Jacqueline Hughes
Chapter 31 © Clare Williams and
  Steven P. Wainwright
Chapter 32 © Sarah Nettleton
Chapter 33 © Mary Ann Elston and
  Jonathan Gabe
Chapter 34 © Jonathan Gabe
Chapter 35 © Abbey Hyde
Chapter 36 © Catherine Theodosius
Chapter 37 © Ivy Lynn Bourgeault
Chapter 38 © Michael Hardey
Chapter 39 © Catherine Theodosius
Chapter 40 © Sue Hollinrake
Chapter 41 © Per Måseide
Chapter 42 © Jonathan Gabe
Chapter 43 © Jonathan Gabe
Chapter 44 © Jonathan Gabe
Chapter 45 © Gareth H. Williams
Chapter 46 © Nick Crossley
Chapter 47 © Jonathan Gabe
Chapter 48 © Nicholas Mays
Chapter 49 © Jonathan Gabe

Reprinted 2005, 2006, 2007, 2008, 2009, 2010 (twice) and 2011.
This edition first published 2013

Library of Congress Control Number: 2012946546

British Library Cataloguing in Publication data

A catalogue record for this book is available from
the British Library

ISBN 978-0-85702-477-0
ISBN 978-0-85702-478-7 (pbk)

contents

key concepts in
medical sociology

contents

key concepts in
medical sociology

about the authors

EDITORS

Jonathan Gabe is Professor of Sociology in the Centre for Criminology and Sociology at Royal Holloway, University of London. He has considerable experience of teaching undergraduate and postgraduate students and in recent years has taught modules on Health, Medicine and Society and Introduction to Sociology to undergraduate students and Sociology of Health and Illness and Health Care Organization to Master's students. He also co-teaches a course on Professions in Context to students taking a Professional Doctorate in Health and Social Care. His current research interests include pharmaceuticals – especially for sleep and wakefulness, health professions and chronic illness. He has published 14 edited books and monographs, the latest being *The New Sociology of the Health Service* (Routledge, 2009, edited with Michael Calnan), and *Pharmaceuticals and Society* (Wiley-Blackwell, 2009, edited with Simon Williams and Peter Davis). He has been an editor of the international journal *Sociology of Health & Illness* on two occasions, most recently between 2006 and 2012.

Lee F. Monaghan is Senior Lecturer in Sociology, University of Limerick. He teaches on various modules, such as Classical and Contemporary Sociological Theory, Researching Social Change and The Sociology of the Body. He also teaches The Sociology of Health and Illness to students in the social sciences, nursing and medicine. His research explores issues relating to: the body/embodiment; gender; risk; neoliberalism; and financial capitalism. He has published in various international journals on health matters, including: *Sociology of Health & Illness*; *Social Science & Medicine*; *Social Theory & Health*; *Addiction*; *Health, Risk & Society*; and *Critical Public Health*. His books include *Bodybuilding, Drugs and Risk* (Routledge, 2001), *Men and the War on Obesity* (Routledge, 2008), and *Debating Obesity* (Palgrave, 2011; edited with E. Rich and L. Aphramor). He is currently working on *Challenging Masculinity Myths* (Ashgate, with Michael Atkinson), and researching the causes and consequences of the current financial and economic crisis.

CONTRIBUTORS

Ellen Annandale, Professor of Sociology, Department of Sociology, University of York.

Gillian Bendelow, Professor of Sociology, School of Law, Politics and Sociology, University of Sussex.

Antonia Bifulco, Professor of Lifespan Psychology and Social Science, Lifespan Research Group, Centre for Abuse and Trauma Studies, Kingston University.

Mary Boulton, Professor of Health Sociology, Department of Clinical Health Care, Oxford Brookes University.

Ivy Lynn Bourgeault, Professor in the Interdisciplinary School of Health Sciences, University of Ottawa, and the Canadian Institute of Health Research Chair in Health Human Resource Policy.

Mike Bury, Emeritus Professor of Sociology, Royal Holloway, University of London.

Tarani Chandola, Professor of Medical Sociology, School of Social Sciences, University of Manchester.

Nick Crossley, Professor of Sociology, School of Social Sciences, University of Manchester.

Roberto De Vogli, Associate Professor in Global Health, School of Public Health, University of Michigan; and Senior Lecturer in Social Epidemiology, Department of Epidemiology and Public Health, University College London, Division of Population Health.

Rebecca Dimond, Research Associate, School of Social Sciences, Cardiff University.

Anne Ellaway, Senior Research Scientist and Programme Leader, Neighbourhoods and Health, MRC Social and Public Health Sciences Unit, University of Glasgow.

Mary Ann Elston, Reader Emerita in Sociology, Centre for Criminology and Sociology, Royal Holloway, University of London.

Alex Faulkner, Reader in Global Health Policy, School of Global Studies, University of Sussex.

Michael Hardey (1950–2012) was Co-Director of the Science and Technology Unit, University of York, and Reader in Medical Sociology, Hull–York Medical School.

Sue Hollinrake, Programme Leader and Senior Lecturer in Social Work, School of Applied Social Sciences, University Campus Suffolk.

Jacqueline Hughes, Research Associate, Department of Social and Community Medicine, Bristol University.

Abbey Hyde, Associate Professor, School of Nursing, Midwifery and Health Sciences, University College Dublin.

Ronald Labonté, Canada Research Chair in Globalization and Health Equity, Institute of Population Health, and Professor, Department of Epidemiology and Community Medicine, University of Ottawa.

Sally Macintyre, Director of the Institute of Health and Wellbeing, University of Glasgow, and Honorary Director of the MRC/CSO Social and Public Health Sciences Unit, Glasgow.

Per Måseide, Professor of Sociology, Faculty of Social Sciences, University of Nordland.

Nicholas Mays, Professor of Health Policy and Director of the DH Policy Research Unit in Policy Innovation Research, Department of Health Services Research and Policy, London School of Hygiene and Tropical Medicine, University of London.

Orla McDonnell, Lecturer in Sociology, Department of Sociology, University of Limerick.

James Y. Nazroo, Professor of Sociology and Director of the Cathie Marsh Centre for Census and Survey Research, School of Social Sciences, University of Manchester.

Sarah Nettleton, Reader in Sociology, Department of Sociology, University of York.

Alison Pilnick, Professor of Language, Medicine and Society, School of Sociology and Social Policy, University of Nottingham.

Jane Sandall, Professor of Social Science and Women's Health, Division of Women's Health, School of Medicine, King's College London, University of London.

Graham Scambler, Professor of Medical Sociology and Chair of the UCL Sociology Network, University College London.

Ted Schrecker, Clinical Scientist, Bruyère Research Institute in Ottawa, Canada; Adjunct Professor of Epidemiology and Community Medicine, University of Ottawa; and a Principal Scientist at the University's Institute of Population Health.

Catherine Theodosius, Senior Lecturer in Adult Nursing, School of Nursing and Midwifery, University of Brighton.

Steven P. Wainwright, Professor of Sociology of Science, Health and Culture and Deputy Director of the Centre for Biomedicine and Society, School of Social Sciences, Brunel University, London.

Nicholas Watson, Professor of Disability Studies and Director of the Strathclyde Centre for Disability Research, School of Social and Political Sciences, University of Glasgow.

Clare Williams, Professor of Medical Sociology and Director of the Centre for Biomedicine and Society, School of Social Sciences, Brunel University, London.

Gareth H. Williams, Professor of Sociology and Co-Director of the Cardiff Institute of Society and Health, School of Social Sciences, Cardiff University.

Simon J. Williams, Professor of Sociology, Department of Sociology, University of Warwick.

about the authors

introduction[1]

The first edition of *Key Concepts in Medical Sociology*, published in 2004, was a huge success. The text proved popular among students of sociology and cognate subjects, as well as those undertaking professional training in health-related disciplines. For instance, students of medicine and nursing are increasingly being exposed to socio-logical insights into the relationships between social structures and health inequal-ities, stigma, the social aspects of bodies or embodiment, death and chronic illness. Hence, as with our own teaching of under- and postgraduate students in the social sciences and future clinicians, we have found it useful to include the first edition of this text as a key reference on our class reading lists.

Nine years have passed since that first edition was published, and, as might be anticipated amidst broader social transformations, the domains of health and illness continue to represent rapidly moving objects for and subjects of sociological analy-sis. Health issues demand ongoing consideration amidst increasing complexity and controversy, or at least people's growing awareness that health, illness and care can-not be taken for granted. McDonnell et al. (2009), for example, flag such concerns in relation to the internet and heightened sensitivity to medical risk (iatrogenesis), citing controversies surrounding the putative safety of vaccinations for children. We could, of course, add to this, drawing from health inequalities literature which elu-cidates the impact of neoliberal globalization as Western capitalism lurches from one crisis to the next. At the current historical juncture, we certainly remain mind-ful of the pressing salience of sociology in understanding class divisions (in inter-action with gender and ethnicity, for instance) and their relation to (growing) health inequalities in the UK and beyond. When considering people's private troubles, especially in health contexts, attention cannot veer too far from larger social structures and what C. Wright Mills (1959) termed public issues.

Other popular medical sociology texts, which this book seeks to complement, are similarly revised and updated under rapidly changing social conditions (e.g. Nettleton, 2006). Such updates are welcomed insofar as sociology is a living and breathing discipline, dealing with the stuff of our everyday shared existence and ultimate demise. In short, the sociological community must continually revisit its knowledge base. This book aims to satisfy that mandate, adding to the learning resources available to students via a collection of short, highly focused essays on particular topics. As will be seen, contributors have elaborated on, debated and critiqued ideas within what continues to be a lively, thriving, and at times contro-versial area of study. The ongoing theorization of concepts such as 'embodiment', 'risk' and 'social class' clearly demonstrates that medical sociology is in good health, so to speak, and as relevant as ever in the new millennium. New concepts are also included in this edition, such as 'eHealth', as contributors explore phenomena that

---

[1]This is a revised and updated version of the introduction from the first edition of *Key Concepts in Medical Sociology*, edited by Jonathan Gabe, Mike Bury and Mary Ann Elston.

have hitherto escaped sustained sociological scrutiny. As environments, technologies, debates and other social concerns emerge, evolve and morph, sociologists' interests also develop while remaining connected with, and indebted to, an established canon of key concepts, research and theory.

The aim behind the 'key concepts' approach is to provide readers with systematic, easily accessible information about the building blocks of medical sociology. Our priority has been to present those key concepts (loosely defined here to include substantive issues) that have preoccupied medical sociologists and shaped the field as it exists today. For each one of these concepts, contributors have presented an entry that covers its origin or the background to the issue, an account of its subsequent development and, where relevant, an assessment of its significance to the field. In order to orientate readers, each entry is preceded by a working definition. These were not always easy to write because some of the concepts remain contested within the literature. Each entry then elaborates on the definition, identifying controversies, variations in use and, if relevant, more recent developments in the literature. The entries thus go beyond the inevitable oversimplification of a dictionary, or the passing references that many concepts receive in textbooks. By following cross-references, a picture of the relationship between different concepts can be built up. The short list of references given at the end of each entry provides suggestions for further reading. Our hope is that this book helps guide readers through some of the complexities of the field, encouraging further study and equipping them with the knowledge to understand health and illness, whether as a sociology student, a health care professional in training, or an already experienced practitioner.

Before we describe the contents of the book in more detail, we present a short account of the recent development of medical sociology, highlighting its dual orientation towards sociology and health care. We hope that this will help the reader to understand the context in which the field and its key concepts have been shaped.

MEDICAL SOCIOLOGY AND ITS DEVELOPMENT

When thinking sociologically it is possible to relate to health and illness in at least two different ways (Bury, 1997). On the one hand, a sociological perspective can be applied to the experience and social distribution of health (disorders) and to the institutions through which care and cures are provided. In this sense, medical sociology can have an applied orientation to understanding and improving health, and can also be seen as one among many disciplines that might appropriately be studied by health care providers. On the other hand, the sociological study of health, illness and institutions of health care can stand alongside analysis of other significant social experiences and institutions, as a means of understanding the society under study. Thus, medical sociology is also a theoretically orientated field, committed to explaining large-scale social transformations and their implications, as well as interactions in everyday settings that bear upon health. These two aspects of medical sociology have, in a well-worn phrase, been characterized as sociology *in* medicine and sociology *of* medicine (Straus, 1957). This double-edged character is, in our view, one of the reasons why medical sociology is such an exciting, challenging and rewarding field to work in.

The attractions and challenges of medical sociology have a history. In the mid-twentieth century, medical sociology was a scarcely known subfield of the then controversial but expanding discipline of sociology. Those calling themselves medical sociologists were few and far between. Moreover, they were usually working on applied projects related to public health and social aspects of medicine, often located in medical schools. These sociologists were continuing a long, diverse tradition of research into the relationship between social factors and health in Europe and North America (Bloom, 2000). However, as academic departments of sociology grew in the 1960s, and developed a strongly theoretical orientation, the study of health and illness was sometimes regarded with disdain as being 'an applied activity ... lacking in theoretical substance' (Bird et al., 2000: 1). Yet today, medical sociology is the largest specialist professional study group within both British and North American sociology, and thrives in many other parts of the world, notably Australia, New Zealand and the Nordic countries. Sometimes it will be found under alternative designations, such as the 'sociology of health and illness', with the term 'medical' being regarded by some as evoking too strong an association with one particular health care profession and with pathology rather than health. But whatever the terminology (and in this volume we have chosen to retain the older title), courses which examine sociological aspects of health, disease and health care are now almost ubiquitous offerings within undergraduate sociology programmes, as marked by the number of textbooks (e.g. Barry and Yuill, 2008; Bradby, 2009) and readers (e.g. Albrecht et al., 2003; Bird et al., 2010) that are available.

As a result medical sociology can no longer be regarded as an isolated and applied specialism within its parent discipline. In recent years there has been an increasing rapprochement between long-standing analytical concerns of medical sociology and new issues in sociological theory, most notably in the growing theoretical interest in embodiment (e.g. Turner, 2008), emotions (e.g. Bendelow, 2009) and risk (e.g. Gabe, 1995; Monaghan, 2001). Indeed, we are reminded of Turner's (1992) contention that medical sociology, with its attention to corporeal matters, has the potential to become the 'leading edge of contemporary sociological theory' (p. 163). And it is this concern with sociological theory, or formal conceptual matters, which serves as a central defining characteristic of medical sociology. Cockerham (2007: 291) writes: 'what makes medical sociology most distinct in relation to other disciplines – like public health and health services research – is its use of sociological theory'. At the same time, medical sociologists have been increasingly working across the boundaries with other sociological or interdisciplinary fields, for example, criminology (Timmermans and Gabe, 2003) and social studies of science and technology (Faulkner, 2009).

Another growing area of medical sociology research, which travels across disciplinary borderlands, is the study of health care organization and health policy. The accessibility and quality of health care are significant issues for citizens of any country and, at least in relatively affluent nations, health care (public and/or private) is a major component of the domestic economy and one of the largest employers. Moreover, almost all economically developed and many less developed countries have experienced major reforms to their health care systems since the 1970s. Sociological analysis of these changes and their significance has brought new vigour to the academic study of health policy (Gabe and Calnan, 2009).

Medical sociology has thus now established a secure and prominent place in the social science academe, but not at the expense of its applied institutional roots. In the 1960s and early 1970s, although medical sociologists were mainly to be found in medical schools, their position there was generally a marginal one. In this new millennium, the place of social science is far more central in radically revised medical curricula. Sociology textbooks for medical students and other health professionals are now well established and regularly updated (e.g. Scambler, 2008). And, with the increasing incorporation of professional education for nurses and professions allied to medicine within universities, there has been a burgeoning of medical sociology courses for a wider range of health care students. The same holds for qualified professionals, for example through the distance learning programmes of institutions such as the Open University in the UK (similarly, for the USA, see Bloom, 2000).

Today, then, medical sociology is studied by a wide range of students, with some intent on pursuing a career in one of the health professions, and others, at the opposite end of the spectrum, with strong theoretical interests in the constitution of society. One of the impetuses behind this book was our concern that all such students should have the opportunity to learn about the building blocks of their chosen subject.

EDITORIAL DECISIONS

When editing this text we decided to keep its original structure, as described further below, while either seeking updates or deleting previous entries. We also commissioned and (co-)authored new material. This edition contains new entries on, for instance, 'health professional migration', 'bioethics', 'eHealth', 'emotions', 'awareness contexts' and 'trust in medicine'. To inform our editorial decisions we not only drew on our pre-existing knowledge of medical sociology, we also surveyed leading journals (for example, *Sociology of Health & Illness* and *Social Science & Medicine*) and sought the views of colleagues who are established experts in this field. We asked each contributor to the first edition whether they thought an update of their original entry was needed and, if so, whether they were in a position to undertake that task. Sometimes entries were written afresh by new contributors. If necessary, we updated entries ourselves, either in collaboration with or with the prior agreement of their original authors. For instance, we revised concepts such as 'the sick role', 'stigma' and 'illness narratives' in light of more recent literature. Throughout, each contributor was asked where possible to attend to an international and increasingly global context.

When deciding to retain and update concepts, a key criterion was the continuing discussion about each concept within the broader community of medical sociologists.

Often, concepts were retained if there was also scope for their further development and application. For example, while 'medicalization' was well defined and explained in the first edition, we have retained and updated it here given, among other things, writings on biomedicalization. The latter concept has been defined as 'the increasingly complex, multisited, multidirectional processes of medicalization, both extended and reconstituted through the new social forms of highly techno-scientific biomedicine' (Clarke et al., 2003: 161). 'Illness behaviour' has also been retained from the first edition, though it has now been combined with a discussion on 'health-related behaviour' as part of a critical reflection on these concepts within and beyond medical sociology.

As noted above, we also excised some entries. In part, this was a pragmatic decision given the exigencies of space and our wish to include some new material. Excisions were nonetheless informed by several considerations, including the need to make the text more internationally relevant. Some new entries have effectively replaced old ones and have been included in order to capture particular issues and processes in a politicized global context. Thus, we decided the previous entry on 'health and development' should be replaced by an entry on 'neoliberal globalization and health inequalities'. And, while some entries have been deleted, relevant discussion is often subsumed under particular concepts that are becoming increasingly visible in health debates and policy; for example, 'social support' has been replaced with a critical entry on 'social capital'. Some entries from the first edition have also been combined and condensed, with this text featuring entries on 'ageing and the lifecourse' and 'medical autonomy, dominance and decline' (thereby effectively replacing four entries with two).

Selecting our key concepts has involved some difficult decisions about what to omit. Other medical sociologists' final list might have looked different, but, we believe, only a little. Most of our colleagues would agree, we think, that the topics we have chosen are ones that have significantly shaped the discipline and/or are of obvious contemporary importance, even if we have not been able to include all possible candidates for this accolade. In line with our commitment to giving the reader a sense of how medical sociology has developed, we have emphasized classic concepts rather than opt only for those of obvious current (and possibly ephemeral) interest. Talking only in terms of 'concepts' is less than ideal, but in selecting topics we have recognized that, in addition to the key concepts that have been regularly used in medical sociological analysis, there are recurrent substantive issues or particular approaches which cannot easily be captured by single concepts.

STRUCTURE AND CONTENTS OF THE BOOK

Entries are organized under five pre-defined themes: (1) the social patterning of health; (2) the experience of health and illness; (3) health, knowledge and practice; (4) health work and the division of labour; and (5) health care organization and policy. These themes cover a substantial proportion of medical sociological research and scholarship. There is, of course, some overlap between them, as reflected in the cross-references made between entries. We will outline each of these themes below.

Part 1 focuses on the social patterning of health and includes entries on health inequalities and the social causation of (ill) health. Entries set out the ways in which social divisions, such as 'social class', are associated with various measures of health status, and discuss the ways in which such concepts have been operation-alized. The study of inequalities in relation to occupational 'social class' has been particularly prominent in the UK, for instance. However, as the other entries in this section show, the distribution of life chances and health within and between nations are also structured by 'age', 'gender', 'ethnicity', 'place of residence' and 'neoliberal globalization'. Furthermore, these entries illustrate how research deploying these concepts has developed through collaborating with other disci-plines, such as epidemiology. At the same time, understanding how this social pat-terning of health comes about requires moving beyond statistical correlations. Hence, entries in Part 1 include conceptual approaches that have been used to study the causes of health inequalities. One of the striking aspects of this section is how clearly the different approaches can be related to classic sociological debates. The relative role in health causation of ideas and values compared to material factors in shaping social change and individual behaviour, and the signifi-cance of social integration for health, are concerns that would be recognizable to sociology's founding European triumvirate: namely Karl Marx, Max Weber and Emile Durkheim.

The themes taken up in Part 2 derive more directly from North American tra-ditions of sociology, in the form of functionalism and symbolic interactionism, with the conception of illness as a form of deviance linking the two. Sociological studies of the experience and meanings of illness and people's interactions with health professionals have, indubitably, generated concepts that have had a pro-found impact on both sociology as a discipline and the delivery of care. Arguably, the concepts of 'stigma', 'chronic illness' and 'quality of life' have become so taken-for-granted in discussions of health care that their origins in particular con-cerns and the ways in which their use may have changed can be overlooked. Few sociology students go back, for example, to Parsons' (1951) original formulation of 'the sick role' and, as a result, often fail to appreciate fully either the context in which Parsons wrote or that this concept was a depiction of normative expec-tations and not actual behaviours. Other contributions to this section cover con-cepts that have risen to prominence more recently, such as 'illness narratives', 'embodiment', 'risk' and 'emotions'. In developing and using these concepts, medical sociology has sought to move beyond one-dimensional accounts of illness as deviance to link up with more general concerns with self-identity and cultural meaning that characterize late modern societies. The experience of illness can therefore be seen to reflect and contribute to the shaping of contemporary cul-tures. The emphasis on personal narratives has expressed this central motif, both for sociology and the wider society.

Part 3 focuses on knowledge of and practice about health. Here the entries begin by discussing what has, at times, been regarded as not so much a useful analytical concept, but more an object to be attacked: 'the medical model'. Underpinning this model is scientific knowledge about the working of the human body and the next two entries examine recurrent concerns within medical sociology: the social shaping of this scientific knowledge and its relationship with lay people's knowledge and understanding of health and illness. In health care, scientific knowledge and technologies are combined to create forms of practice in which professionals and lay people interact. In recent years, there has been growing sociological interest in how this interaction is shaped, particularly in relation to innovative technologies such as those increasingly involved in the management of 'reproduction' and in genetic medicine or 'geneticization'. New entries on 'eHealth' and 'bioethics' are also included here. Finally, reflecting the influence of the French social thinker, Michel Foucault, on medical sociology, another growing area of practice is examined – that which is concerned with monitoring and promoting population health. Discussion in this area focuses on the tension between promoting the welfare of patients and the role of health care – especially health promotion – in effecting surveillance and disciplinary power over lay people's behaviour. At the same time, modern health care is a highly developed set of social processes, involving many different forms of activity, and is provided by many actors, from highly trained professionals to self-care. This complex division of labour is, therefore, the focus of Part 4.

Until relatively recently, medical sociology was preoccupied with doctors, as members of an archetypal, autonomous profession of a particular occupational form and as the dominant occupational group in health care provision. The first two entries in Part 4 cover such issues. However, in recent decades, sociological research on health care providers has developed beyond the study of doctors. This has evolved in three main ways. First, there has been a certain, albeit limited, increase in research on other health care occupations such as nursing and midwifery. Second, particularly since the mid-1980s, sociologists' interest in the rise of medical power and authority has been superseded by a consideration of their putative decline. One possible indication of this is the apparent growth in resorting to non-orthodox medicine, which has revived sociological interest in the concept of 'medical pluralism' (subsumed in this text under an entry on 'complementary and alternative medicine'). Third, there has been a shift in emphasis away from specific occupations towards the division of labour itself and the character of health care work, wherever it is undertaken. Alongside micro-sociological studies of inter-professional interactions and boundary work, feminism has had an important influence on medical sociology research in this area since the 1970s. On the one hand, it has led to recognition of the value of 'emotional labour' as a relevant concept when studying health care as a form of people-processing. On the other hand, it has resulted in a wider conception of the location of health and the division of labour, including 'informal care' which takes place in the home. We would add, as with the entry on 'health professional migration', that such labour needs to be examined with a close eye on global power relations. Hence, sociological attention should focus not only on relations between health workers and their recipients of care but also on relations between higher and lower income nations, with care delivered in the former often leaving deficits in the latter.

The final section, Part 5, considers some of the key concepts and issues that have shaped medical sociological research on health care organization and policy. As might be inferred from the above discussion, such studies can be focused on different levels: the macro, societal level; the meso level of the formal organizational structure; and the micro interactional level. A concern with these different yet interconnected levels is reflected in our choice of topics, ranging from the hospital and what unfolds therein to the political economy of medicine and the legal systems surrounding health care. The key concepts and issues reviewed here fall into three main, albeit overlapping, categories. First are the theoretical concepts used to analyse the major shifts that are currently occurring in health care across much of the relatively affluent world, such as 'privatization', 'managerialism', 'consumerism', and the reconfiguration of 'citizenship' in relation to health care entitlement. Second, there are sociological concepts that have been deployed in the analysis of how some issues become health policy concerns, as exemplified in relation to 'social movements'. Finally, there are concepts relating to institutional processes and organizations that are increasingly prominent in contemporary health care, such as 'medicines regulation', 'evaluation' and 'malpractice'. These latter concepts feed back into the discussion of the possible decline of an autonomous and all-powerful medical profession.

REFERENCES

Albrecht, G.L., Fitzpatrick, R. and Scrimshaw, S.C. (eds) (2003) *Handbook of Social Studies in Health & Medicine*. London: Sage.

Barry, A.M. and Yuill, C. (2008) *Understanding the Sociology of Health*, 2nd edn. London: Sage.

Bendelow, G. (2009) *Health, Emotion and the Body*. Cambridge: Polity Press.

Bird, C.E., Conrad, P. and Fremont, A.M. (2000) 'Medical sociology at the millennium', in C.E. Bird, P. Conrad and A.M. Fremont (eds), *Handbook of Medical Sociology*, 5th edn. Upper Saddle River, NJ: Prentice Hall.

Bird, C.E., Conrad, P., Fremont, A.M. and Timmermans, S. (eds) (2010) *Handbook of Medical Sociology*, 6th edn. Nashville, TN: Vanderbilt University Press.

Bloom, S. (2000) 'The institutionalization of medical sociology in the United States, 1920–1980', in C.E. Bird, P. Conrad and A.M. Fremont (eds), *Handbook of Medical Sociology*, 5th edn. Upper Saddle River, NJ: Prentice Hall.

Bradby, H. (2009) *Medical Sociology: An Introduction*. London: Sage.

Bury, M. (1997) *Health and Illness in a Changing Society*. London: Routledge.

Clarke, A.E., Mamo, L., Fishman, J.R., Shim, J.K. and Fosket, J.R. (2003) 'Biomedicalization: techno-scientific transformations of health, illness, and US biomedicine', *American Sociological Review*, 68: 161–94.

Cockerham, W.C. (2007) 'A note on the failure of postmodern theory and its failure to meet the basic requirements for success in medical sociology', *Social Theory & Health*, 5 (4): 285–96.

Faulkner, A. (2009) *Medical Technology in Healthcare and Society: A Sociology of Devices, Innovation and Governance*. Basingstoke: Palgrave Macmillan.

Gabe, J. (ed.) (1995) *Medicine, Health and Risk*. Oxford: Blackwell.

Gabe, J. and Calnan, M. (eds) (2009) *The New Sociology of the Health Service*. London: Routledge.

McDonnell, O., Lohan, M., Hyde, A. and Porter, S. (2009) *Social Theory, Health and Healthcare*. Basingstoke: Palgrave Macmillan.

Mills, C. Wright (1959) *The Sociological Imagination*. New York: Oxford University Press.

Monaghan, L.F. (2001) *Bodybuilding, Drugs and Risk*. London: Routledge.

Nettleton, S. (2006) *The Sociology of Health and Illness*, 2nd edn. Cambridge: Polity Press.

Parsons, T. (1951) *The Social System*. New York: The Free Press.

Scambler, G. (ed.) (2008) *Sociology as Applied to Medicine*, 6th edn. Edinburgh: Saunders.

Straus, R. (1957) 'The nature and status of medical sociology', *American Sociological Review*, 22: 200–4.

Timmermans, S. and Gabe, J. (eds) (2003) *Partners in Health, Partners in Crime*. Oxford: Blackwell.

Turner, B.S. (1992) *Regulating Bodies: Essays in Medical Sociology*. London: Routledge.

Turner, B.S. (2008) *The Body & Society*, 3rd edn. London: Sage.

Jonathan Gabe and Lee F. Monaghan

key concepts in
medical sociology

Part 1
Social Patterning of Health

Social Class

Social classes are strata of society defined in terms of (1) the relationship between capital and labour, extending to (2) aspects of labour market position and work characteristics.

With the possible exception of the earliest or pre-Neolithic societies, human sociability has consistently shown evidence of enduring hierarchy or strata. This division of social formations by hierarchy or strata is usually referred to as 'social stratification'. Even in post-Neolithic but still traditional or pre-modern societies, stratification was more complex than simple oppositions between 'master and slave' and 'lord and serf' suggest. In highly differentiated modern societies, stratification is invariably multi-dimensional. While social class is the dimension of stratification that has been most often highlighted and debated, it is far from being the only one. Moreover, as the historian Braudel (1984) has so painstakingly shown in his study of Europe from 1400 to 1800, transitions from pre-modern to modern were invariably slow and uneven: no modern or capitalist society is without its pre-modern or feudal residue.

Neither the concept of social class nor the phenomena it denotes originated with Marx, but his contribution remains influential. While recognizing the dynamic, complex and multi-dimensional nature of stratification in modern societies, he insisted: (1) that class is fundamental, and (2) that there would develop an antagonistic polarization between two 'basic' classes – the *bourgeoisie* (the owners of capital) and the *proletariat* (the wage-labourers) – that would ultimately lead to revolutionary or transformatory change. Opinion remains divided on whether Marx simply got it wrong – the polarization he anticipated in the industrialized West, leading to a revolutionary shift in favour of the proletariat, has yet to occur – or whether his analysis was convincing but his timing was out. Weber took a lot of what Marx argued about class on board but disassociated himself from any sense of historical inevitability, emphasizing the salience of class-based life chances or opportunities and contending that other dimensions of stratification than class, notably 'honour' (or status) and 'party' (or political organization around agendas for change), remained important in their own right and could and do vary independent of class.

The classical Marx–Weber debate lives on but has been joined by a plethora of rival theories of class in modern society, and more recently by theories about the demise of class in post-modern societies. There is space here only to comment on ideas regarding the 'death of class'. Some have argued that the 'discourse of class' that came to prevail in modern society was never truly warranted; others have held that while class was a, or even *the*, fundamental form of stratification in modern society, this is no longer true of post-modern society (Pakulski and Waters, 1996). For the latter, class has been complemented, and even displaced, both by the likes of gender, ethnicity, sexuality and so on, and by a novel cultural shift towards the increasingly individualistic, open, and hybrid business of identity-formation. In other words, class is not what it was – either objectively or subjectively. An alternative position is that class remains significant *objectively* but has become less significant *subjectively*: namely, class continues to mould individuals' experiences, although they are less likely than even a generation ago either to recognize this or to construct their identities in terms of class (Scambler, 2002).

A gap is also apparent between the concepts of class found in theories and those encountered in the research domain. Socio-economic classifications (SECs), often presented as proxies for class, have routinely shown a strong inverse association between occupational standing and health status and longevity. Mention might be made here of a relatively subtle SEC, the broadly neo-Weberian National Statistics Socio-economic Classification (NS-SEC) scheme introduced in England and Wales (see Rose and O'Reilly, 1997). In this scheme, occupations are differentiated in terms of reward mechanisms, promotion prospects, autonomy and job security. It comprises the following: senior professionals/senior managers; associate professionals/junior managers; other administrative and clerical workers; own account non-professionals; supervisors, technicians and related workers; intermediate workers; other workers; and never worked/other inactive. The most advantaged NS-SEC 'classes' typically exhibit personalized reward structures, have good opportunities for advancement and relatively high levels of autonomy within the job, and are relatively secure (these attributes tending to be reversed for the most disadvantaged or routine 'classes') (Langford and Johnson, 2010).

As far as England and Wales are concerned, the changes captured through studies of a succession of SECs on the one hand, and, say, life expectancy on the other, are unambiguous. They show an upward trend in life expectancy for men and women across the SEC spectrum. However, the improvement in life expectancy has been more rapid among those at the top than among those at the bottom of the 'socio-economic hierarchy' (Graham, 2009). The same pattern is found in other developed or high-income countries (Mackenbach, 2005).

Data in this vein also testify to the existence of a 'social gradient' – that is to say, the relationships between SECs and measures of health and longevity are finely graded. Not only are there considerable differences between the best- and worst-off in England and Wales, but the higher one's social position is (or level of education, occupational status or housing conditions) the better one's health is likely to be. The authors of the Marmot Review (2010: 16) write:

> These serious health inequalities do not arise by chance, and they cannot be attributed simply to genetic makeup, 'bad', unhealthy behaviour, or difficulties in access to health care, important as these factors may be. Social and economic differences in health status reflect, and are caused by, social and economic inequalities in society.

There is a paucity of material for developing societies, certainly as far as social gradients are concerned. However, there is ample evidence for ubiquitous inter- and intra-national health inequalities, the most dramatic of which appear across the developed/developing and North/South divides (WHO, 2008).

There is no doubting the sociological utility of SECs like NS-SEC, but do they catch enough of the ongoing contradictions between capital and labour that are so pivotal not only for Marx but also for many mainstream sociologists? Indicators of or proxies for class, like the NS-SEC, have raised important issues around the (nature of the) causal relationship between class and health. To some extent the disciplinary boundary between social epidemiology and medical sociology has been obscured here. Positively, this might be interpreted as a victory for 'inter-disciplinarity'; negatively, it might be seen as social epidemiology's co-option of medical sociology. Most probably the answer lies somewhere in the middle. Much depends, however, on whether class theory has any purchase in the here-and-now. If it does, then it falls on sociologists to do it justice.

The statistical linkages between occupational standing (or other SECs developed across the globe) and health have led to a number of sociological models, many of them focusing on the causal role of material, behavioural and psychosocial factors for health, and many also using the notion of the lifecourse as a vehicle (see Graham, 2009). These could be defined as 'middle range' sociological models since they focus on measurable aspects of social phenomena and observed empirical regularities. However, measures like that of the NS-SEC neither purport to be nor are substitutes for Marxian models of class. This gives rise to two questions. First, is it premature to write neo-Marxist concepts of class out of the medical-sociological script? And second, does class, thus understood, have some causal bearing on the enduring statistical associations between SECs and health/longevity?

Navarro (2002) has long argued against neglecting Marx's theories, holding class relations accountable not just for inter- and intra-national health inequalities but also for the near-ubiquitous failure of governments to tackle them effectively and for the flaws found in many health care systems. A related thesis is that class relations understood in this way are largely responsible for the consistent and long-standing associations between SECs and health. It is class relations, in short, that 'lock' people into their SEC (and the parsimony of post-war social or inter-SEC mobility is indeed remarkable). In an extension of this thesis, it has been suggested that the attention of researchers should switch from its past and present focus on the poor health behaviours and prospects of the poor and powerless to concentrate on the behaviours of the rich and powerful. The polemically-named 'greedy bastards hypothesis' (or GBH) claims that it is the behaviours of a small, hardcore group of thoroughly global capitalists who are active in the UK (the chief executive officers of major and multi-national corporations, financiers, rentiers and so on) – increasingly and significantly *favoured* since the mid-1970s by the globali*zing* power elite of the state – that provide the principal causal motor for (1) the enduring nature, and even deepening, of health inequalities in the UK, and (2) the persistent failure to properly address these (Scambler, 2002). Implicit in the GBH is a critique of the abandonment of sociology's classic focus on social structures or relations. It sees the maldistribution of wealth and income as – directly and indirectly – pivotal for health inequalities, and defines both this maldistribution *and its near-systematic neglect* as a function of class relations. The rich, it suggests, engage in forms of 'illness behaviour' with profound implications for the poor, while it is the illness behaviour of the poor that is the more-or-less exclusive object of current (funded) research programmes. The bulk of research funding comes directly or indirectly from the state.

Arguably it is not simply a matter of choosing *either* middle-range theories consonant with known statistical linkages between SECs and health *or* a more traditional or modern sociological emphasis on social structure. Both can contribute to our understanding of how people's social positions and behaviours will have ramifications for their health status and life expectancy. Graham (1995) seminally showed, Durkheim-like, how seemingly individual decisions to engage in 'risk behaviours' like smoking can be rational by-products of the structured circumstances in which women happen, unwittingly, to find themselves. The challenge of the next decade may be to discover more effective ways of (1) integrating macro-, meso- and micro-sociological theories of health inequalities, (2) facilitating genuinely interdisciplinary – sociological, psychological and biological – approaches to health inequalities, and (3) propagating policies to tackle health inequalities. Arguably, none of these projects can be comprehensively pursued in the absence of a classic modern theory of relations of class.

See also: *Material and Cultural Factors; Neoliberal Globalization and Health Inequalities*

REFERENCES

Braudel, F. (1984) *The Perspective of the World*. London: Collins.
Graham, H. (1995) 'Cigarette smoking: a light on gender and class inequality in Britain', *Journal of Social Policy*, 24: 509–27.
Graham, H. (2009) *Unequal Lives: Health and Socioeconomic Inequalities*. Maidenhead: Open University Press.
Langford, A. and Johnson, B. (2010) 'Trends in health inequalities in male mortality, 2001–08: intercensual estimates for England and Wales', *Health Statistics Quarterly*, 47 (1): 1–28.
Mackenbach, J. (2005) *Health Inequalities: Europe in Profile*. Rotterdam: Erasmus MC University Medical Centre.
The Marmot Review (2010) *Post-2010 Strategic Review of Health Inequalities* (The Marmot Review). London: The Marmot Review.
Navarro, V. (ed.) (2002) *The Political Economy of Social Inequalities: Consequences for Health and Quality of Life*. New York: Baywood Publishing Company.
Pakulski, J. and Waters, M. (1996) *The Death of Class*. London: Sage.
Rose, D. and O'Reilly, K. (eds) (1997) *Constructing Classes: Towards a New Social Classification for the UK*. London: Office of National Statistics.
Scambler, G. (2002) *Health and Social Change: A Critical Theory*. Buckingham: Open University Press.
World Health Organization (WHO) (2008) *Commission on Social Determinants of Health (CSDH) – Closing the Gap in a Generation: Health Equity through Action on Social Determinants of Health*. Geneva: WHO.

Graham Scambler

> *Gender concerns the social relations within and between groups of men and women, boys and girls; it is an interactive process that also has health implications.*

'Being a man or a woman', writes Connell (2009: 5), 'is not a pre-determined state. It is a *becoming*, a condition actively under construction'. The social construction of gender has implications for health. Health is socially patterned while remaining dynamic and sensitive to changes in the social relations of gender within and between societies over time.

The distinction between biological sex and social gender has been indispensable for the study of gender and health. However, sex and gender tend to be treated as competing explanations when – more often than not – they *both* matter and it is their interaction that is important. Male sex makes men vulnerable to prostate disease and female sex makes women vulnerable to cervical cancer and cancer of the womb. Biology also has a role in conditions which *both* men and women experience. Lung function matures more slowly in the male foetus which gives rise to more respiratory distress syndromes and lung-related injuries in newborns. Female sex hormones reduce the risk of coronary heart disease in women in their 'reproductive years'. But biological factors do not *determine* the health of men and women, boys and girls. Social factors can overrule or even cancel out biological propensities. For example, in HIV infection the biological body puts women at a higher risk of seroconversion during unprotected sex with an infected male partner since, amongst other things, the greater area of mucus membrane exposed during sex provides a fertile ground for the virus to enter the body, and micro-tears in vaginal tissue increase the risk of male-to-female transmission. But, crucially, around the world, it is the *social* relations of gender – especially women's relative lack of control over sexual activity – that matter most because these are what put women at risk of exposure to the virus in the first place (Gilbert and Selikow, 2010).

In other words, gender relations interact with the biological body to produce particular patterns of morbidity and mortality at different times and in different places. We can see this in international differences in life expectancy. Today women outlive men in virtually all countries of the world. However, the extent of this longevity has fluctuated considerably over time and presently there are large variations across societies, from just one year in the Sudan, to four to five years in the UK and the USA, and twelve years in the Russian Federation (WHO, 2010).

The late 1800s to around the 1970s saw the gradual emergence of the current female longevity advantage in the West. For example, in England and Wales, the number of 'extra years', on average, that a female might expect to live at birth compared to a male rose from around two years for those born in 1841 to 6.3 years for those born in 1969/1970. Life expectancy continues to grow for males and females alike, but the 'gender gap' between them has been decreasing since around the 1970s. This is accounted for by larger 'male gains' at all age points. Between 1980 and 2003, the life expectancy of Western European men as a whole increased by 6.5 per cent and that of women by only 3.5 per cent (White and Cash, 2004), and while these differences seem small, they mark a new historical trend.

Gender distinctions have been breaking down in the West as women's educational and workforce participation has risen and social attitudes about what is gender-appropriate behaviour have loosened for both women and men. Men's health emerged from the shadows of gender and health research in the 1990s as the spotlight turned upon the health-damaging effects of a 'hegemonic' – or dominant, controlling – masculinity. The corollary is that if men cast off their traditional masculinity and/or women take it on, we might expect the differences in life expectancy to decrease. This expectation appears to have been borne out. To take the UK as an example, although the rates of major causes of death remain higher for men, they have experienced swifter declines in heart disease and stroke mortality in recent decades. Lung cancer incidence rates remain higher for men than for women, but they have declined since the mid-1970s while women's have risen. These health conditions are associated with the very lifestyle and health behaviour changes that have accompanied so-called gender convergence. An obvious example is lung cancer where past and current smoking patterns are showing up as men's and women's life-time risks of lung cancer start to narrow, and in some countries even reverse. These changes are not however a simple matter of individual lifestyle choice – rather they are forged within the complex social relations of gender, class, age and ethnicity that influence the lives of men and women (Annandale, 2009).

Many countries in Sub-Saharan Africa have also experienced a decreasing 'gender gap', to the point that in some, such as Mozambique and Zimbabwe, there is now no difference in average life expectancy (WHO, 2010). In Sub-Saharan Africa, the poorest region in the world, any biological advantage women may have in life expectancy is easily diminished as they bear the brunt of the harsh neoliberal economic policies that accompany globalization, alongside gender discrimination. Women in the region are at an exceptionally high risk of premature death from AIDS-related human rights abuses and from sexual violence during armed conflict.

Yet some countries, as distinct from the West and Sub-Saharan Africa, have experienced an *increasing* 'gender gap' in life expectancy. For example, as with their counterparts elsewhere in the world, Russian women have longer average life expectancies than men. However, the life expectancies of both men and women worsened between 1980 and 2002 with men's worsening more than women's. And by 2008 the average life expectancy of 74 years for women, and 62 years for men, represented the largest 'gender gap' in the world (WHO, 2010). Heart disease mortality has been increasing, especially for men, and there has also been a dramatic rise in all forms of violent deaths (including alcohol-related). Pietilä and Rytkönen (2008: 1082) found that even though their Russian respondents attributed this gap more to changing structural conditions in their country than to individual behaviours, they drew heavily on the notion of gender roles as natural: 'a kind of haven, standing for something permanent and stable in the context of rapid social change'.

Situating global variations in life expectancy within their societal and global contexts helps to explain the social patterning of mortality. Yet it tells us little about a person's health during their lifetime. As Arber (2004) explained in the first edition of *Key Concepts in Medical Sociology*, research has been concerned with the apparent paradox that 'women are sicker but men die quicker' (or why, on average, in most countries of the world, women still live longer than men, but they are also – or appear to be – sicker during their lives). However, the first aspect of the 'gender paradox' has been questioned.

From the mid-1990s, research has shown that self-reported gender differences in general health status and longstanding illness appear to be relatively small amongst adults in the West. Nevertheless, women generally suffer more from chronic conditions such as arthritis and rheumatism. Although rates of mental illness do not differ much overall, depression and anxiety tend to be higher amongst women and personality disorder and suicide higher amongst men. In light of these findings, the 'gender paradox' is often resolved by the deduction that although any 'excess' morbidity experienced by women is debilitating, it typically does not result in an early death. However, it needs to be appreciated that since doing health is also part of doing gender (Saltonstall, 1993), self-assessments of health and gender are intricately connected and cause and effect are not easily disentangled.

The 'men die quicker' side of the equation has been linked to their more danger-ous employment conditions, life chances, risk-taking, and seeming reluctance to seek help when ill. The latter in particular is interpreted as part of 'doing masculin-ity': for example, Courtenay highlights that 'when a man brags "I haven't been to a doctor in years", he is simultaneously describing a health practice and situating himself in a masculine arena' (2009: 15). However, masculinity is plural: men in more marginalized and subordinated positions bear the brunt of those who are in hegemonic positions, as do many women (Connell, 2009). Moreover, for many people, seeking care in the first place hinges on an ability to pay for this. In low income countries, and in economically deprived communities in high income countries, girls and women often cannot afford to seek formal health care and families invest less in their care even though their needs may be greater than those of males.

So while the lives of some groups of men and women may be converging, important differences remain which subject them to different social and material exposures. In spite of Western women's increased labour force participation, hori-zontal and vertical segregation remains. This means that on average women are paid less than men and they are still mainly responsible for childcare and the home. Meanwhile, large numbers of women and girls from the global South migrate to find work as lowly paid domestic and care workers which enables the careers of wealthier women of the North (Sen et al., 2007).

Research generally finds that the magnitude of socioeconomic gradients in health in the West is sharper amongst men than amongst women. Since it is hard to imag-ine that socioeconomic inequality matters less for the health of women than for men, it is possible that the shallower gradient is an artefact of how socioeconomic status is measured. Occupationally-based measures are problematic because they are usually based on a male occupational structure and consequently fail to differentiate between the jobs that women do. To fully capture the relationship between gender, socioeconomic status and health we need to move beyond individual characteristics and take the gendered context of the places people live in – such as municipalities, states and countries – into account. Such research has been limited to date, although there is some evidence from a study by Chen and colleagues (2005) that in a very unequal nation such as the USA, living in a more equal (as compared to unequal) state benefits the mental health of women. The authors report that this could be because those states where women's status is higher may provide better material and social resources, such as higher wages and family-friendly policies. Living in a more equal state may also have psychosocial effects, reducing the stress associated with overt and covert discrimination. Other research has found that high levels of patriarchy are associated with higher male mortality in many societies (Stanistreet et al., 2005).

In conclusion, on average, women still live longer than men in most countries. However, the social patterning of gender and health is exceedingly complex and highly responsive to social contexts and to social change. This is evident in the decreasing and increasing 'gender gaps' in life expectancy in different parts of the world. The conventional assumption that women are sicker during their lives is questionable and in need of further research. Finally, gender does not stand alone as an influence upon health; rather, it intersects in complex and in as yet relatively unexplored ways with other factors such as socioeconomic status.

See also: *Social Class; Neoliberal Globalization and Health Inequalities*

REFERENCES

Annandale, E. (2009) *Women's Health and Social Change*. London: Routledge.
Arber, S. (2004) 'Gender', in J. Gabe, M. Bury and M.A. Elston (eds), *Key Concepts in Medical Sociology*. London: Sage.
Chen, Y., Subramanian, S.V., Acevedo-Garcia, D. and Kawachi, I. (2005) 'Women's status and depressive symptoms: a multilevel analysis', *Social Science & Medicine*, 60: 49–60.
Connell, R. (2009) *Gender*, 2nd edn. Cambridge: Polity Press.
Courtenay, W. (2009) 'Theorising masculinity and men's health', in A. Broom and P. Tovey (eds), *Men's Health: Body, Identity and Social Context*. London: Wiley-Blackwell.
Gilbert, L. and Selikow, T. (2010) 'HIV/AIDS and Gender', in E. Kuhlmann and E. Annandale (eds), *The Palgrave Handbook of Gender and Healthcare*. London: Palgrave.
Pietilä, I. and Rytkönen, M. (2008) '"Health is not a man's domain": lay accounts of gender difference in life-expectancy in Russia', *Sociology of Health & Illness*, 30: 1070–83.
Saltonstall, R. (1993) 'Healthy bodies, social bodies: men's and women's concepts and practices of everyday health', *Social Science & Medicine*, 36: 7–14.
Sen, G., Ostlin, P. and George, A. (2007) *Unequal, Unfair, Ineffective and Inefficient: Gender Inequity in Health – Why It Exists and How We Can Change It*. Final report to the WHO Commission on Social Determinants of Health by the Women and Gender Equity Knowledge Network. Online: http://www.who.int/social_determinants/resources/csdh_media/wgekn_final_report_07.pdf
Stanistreet, D., Bambra, C. and Scott-Samuel, A. (2005) 'Is patriarchy the source of men's higher mortality?', *Journal of Epidemiology and Community Health*, 59: 873–6.

White, A. and Cash, K. (2004) 'The state of men's health in Europe', *Journal of Men's Health and Gender*, 1: 60–6.

World Health Organization (WHO) (2010) *World Health Statistics 2010*. Online: http://www.who.int/whosis/whostat/EN_WHS10_Full.pdf

Ellen Annandale

Ethnicity

> *Ethnicity refers to people's identification with a social group – membership of a collectivity – on the basis of shared values, beliefs, customs, traditions, language and lifestyles.*

A consideration of what is meant by the term 'ethnicity', and the more contentious term 'race', is, of course, central to any discussion of ethnic inequalities in health. There is a wide sociological literature on ethnicity and 'race', which can be broadly defined as concerned with understanding how ethnic and racial groups become social realities, the relationships between them, and the causes and extent of social inequalities between them. Within this work there is agreement that the concept of 'race', reflecting genetically distinct groupings, does not have scientific validity – that people cannot be divided into races on the basis of genetic differences – and hence the almost universal use of quotation marks around 'race'.

In contrast, most commentators give credence to a notion of ethnicity that reflects an identification with cultural traditions that provide (fluid) boundaries between groups. Ethnic groups are 'real collectivities, [with] common and distinctive forms of thinking and behaviour, of language, custom, religion and so on; not just modes of oppression but modes of being' (Modood, 1996: 95). However, it is important to consider how these cultural traditions are historically located and context dependent, that is, how they, and the social significance of particular categories that they mark – such as 'Muslim' – change over time and place. In addition, ethnicity is only one element of social identity. For example, gender and class are also important and in certain situations may be more so than ethnic identity. Central to this 'instability' of cultural identity is the way in which geographical boundaries have become less fixed over time, both in terms of the movement of populations across them and the globalization of media. This has brought differing cultural traditions into close contact and, inevitably, has also resulted in the transformation of these traditions, though not necessarily in a straightforward way. For example, Hall (1992) argues that globalization can lead to a strengthening of cultural traditions, on the one hand, and their transformation and the formation of new – hybrid – traditions, on the other.

Some elements of these discussions of ethnicity and 'race' have been adopted by research on ethnicity and health. For example, within the UK, 'race' is never explicitly measured and 'ethnicity' is clearly the favoured term. However, the quantitative nature of much health (rather than social) research, with a need for easily used and repeatable measures, often results in the concepts of ethnicity and 'race' not being clearly distinguished and the dynamic and contextual nature of ethnicity being ignored in the operationalization of ethnic categories. Therefore the term 'ethnic' is frequently used to refer to supposed genetic and cultural features of the population under investigation that are considered to be stable and to mark them out as different.

The fact that even at a descriptive level ethnic inequalities in health are complex aggravates this situation. Differences in health across ethnic groups, in terms of both morbidity and mortality, have been repeatedly documented in both the USA (Rogers, 1992) and the UK (Marmot et al., 1984; Nazroo, 2001; Sproston and Mindell, 2006). When looking at these data, the initial picture is one of uniform disadvantage for ethnic minority groups, with higher mortality (death) and morbidity (illness) rates. However, closer examination of the data suggests great diversity, with the extent of any health disadvantage varying across ethnic groups and by condition. For example, survey evidence from the UK suggests that within the ethnic minority group that is broadly described as South Asian, Pakistani and Bangladeshi people have very poor health, while Indian people have levels of health that are comparable to the general population (Nazroo, 2001). And while Pakistani and Bangladeshi people have very poor health generally, their respiratory health is better than that of the general population (2001). Mortality data also vary by condition and ethnic group. For conditions affecting the cardiovascular system, for example, in the UK those who were born in South Asia have markedly higher death rates from ischaemic heart disease, while those born in the Caribbean have average or low death rates from ischaemic heart disease, but high death rates from strokes and other diseases related to hypertension (Marmot et al., 1984).

Rather than complex explanations for such diversity in the patterning of ethnic inequalities in health, the dominant set of explanations has been straightforwardly based on the premise of genetic and cultural differences between ethnic groups. This is at least partly a consequence of the ease with which such meanings are imposed on ethnic categorizations – ethnic difference, no matter how complex, is easily equated with fixed genetic or cultural difference, despite the obvious problems that have been outlined above. The central problem with such an approach is not that genetic or cultural explanations should be rejected out of hand, but that they are universally invoked with little supporting empirical evidence. In particular, they become explanations by exclusion – they remain once other explanations are ruled out, but are not formally tested themselves.

This lack of supporting evidence is, of course, partly a consequence of the difficulty in identifying contributing genes and behaviours and subsequently measuring them in population samples. But it is also a consequence of the assumption that other, competing, explanations are either irrelevant or have been adequately accounted for in the data, so all that remains must be a result of genetic or cultural differences. There are, in fact, several alternative explanations for ethnic inequalities in health. The most frequently considered is the possibility that they are a consequence of socio-economic differences between ethnic groups. Given the large socio-economic inequalities faced by most ethnic minority groups in the UK and the USA (Modood et al., 1997), such an explanation for ethnic inequalities in health is clearly worth exploring. Although initial studies in the UK suggested that socio-economic differences did not contribute to ethnic inequalities in health (Marmot et al., 1984), work in the USA (Rogers, 1992) and more recent work in the UK (Nazroo, 2001) have suggested that material factors make the key contribution to differences in health between different ethnic groups (Nazroo and Williams, 2005).

Across a variety of outcomes, and for all ethnic minority groups in the UK, careful adjustment for socio-economic differences reduces the health disadvantage in comparison with the general population (Nazroo and Williams, 2005). Such careful adjustment for socio-economic indicators is not straightforward, however. For example, occupational class is commonly taken as an indicator of socio-economic position, but within an occupational class ethnic minority people are more likely to be found in lower or less prestigious occupational grades, to have poorer job security, to endure more stressful working conditions, and to be more likely to work unsocial hours. Data from a national survey in the UK have shown that for the poorest ethnic groupings – Pakistani and Bangladeshi people – the average household income is half that of white people within each occupational class, and that the average income in the highest class group for Pakistani and Bangladeshi people is equivalent to that for the lowest class group for white people (Nazroo, 2001; Nazroo and Williams, 2005). Indeed, even a careful adjustment for socio-economic position still does not account for the numerous other forms of social disadvantage that ethnic minority people face, such as their geographical concentration in poor and poorly serviced areas, discrimination and racial harassment. And there is growing evidence to suggest that such forms of disadvantage are related to poor health. For example, Karlsen and Nazroo (2002) have shown that both the experience of racial harassment and the perception of the UK as a racist society are strongly related to poor health. Surprisingly, perhaps, this does not appear to extend to the UK's NHS, where outcomes of care for ethnic minority people are similar to those for white people, although this is not the same in other health-system contexts, such as that of the USA (Nazroo et al., 2009).

So, evidence from studies that have used adequate indicators of socio-economic position suggests that socio-economic factors make a large contribution to ethnic inequalities in health. And studies exploring the relationship between racial discrimination and harassment and health suggest that these experiences are also related to poor health for ethnic minority people. However, as described earlier, the ethnic patterning of health is not one of uniform disadvantage across minority groups and outcomes. There are key differences between ethnic minority groups, the patterns are different for particular outcomes, and these cannot be easily explained by a crude 'ethnic disadvantage' hypothesis. Of course, the social patterning of ethnic disadvantage is also complex (Modood et al., 1997). It is likely that other factors are important and that the relative significance of particular factors in determining ethnic inequalities in health might vary according to the type of illness actually being considered.

There remains the possibility that cultural and biological differences do contribute to ethnic inequalities in health and it is tempting to consider such explanations when ethnic disadvantage does not easily fit the pattern of inequality for a particular illness or ethnic group. However, when doing this, it is necessary to recognize that neither cultural practices nor biology are static. Over time, environmental factors become reflected in current biological measures, so biological differences may be a consequence of both genetic and environmental determinants. Furthermore, ethnic identity changes over time and is dependent on social context and other elements of identity also contribute to cultural practices. The marked ethnic differences in the prevalence of smoking in the UK provide a good illustration of this point (Nazroo, 2001). Among those people broadly classified as South Asian, there are low rates of smoking among Indian people, and relatively high rates among Pakistani and Bangladeshi people. And for Indian people, smoking is strongly related to religion, with Sikhs having very low rates and Muslims having high rates. Smoking is also strongly related to gender for South Asian people, with women having very low rates regardless of their country of origin or religion. And as for the general population, it is also strongly related to class for South Asian people, with those in manual classes having higher rates than those in non-manual classes. But perhaps most importantly, smoking rates are strongly related to age on migration to the UK, with those migrating at younger ages, or born there, having higher rates of smoking than those migrating at older ages. In fact, recent work suggests that changes across generations in both cultural practice and socio-economic position are relevant to ethnic inequalities in health (Smith et al., 2009).

Overall, then, a more complex approach to the factors underlying ethnic differences in health is required than simply considering them to be socio-economic, or cultural, or genetic – such factors are unlikely to operate in isolation. Racism is of central importance here. First, ethnic identity and ethnic boundaries are assigned as well as adopted, and assigned on the basis of power relations. Second, the socio-economic differences between ethnic groups should not be considered as somehow autonomous. Rather, the socio-economic disadvantage of ethnic minority people is the outcome of a long history of institutional racism and discrimination that has produced the current levels of disadvantage.

See also: *Social Class; Material and Cultural Factors*

REFERENCES

Hall, S. (1992) 'The question of cultural identity', in S. Hall, D. Held and T. McGrew (eds), *Modernity and its Futures*. Cambridge: Polity Press.

Karlsen, S. and Nazroo, J.Y. (2002) 'The relationship between racial discrimination, social class and health among ethnic minority groups', *American Journal of Public Health*, 92 (4): 624–31.

Marmot, M.G., Adelstein, A.M., Bulusu, L. and OPCS (1984) *Immigrant Mortality in England and Wales 1970–78: Causes of Death by Country of Birth*. London: HMSO.

Modood, T. (1996) 'If races don't exist, then what does? Racial categorisation and ethnic realities', in R. Barot (ed.), *The Racism Problematic: Contemporary Sociological Debates on Race and Ethnicity*. Lewiston, NY: The Edwin Mellen Press.

Modood, T., Berthoud, R., Lakey, J., Nazroo, J., Smith, P., Virdee, S. and Beishon, S. (1997) *Ethnic Minorities in Britain: Diversity and Disadvantage*. London: Policy Studies Institute.

Nazroo, J.Y. (2001) *Ethnicity, Class and Health*. London: Policy Studies Institute.

Nazroo, J.Y. and Williams, D.R. (2005) 'The social determination of ethnic/racial inequalities in health', in M. Marmot and R.G. Wilkinson (eds), *Social Determinants of Health*, 2nd edn. Oxford: Oxford University Press.

Nazroo, J., Falaschetti, E., Pierce, M. and Primatesta, P. (2009) 'Ethnic inequalities in access to and outcomes of healthcare: analysis of the Health Survey for England', *Journal of Epidemiology and Community Health*, 63 (12): 1022–7.

Rogers, R.G. (1992) 'Living and dying in the USA: socio-demographic determinants of death among blacks and whites', *Demography*, 29: 287–303.

Smith, N.R., Kelly, Y.J. and Nazroo, J.Y. (2009) 'Intergenerational continuities of ethnic inequalities in general health in England', *Journal of Epidemiology and Community Health*, 63: 253–8.

Sproston, K. and Mindell, J. (2006) *Health Survey for England 2004: The Health of Minority Ethnic Groups*. London: The Information Centre.

James Y. Nazroo

Place

Place refers to a socially significant or socially constructed location in geographical space.

place

While there is a classic heritage of sociology that considers the interrelationships between place and health, place has, perhaps understandably, received more sustained attention within disciplines such as geography. There is no single definition within medical geography, but geographers have tended to define space as being a natural and physical construct relating to geometric location, and places as being socio-cultural locations in space. According to Gesler, 'place is studied with an eye to its meanings for people; space is analysed in terms of its quantifiable attributes and patterns' or, in other words, place is 'a space filled with people acting out their lives' (quoted in Kearns and Joseph, 1993: 712). More colloquially, place can also be used in a metaphorical or purely social sense, as relating to one's position in life, in a social hierarchy, or a family, or as in 'I know my place'. Here, however, the focus will be on place as having a physical locational element, and particularly on place of residence. After a passing reference to some historical texts, and some attention given to the concerns of other disciplines (for example, epidemiology), we will highlight the ongoing relevance of the concept of 'place' in medical sociology with reference to some recent research.

An early text on the influence of place on health was Hippocrates' *Airs, Waters, Places*, written in the fifth century BC. The three elements in the title referred to features of climate and topography, which were believed to influence the prevalence and types of disease likely to be found in different places. In Britain social regularities in death rates were first studied systematically in the seventeenth century by John Graunt, whose 'Natural and political observations upon the Bills of Mortality' was published in 1662. Graunt was interested not only in the direct effects of the environment on physical health, but also in effects on mental health and human behaviour; for example, he believed that adultery and fornication, and anxieties resulting from concerns with business, were more prevalent in London than in the country. The health effects of industrialisation in the nineteenth century prompted a considerable amount of interest in the UK and USA in the social and geographical patterning of disease. In Britain, for example, William Farr examined the social patterning of mortality by comparing the death rates of different localities. He drew up life tables for 'healthy districts' which could be compared, and as a basis for inferring that much premature mortality was due to environmental conditions and was therefore preventable. Engels' work on the conditions of the working class in England was similarly undertaken in the spirit of scientific discovery, social justice and change.

Following the decline in infectious diseases and improvements to the environment in the nineteenth and twentieth centuries in many Western industrial nations, interest in the direct effects of the local environment on physical health decreased. In the latter half of the twentieth century, much epidemiology mainly used geographical data as a proxy for individual data. Individual exposure to some pathogen in the environment, or individual levels of material disadvantage, were inferred from information about someone's place of residence. Because individual-level data on socio-economic status or income are frequently not available on a large scale, material advantage or disadvantage is often measured indirectly from someone's address in the UK, using deprivation indices based on postal or census geography, and in the USA by measures such as aggregate income in census areas. Thus, while there have been many epidemiological studies of area variations in morbidity and mortality, most have used place of residence as a vehicle for exploring hypotheses about the role of individual physical exposure or material deprivation as determinants of health, rather than focusing more directly on the role of place itself (Macintyre and Ellaway, 2000).

Exceptions can be found in early sociological work on mental health. Classic studies, such as those in the 1930s of the spatial patterning of schizophrenia in Chicago (Faris and Dunham, 1939), generated competing hypotheses about the relative importance of the 'breeder' and 'drift' communities. The 'breeder' hypothesis suggests that such areas generate illness in their residents, while the 'drift' hypothesis suggests that ill individuals gravitate towards such areas.

During the period from the end of the Second World War to the early 1990s, epidemiology, medical geography and medical sociology tended not to study directly the impact of the local social or physical environment on human health, despite there being many community studies exploring life and health or health-related experiences in particular localities. One reason for the relative neglect of the role of place in medical sociology during that period was fear of the eco-logical fallacy. This fallacy involves inferring individual-level relationships from associations observed at the aggregate level, and a number of influential socio-logical papers in the 1950s warned that this could lead to entirely incorrect inferences being made, because ecological and individual correlations between the same variables can differ markedly, even in different directions. As a result, ecological approaches were shunned in sociology and epidemiology (Macintyre and Ellaway, 2000).

Another reason was the dominance of methodological, conceptual and political individualism in many industrialised countries from the mid-1950s. This emphasis on individualism in health research emerged partly from analyses of the epidemio-logical transition. Such work prioritised the role in chronic disease of individual lifestyle choices (particularly the 'big four' of smoking, drinking, diet and exercise), rather than the structural and environmental conditions which were believed to influence patterns of infectious disease or diseases of extreme want. With the rediscovery of health inequalities in the 1980s in the UK, and in the 1990s in North America and Australasia, attention initially tended to focus on the proper-ties of individuals and families such as low income or unemployment rather than on the environments (physical or social) to which individuals or families are exposed. Debates about the relative importance of health selection versus social causation echoed earlier discussions about the drift and breeder hypotheses but rarely cited this earlier literature.

Since the early 1990s there has been a resurgence of interest in the role of place on people's health, and a new debate within medical sociology has devel-oped about the relative importance of people or place characteristics. A distinc-tion is often made between compositional and contextual explanations for observed associations between place of residence and health. A compositional explanation is that the characteristics of individual residents in a particular area (for example, their collective age, sex and socio-economic status) explain area dif-ferences in health; a contextual explanation is that characteristics of the area (such as access to amenities and facilities to support a healthy life), over and above those of resident individuals, can help to explain area differences. Compositional explanations would suggest that individuals with particular char-acteristics would have the same levels of health wherever they live; the contex-tual explanation would suggest the health experiences of individuals will depend partly on the characteristics of the area in which they live (Curtis and Rees Jones, 1998). Compositional explanations have usually been preferred, partly because of the above-mentioned fears about the ecological fallacy. However, a number of socio-epidemiological studies in the UK and USA, often using multilevel statistical modelling techniques, have found residual effects of area of residence over and above the predictive value of individual or household characteristics (Riva et al., 2007).

Although there is now some empirical evidence for the role of place of residence in influencing health, the pathways by which place might influence health have been somewhat under-theorized (Diez Roux and Mair, 2010). Place effects have often been treated as a black box of the residual variation in statistical models left over when one has controlled for every conceivable individual variable. However, there are now some attempts to improve the conceptualisation of place and its effects. One suggestion has been to develop a model of what residents need in the local residential environment in order to lead healthy lives. Human needs range along a hierarchy from air, water, food, shelter, etc. to facilities for religious expression, collective activities and play. The aim would then be to operationalise and measure these and explore how features of the local environment might individually or collectively relate to different aspects of health (Macintyre et al., 2002). An influence on recent theorizing on how place might influence health has been a debate within the broader field of inequalities in health. This debate addresses the relative importance of psychosocial as compared to material influences on health (Lynch et al., 2000) and the social processes within places (Sampson et al., 2002). Others argue that the conceptualisation and measurement of 'place' needs to encompass a historical perspective and a consideration of the experiences of people who live or are connected with a 'place' (Popay et al., 1998). There has also been a substantial recent increase in studies exploring how the features of place of residence influence health outcomes, such as obesity and its determinants (Lake and Townshend, 2006), with concomitant debates on the contested nature of the measurement and meaning of 'obesity' within and outside of sociology (Rich et al., 2011).

While this entry has focused on place of residence, it should be noted that the concept of place has been widely applied to a number of other settings (for example, health care settings, and therapeutic environments including landscapes, schools, workplaces and churches); to a number of other health-related outcome variables (such as preventive health behaviours, health risk behaviours, access and use of health care); and to more abstract concepts such as 'a sense of place'. If places are socially constructed and have social significance, then medical sociologists should be interested in them as social contexts within which people's lives and health-related experiences are played out. Whereas sociologists conducted many of the early health-related community studies, sociology and sociological theory have been less apparent in the recent literature on the role of place and health, which has been dominated by epidemiologists and medical geographers. Future work in medical sociology, we would argue, should therefore pay heed to its classic heritage and not leave the concept of 'place' solely to other disciplines.

See also: *Material and Cultural Factors; Psychosocial Factors*

REFERENCES

Curtis, S. and Rees Jones, I. (1998) 'Is there a place for geography in the analysis of health inequality?' *Sociology of Health & Illness*, 20 (5): 645–72.

Diez Roux, A. and Mair, C. (2010) 'Neighborhoods and health', *Annals of the New York Academy of Sciences*, 1186: 125–45.

Faris, R. and Dunham, H. (1939) *Mental Disorders in Urban Areas*. Chicago: University of Chicago Press.

Kearns, R.A. and Joseph, A.E. (1993) 'Space in its place: developing the link in medical geography', *Social Science & Medicine*, 37 (6): 711–17.

Lake, A. and Townshend, T. (2006) 'Obesogenic environments: exploring the built and food environments', *Journal of the Royal Society for Health*, 126 (6): 262–7.

Lynch, J., Davey Smith, G., Kaplan, G. and House, J. (2000) 'Income inequality and mortality: importance to health of individual income, psychosocial environment, or material conditions', *British Medical Journal*, 320: 1200–4.

Macintyre, S. and Ellaway, A. (2000) 'Ecological approaches: rediscovering the role of the physical and social environment', in L. Berkman and I. Kawachi (eds), *Social Epidemiology*. Oxford: Oxford University Press.

Macintyre, S., Ellaway, A. and Cummins, S. (2002) 'Place effects on health: how can we conceptualise, operationalise and measure them?', *Social Science & Medicine*, 55: 125–39.

Popay, J. Williams, G., Thomas, C. and Gatrell, A. (1998) 'Theorising inequalities in health: the place of lay knowledge', *Sociology of Health & Illness*, 20 (5): 619–44.

Rich, E., Monaghan, L.F. and Aphramor, L. (eds) (2011) *Debating Obesity: Critical Perspectives*. Basingstoke: Palgrave Macmillan.

Riva, M., Gauvin, L. and Barne, T.A. (2007) 'Toward the next generation of research into small area effects on health: a synthesis of multilevel investigations published since July 1998', *Journal of Epidemiology and Community Health*, 61: 853–61.

Sampson, R., Morenoff, J.D. and Gannon-Rowley, T. (2002) 'Assessing "neighbourhood effects": social processes and new directions in research', *Annual Review of Sociology*, 28: 443–78.

Sally Macintyre and Anne Ellaway

Material and Cultural Factors

Material factors refer to those natural or social structures that can have a causal bearing on population and individual health and longevity, while cultural factors denote the 'frames' in terms of which groups and individuals make sense of their lives and take decisions that can similarly impact on their own and the population's health.

The publication of the Black Report (DHSS, 1980) marked a turning point in the understanding of health inequalities in the UK and beyond, not least for sociologists. Charged not only with documenting but also explaining health inequalities, Black and his colleagues ranked material factors as being of the first importance, with cultural factors (giving rise to individual 'risk behaviours' for health) coming second. In short, the Black Report gave a higher priority to the 'hard' material underpinnings to people's lives (for example, their incomes, neighbourhoods, housing) than to the 'soft' business of healthy versus unhealthy lifestyles. This hard/soft division has political overtones. Through the 1980s and beyond, the UK, the USA and most other developed societies have been characterized by party political divisions between a social democratic or 'left-of-centre' focus on hard material factors and a neoliberal or 'right-of-centre' focus on soft cultural factors. The logics are transparent: political parties presenting as social democratic/left-of-centre express a commitment to *collectivist* government interventions aimed at material redistribution, while those presenting as neoliberal/right-of-centre espouse a philosophy of *individualism* predisposed to allow individuals to assume personal responsibility for their health-related behaviours.

The material/cultural distinction might work analytically, and for a while it brought to the surface rival political orientations, but it has also been subjected to growing academic scrutiny and critique (see Cockerham, 2010). Health inequalities research since 1980 has shown that if people's day-to-day circumstances and health behaviours are examined in detail, it is neither natural nor sensible to draw a hard-and-fast distinction between the causal contributions of material *versus* cultural factors. Apparently individual decisions to smoke, consume *cheap* 'fast foods', adopt sedentary lifestyles, take drugs and so on, have a lot to do with people's differential access to material resources, both in the present and in the futures they can anticipate. Smoking can be a relatively cheap and rational way of getting by if you are a single mum with three children under 5 subsisting on those benefits still on offer in the post-welfare state era. Fast foods are cheaper than many organic alternatives.

It does not follow that cultural factors collapse into or can be reduced to material factors, which is manifestly not the case. Quah (2010) rightly insists that culture is pervasive and that cultural values and norms inevitably frame and influence day-to-day preventive health behaviour, illness behaviour and sick-role behaviour among individuals and groups as well as at the macro-level of healing systems. She makes three other general points about the study of culture in health and illness. The first concerns the need, well attested in theory and research, to recognize culture as an independent phenomenon, if not an entirely autonomous one. The second is to note the divergence to be found *within* as well as between healing systems; many systems lack internal consistency, with the different subgroups within them (for example, doctors, nurses and managers) having quite different interpretations of its core values or principles and how these might best be implemented (i.e. possessing their own distinctive subcultures). Quah refers, third, to 'pragmatic acculturation', or the borrowing from other cultures of 'elements, ways of thinking, and ways of doing things, with the objective of solving specific or practical problems' (p. 41); this, she suggests, is found in all aspects of behaviour around health and illness.

If the possession of material resources or goods seems fairly straightforward to understand and define (for example, net household income), it is less obvious how the possession of cultural resources might be defined. What, first, *is* culture? It is generally taken to refer to a reasonably coherent set of beliefs, values, attitudes and habits or behavioural predispositions. A given society might have a recognizable cultural 'profile', but it will also be comprised of overlapping subcultures: an Afro-American or Afro-Caribbean teenager from a household with no family member having been in employment for a decade may have remarkably little in common with the son or daughter of a white lawyer or doctor. To acknowledge this is not to sign up to cultural 'stereotypes'. Stereotypes – for example, associating (material and) cultural disadvantage or impoverishment with risk behaviours for health – always embody errors of omission and commission; moreover, they gloss over exceptions. Teenagers from 'disadvantaged' or 'impoverished' households can and do become lawyers and doctors *even if this is statistically exceptional*. It is one thing to uncover and report statistical trends and quite another, and altogether more complex, matter to provide sociological explanations for what is going on, and why.

Conventionally, sociologists have tended to focus on material factors, and often on their roots in social structures as well, while anthropologists have paid most attention to cultural factors. Some of the recent socio-epidemiological and sociological literature on health inequalities, however, has posited culture-based 'psychosocial pathways' as being of pivotal importance. The concept of 'social capital' popularized by Putnam (2000) and referring to the positive, health-bestowing effects of people's supportive networks of family members, friends, neighbours and acquaintances, has been much cited and studied in this connection. Some commentators, like Wilkinson (1996), have contended that material and cultural factors combine to promote health inequalities; he suggests that high income inequality leads to social fragmentation and dislocation and a breakdown of reciprocity and trust in people's dealings with each other, and thenceforth to differential rates of morbidity and mortality (and to many other social pathologies; see Wilkinson and Pickett, 2009).

Others have sought to displace the longstanding emphasis on material factors by attributing unambiguous priority to phenomena like social capital. This replay of material *versus* cultural factors once again has political connotations, brought into sharp focus by politicians' calculated deployment of terms like 'health variations' (in preference to health inequalities) and, more recently, 'social exclusion'. The contribution of material factors to health inequalities slips out of view in such language. To reiterate, taken in the round, sociological research makes it clear that it makes no sense to choose *between* material and cultural factors in accounting for health inequalities: it is not a matter of either/or.

One way of allowing (1) for both material and cultural factors to influence an individual's life chances and prospects for health and longevity, and (2) for their relative contributions to vary over time is via the concept of capital or *asset flows*. Scambler (2002) lists the following asset flows as being of known salience for health:

- biological (positive/negative 'body capital');
- psychological (resilient/vulnerable);
- social (networked/socially isolated);
- cultural (favourably/unfavourably positioned);
- spatial (depressed/affluent neighbourhood);
- material (high income/low income household).

Even the flow of biological assets can be influenced by social factors: women from low-income households are more likely than their more affluent counterparts to have low-birthweight babies, for example; and low-birthweight babies seem prone to health problems well beyond infancy. More significantly, it is consistent with research findings to suggest that a 'strong' flow of one asset (for example, biological) can *compensate* for a 'weak' flow of another (for example, material). In many an individual lifecourse, flows of assets are variable and they can and do vary independent of each other.

So there is evidence that material and cultural factors *both* affect health and longevity, even if there is an ongoing discussion and dispute about their relative contributions and interrelations. However, surprisingly few of the heady mainstream sociological discussions on precisely how structure and culture might best be theorized have impacted on substantive medical sociological research, and to structure and culture should be added a third candidate, agency (or the capacity to choose A rather than B, C, D, etc.).

The work of Bourdieu (1977), whose concept of 'cultural capital' is picked up in Scambler's notion of a 'cultural' asset flow, has a special resonance for those wanting to theorize structure, culture and agency for the more fruitful empirical study of health and longevity. His notion of 'habitus' has particular potential. Initially formulated and applied in relation to social class, Bourdieu maintained that a structural, class-based habitus can be empirically discerned via people's everyday decision making and biographies. Briefly, individuals' day-to-day lives betray sets of behavioural dispositions to decide and act 'this way rather than that way' that only fully make sense in terms of their background experiences: whether aware of it or not, their agency is structured (but not structurally determined), and agency can only ever be exercised in the cultural contexts in which people find themselves. In other words, the 'choices' that we make and the 'symbolic' resources available to us to make them (those pre-established 'cultural' beliefs, values and attitudes we so tellingly encounter during socialization), are more structured, or 'shaped', than we realize. This is a thesis examined sympathetically and in some detail in Cockerham's (2010) discussion of the social bases of apparently individual lifestyle decisions that are of critical importance for health.

See also: *Social Class; Social Capital*

REFERENCES

Bourdieu, P. (1977) *Outline of a Theory of Practice.* Cambridge: Cambridge University Press.
Cockerham, W. (2010) 'Health lifestyles: bringing structure back', in W. Cockerham (ed.), *The New Blackwell Companion to Medical Sociology.* Oxford: Wiley-Blackwell.

DHSS (1980) *Inequalities in Health: Report of a Working Group (The Black Report)*. London: HMSO.

Putnam, R. (2000) *Bowling Alone: The Collapse and Revival of American Community*. New York: Simon and Schuster.

Quah, S. (2010) 'Health and culture', in W. Cockerham (ed.), *The New Blackwell Companion to Medical Sociology*. Oxford: Wiley-Blackwell.

Scambler, G. (2002) *Health and Social Change: A Critical Theory*. Buckingham: Open University Press.

Wilkinson, R. (1996) *Unhealthy Societies: The Afflictions of Inequality*. London: Routledge.

Wilkinson, R. and Pickett, K. (2009) *The Spirit Level*. London: Allen Lane.

Graham Scambler

Psychosocial Factors

Used as a summary label, psychosocial factors characterize socio-environmental and personal conditions and attributes that increase or decrease the risk of illness over the lifecourse.

The study of psychosocial factors has a long history emerging from sociological, psychological and medical disciplines. For example in sociology, William Farr in the mid-1800s noticed different mortality rates in marital groups while Sigmund Freud in psychology some decades later examined the role of adverse early life experiences in the genesis of adult psychopathology. The groundwork for psycho-physiological research was laid down by Walter Cannon in the late 1920s in the study of bodily changes related to emotional arousal, followed by Hans Selye (1956) who identified the physiological correlates of stress in his seminal text, *The Stress of Life*.

Psychosocial factors have been a focus of research on the causation of disease in both medical sociology and health/clinical psychology. Traditionally there has been some polarization with medical sociology emphasizing the role of socio-environmental factors such as socio-cultural instability, rapid social change, social anomie, or low socio-economic status and material deprivation. Focusing more on the individual rather than societal level, health/clinical psychology has stressed the importance of personality (for example, Type A) and cognitive-emotional factors such as coping (for example, locus of control) and self-esteem. These factors are often intertwined and there is increasing investigation of the interaction between the two. Effects can be direct, for example where poor living conditions increase the risk of respiratory infections or the transmission of infectious agents. Others are less direct, for example migrant populations who are at increased health risk through a number of factors including social separation, socio-economic status, social exclusion and changes in dietary habits. A new and flourishing area of study involving both social and psychological factors in illness is the Attachment Framework – the interpersonal style emanating from early life adverse parenting, often the result of deprived material conditions and fragmented families.

Both sociological and psychological lines of enquiry have a common interest in the investigation of adverse childhood experience as a precursor to a worse adult health status. Socio-environmental factors such as loss of a parent, childhood neglect and abuse in deprived family settings have been associated with a range of poor health outcomes, both physical (Leserman et al., 1996) and mental (Bifulco and Moran, 1998). Lifespan psychosocial models show adverse childhood experience is associated with a range of adult risk factors such as a lower socio-economic status, single parent status and domestic violence, a worse education and poorer employment record, as well as lower self-esteem and a poorer ability to relate and to cope with stress (1998). This has led to the development of lifetime models tracing psychosocial risk pathways for psychological disorder that emphasize different trajectories, as well as identify key mediating or moderating factors. The issue has also moved to a discussion of resilience: not only does the threefold increase of psychological disorder in response to childhood adversity need explaining, but also the two-thirds of those with childhood adversity who do not experience disorder (1998).

Health risk behaviours have been studied by representatives of both disciplines. These include smoking (the risk of cardio-vascular and lung disease), alcohol consumption (the risk of diseases of the liver, stomach and central nervous system as well as traffic accidents and suicide), obesity (the risk of diabetes mellitus, cardiovascular disease) and physical activity (the risk of cardiovascular disease). Causes for these have been sought in both socio-environmental (for example, social class, marital status, dietary habits, social support) and psychological (for example, risk-taking behaviour and 'Type A' personality) domains. While there is accruing evidence for the importance of factors in both arenas, some caution is necessary. For instance, sociologists would question the attribution of individual responsibility in lifestyle and health, indicating the substantial role played by socio-economic status, inequality and culture (Graham, 2009). Obesity discourse is also challenged from within and outside of sociology (Rich et al., 2011).

Determining a *causal* role for psychosocial factors involves the following:

Timing: Psychosocial risk factors can act as antecedent, perpetuating or residual factors of ill health. For example, in the work domain job loss can trigger mental or physical health problems, a lack of employment can aggravate existing disorders, and chronic unemployment is often a residue of long-term ill health. Similar distinctions can be made about marital status, where health differences between marital groups can result from both an effect of health on marital status (through the selection of health in partners) and an effect of marital status on health (the stress induced by unhappy relationships leads to health problems).

Varying risk factors: A causal factor is one which, when manipulated, can be shown to change the risk of outcome. In the study of psychosocial factors, an adequate distinction is rarely made between fixed and varying risks. A fixed marker is unchangeable, and encompasses aspects such as 'race', gender and year of birth. Although these might be distally associated with health outcomes, they are unlikely to account for the timing of a disorder, nor can they be manipulated to change a health outcome. Variable risk factors can either change spontaneously within a subject (such as age) or be changed by intervention (for example, self-esteem and marital status). The change potential for psychosocial risks is important not only in understanding the causal agency for disorders but also for devising interventions. The degree to which psychosocial risks are varying is underestimated in many health studies, due to single-time point measurement.

Risk mediation: Although a substantial investigation has been made of a range of psychosocial risks and their association with different health outcomes, relatively little is currently known about the process of risk mediation. It is important to note that the origins and mode of mediation of a risk factor on health are not synonymous. Thus psychosocial risks may be responsible for bringing about certain health outcomes but the mediator of risk is likely to be in the physiological domain. For example, the reasons for smoking are multiple and include personality, cultural factors, social class, deprivation, and access to cigarettes. But risk processes linking smoking with cardio-vascular disease and lung cancer concern the physical influences of carbon monoxide and carcinogenic tars on the body. The origin of the risk factor is of critical importance for sociological and psychological study, but on its own is uninformative about the process of risk mediation.

During the last decade there have been *three* major developments internationally in UK, US and Canadian research, which have indicated complex relationships between psychosocial and biological factors, with swings in emphasis between these. The current position is for the psychosocial and socio-environmental factors to be again seen as driving much of the biological change (see epigenetics below).

Biological factors and genetics: Psychosocial factors are playing an increasing role in understanding the genetic bases of human behaviour in relation to disorder. In the field of behavioural genetics, socio-environmental factors are categorized in terms of whether they are 'shared' or 'non-shared' by family members (Plomin et al., 2001). The effect of a shared or non-shared environment on mental health and development is inferred from the degree to which twins reared together are more similar to one another than would be predicted on genetic grounds alone.

While early formulations gave the greatest weight to a 'non-shared' environment or personal experience over that which was 'shared', the emphasis on genetic interpretations of experience has gained greater weight. Some investigators have concluded that not only is there is an important genetic component in almost all environmental measures, but also that psychosocial research should be rejected as a meaningful way to study health and development in favour of gene–environment interaction. One example is a UK/New Zealand study of the effect of childhood maltreatment on a polymorphism of the MAOA gene, which is associated with violent behaviour in young adult males (Caspi, 2002). Very recent work on epigenetics has argued that the environment can actually shape genetic expression. Thus, DNA methylation is an epigenetic event that affects cell function by altering gene expression. Animal studies in Canada have shown that early life maternal separation can result in a different genetically mediated expression of traits and behaviour (Meaney, 2001). Whilst this latter phenomenon has not been tested in humans, the direction of investigation is to emphasize socio-environmental factors as a driver for a subsequent biological change with implications for disease and disorder.

Attachment Theory: Attachment frameworks bring together a range of social experiences to influence the lifetime risk of a disorder (both physical and mental), through a poor ability to relate to others and the absence of social support (Cassidy and Shaver, 1999). This framework has been adopted internationally, with studies emerging from around the world. It has been shown that early parenting experience leads to changes in the individual's cognitive templates which then determine their responses to making close relationships. Whereas a secure style is adaptive, those insecure styles denoting anxious or avoidant characteristics give rise to different types of difficulty in relating to others. Such styles are known to be associated with a range of psychological disorders (1999) but are also being investigated in Canada and the USA in relation to physical illnesses such as diabetes (Ciechanowski et al., 2002) and service-use issues (Maunder, 2009). However, attachment style is also shown to be associated with cultural factors and social class, as indeed is its genesis in parenting behaviour, showing Attachment Theory to have sociological as well as psychological underpinnings.

Resilience: Whilst the concept of resilience was first investigated in the 1980s, based on the seminal work of Norman Garmezy and Michael Rutter and colleagues in the USA and UK, it has now taken a more central role in health research because of important preventative implications. Resilience approaches provide explanations for why individuals who have experienced disadvantage do not succumb to disorder. These explanations focus on the presence of positive social and psychological experiences in addition to adversity (Rutter, 2007). Within resilience approaches, the relevant psychosocial factors include: social support, a secure attachment style, a high IQ, and religious belief. Benign economic environments are also considered.

The challenges for future investigation include improved measurement adapted for use in the large samples required for investigating multiple factors in different disorders, the identification of causes of time trends in changes in psychosocial risks and their effects, the delineation of a lifetime liability to poorer health outcomes and understanding an individual susceptibility to illness, including genetic influences. Such approaches need to incorporate sociological themes that emphasize the importance of socio-economic status, cultural factors, and how these impact on lifestyle or, perhaps more significantly, life chances. Thus, there is still important research which needs to be done on the role of psychosocial factors in health. Undoubtedly, investigating the protective mechanisms that can *promote* health and heighten resilience is crucial given that health services seek to encourage healthy lifestyles in the expressed hope of decreasing illness incidence or chronicity. However, health and illness need to be recognized as not only involving individual 'choices' or behaviours but also as being a function of (dis)advantage in people's social contexts and circumstances.

See also: *Social Class; Material and Cultural Factors; Life Events; Geneticization*

REFERENCES

Bifulco, A. and Moran, P. (1998) *Wednesday's Child: Research into Women's Experience of Neglect and Abuse in Childhood and Adult Depression*. London and New York: Routledge.

Caspi, A. (2002) 'Role of genotype in the cycle of violence in maltreated children', *Science*, 297: 851–4.

Cassidy, J. and Shaver, P.R. (eds) (1999) *Handbook of Attachment: Theory, Research, and Clinical Applications*. New York: The Guilford Press.

Ciechanowski, P.S., Walker, E.A., Katon, W.J. and Russo, J.E. (2002) 'Attachment theory: a model for health care utilization and somatization', *Psychosomatic Medicine*, 64: 660–7.

Graham, H. (2009) *Unequal Lives: Health and Socioeconomic Inequalities*. Maidenhead: Open University.

Leserman, J., Drossman, D.A., Li, Z., Toomey, T.C. and Hu, Y.J.B. (1996) 'Sexual and physical abuse history in gastroenterology practice: how types of abuse impact health status', *Psychosomatic Medicine*, 58 (1): 4–15.

Maunder, R.G. (2009) 'Assessing patterns of adult attachment in medical patients', *General Hospital Psychiatry*, 31: 123–30.

Meaney, M. (2001) 'Maternal care, gene expression and the transmission of individual differences in stress reactivity across generations', *Annual Review of Neuroscience*, 24: 1161–92.

Plomin, R., Asbury, K. and Dunn, J. (2001) 'Why are children in the same family so different? Non-shared environment a decade later', *Canadian Journal of Psychiatry*, 46: 225–33.

Rich, E., Monaghan, L.F. and Aphramor, L. (eds) (2011) *Debating Obesity: Critical Perspectives*. Basingstoke: Palgrave Macmillan.

Rutter, M. (2007) 'Resilience, competence, coping', *Child Abuse & Neglect*, 31: 205–9.

Selye, H. (1956) *The Stress of Life*. New York: McGraw-Hill.

Antonia Bifulco

> *An environmental circumstance indicating change, often stressful, that has an identifiable onset and ending, and carries a potential for altering an individual's present state of mental or physical well-being.*

There is a long history to the linkage between life events and poor health outcomes. As early as the seventeenth century, Robert Burton described how melancholia was precipitated by environmental adversities, including interpersonal losses. Such observations began to be more systematically documented from the mid-twentieth century onwards. Specifically, clusters of life events were noted to occur prior to the onset of physical and mental illness. Adolf Meyer was the first modern practitioner to argue that life events relate to psychopathology, developing a chart system for recording the temporal association of life experiences and disorder. A substantial amount of research in the 1970s and 1980s in the area of psychiatric epidemiology, allied to medical sociology, examined the full potential of life events as social causes of illness, both physical and mental. The initial conceptualization of the event–illness link emphasized *change* in life circumstances producing stress on the *physical* system to affect its dynamic steady state and increase the likelihood of ill health. Subsequent investigation, however, emphasized the *stressfulness* of events in terms of the social and psychological threat attached and the *cognitive* states mediating between an event, its physiological impact and ill health. The most recent developments have been in examining genetic bases for susceptibility to life events in psychiatric disorder.

The study of life events has progressed furthest in the field of mental health, their role first identified in schizophrenic relapse, but then developed in relation to depression and anxiety states. The research by George Brown and colleagues into social factors in mental health was responsible for many of the developments in measurement and conceptualization that have ensued (Brown and Harris, 1978). This research was subsequently extended to examine the role of life events in physical illness (Brown and Harris, 1989).

An important observation concerning life events is that while common mental disorders such as depression frequently occur shortly after the experience of a severe life event, the majority of individuals who suffer severe life events do not become ill. This has led to five interrelated lines of investigation.

First, the *characteristics of events* which have most potency for causing a disorder have been specified so that the focus of an investigation can be narrowed to those with the highest subsequent rates of illness. Specific types of events which relate to particular illnesses or disorder have been identified (for example, 'loss' to depression and 'danger' to anxiety). At times there is a match between negative aspects of events and the prior commitment, goal attainment or coping endeavours of the individual. Thus, for example, a severe life event in a domain of prior high commitment (such as losing a job in the context of a marked work commitment; or failing a professional exam after sustained effort) will carry an increased risk of affective disorders occurring such as depression. In addition, such events around employment have a greater impact on males that is associated with gender roles and identity. Indeed, when considering unemployment, gender differences in mortality are very pronounced (Roelfs et al., 2011). Thus, what appears to be a similar event on a checklist, can be experienced differently by individuals depending on their context and social divisions.

A second line of investigation has identified those individuals with a greater *susceptibility* to life events. In the 1980s and 1990s the focus of the investigation was on personal vulnerability characteristics – both ongoing and in early life – which would render an individual more susceptible, particularly in relation to depression. Vulnerability factors (such as the lack of a close confidant, the presence of three or more children, the loss of a mother in childhood and the lack of employment) that were identified early on were argued to undermine self-esteem which, in the face of a severe life event, resulted in depression (Brown and Harris, 1978). Further prospective investigation has shown the attributes of such roles to be critical. Thus, negative relationships (including conflict with a partner or child) are associated with low self-esteem and together interact with a severe life event in creating the optimal conditions for depression.

Third, an individual's *response* to an event in terms of appraisal and coping has also proved critical in determining whether a disorder ensues. Researchers writing in the early 1980s, such as Richard Lazarus and Susan Folkman on stress appraisal, and Leonard Pearlin and Carmi Schooler in the late 1970s on types of coping, differentiated phases of response to and coping with stress, such as through an emotion-focused versus a problem-focused response. Findings show that better health outcomes are associated with problem solving and a positive appraisal of coping options following a life event. Worse outcomes are related to coping behaviours such as self-blame, pessimism and denial. Vulnerable individuals typically exhibit poorer coping behaviours in response to severe life events, but the characteristics of the events themselves can also influence people's responses (Bifulco and Brown, 1996).

A fourth line of investigation considers the importance *of life events and difficulties throughout the lifecourse*. Events at different points in early life can influence illness or disorder at later ages; for example, separation from one's mother in childhood, or losing a child as an adult. Such events can have lifelong implications. Early negative experiences of parenting can also lead to higher rates of life events in later life. Although life events are defined by their discrete/acute occurrence, they are frequently related to longer-term stressful circumstances which can precede or follow the event. There is evidence that events arising from chronic difficulties have a greater association with the onset of depressive illness and create a greater propensity towards the chronicity of disorder.

Finally, debate has centred on the *origin of life events*. Life events are not evenly distributed, either by individual or by gender, family, age, socio-economic group or location. As elaborated in other entries in this section of the book, much can be attributed to social class and material deprivation on a global scale, resulting in increased numbers of stressors and lower resources to reduce their impact. However, as one might anticipate under the current conditions of neoliberalization, explanations have also been sought in terms of individuals putatively creating their own high-risk environments by 'generating' events increasingly over the lifecourse. This is effectively an element of victim-blaming which has not, on the whole, been employed by medical sociologists. The association of life events and difficulties with psychiatric disorder has been shown to hold throughout the lifecourse, where it patently makes little sense to blame autonomous individuals. Studies of the lifespan show a long-term trajectory of influence, with childhood adversity relating to greatly increased rates of lifetime difficulties and recurrent disorders such as depression (Bifulco et al., 2000).

Certain methodological issues have dogged the study of life events and illness outcomes and have required sophisticated measurement and prospective study. This is to circumvent the problems of reporting bias, uncertainty about the timing of an event in relation to the onset of a disorder, and determining the context of events in order to ascertain their likely stressful potential. Such errors are more likely with self-report checklists of life events. Semi-structured interviews were thus developed which encouraged narrative accounts of events which, together with extensive probing questions, elicited the full social context of life events and their timing and sequence in relation to a disorder (for example, the Life Events and Difficulties Schedule (LEDS): see Brown and Harris, 1978). The characteristics of these events were rated by the investigators, aided by manuals of precedent examples and consensus agreement to ensure reliability. Events found to provoke depressive disorder were those objectively assessed as involving a high threat or unpleasantness in the longer term, focused on the individual, and independent from the illness itself. The latter is important in avoiding circularity in terms of illness-related events being seen to bring about the disorder.

Research in this field has been through a fallow period in the last decade. The geneticization of disorder investigation in the UK and USA has meant that broader life events, social adversity and depression have no longer been a key focus of medical interest. Many genetic studies of psychiatric disorder and gene–environment interaction have ensued, for example, on clinical depression and the serotonin transporter gene (Caspi et al., 2010). Such studies include the extensive genetic profiling of large patient cohorts; however, for convenience and cost reasons these studies have used brief self-report checklists of the environment, with minimal measurement of social adversity. Unfortunately, such checklists are insensitive to the context of events and present stressors as single-dimensional occurrences (for example, divorces or illnesses), without paying attention to the particulars of an experience which can cover a range of threatening and stressful circumstances. Thus, in recent years psychiatric genetic studies, in focusing on the genetic contributions to mental illness, have tended to marginalize the importance of social adversity represented by life events and life stress. This went largely unremarked until recent reviews noted technical issues around the lack of replicability for key gene–environment interaction findings (Risch et al., 2009). Further commentary has pointed to the conceptualization and measurement of life events as a key factor in the failure of environmental factors to be shown to interact with genetic ones (Monroe and Reid, 2008; Uher, 2008). When studies of life events include the relevant social context and the likely meaning to the individual of the event, the more likely it is the gene–environment interaction will be found. This requires intensive measurement such as that described in the LEDS measure of Brown and Harris above, in order to avoid the high rate of false negatives (i.e. missed events) which result from limited self-report checklists. Obtaining the necessary details needed to uncover context is time intensive, though, as well as expensive and more difficult to undertake with the large sample numbers required for gene–environment studies. This has created something of a quandary in developing the field and exposed some of the biases inherent in the geneticization of the approach, which has been reductionist in relation to social adversity and psychiatric disorder. In order to solve these issues, there is a pressing need for the further development of sensitive in-depth measures of stress which can be administered to large samples, for example via the internet.

The importance of studying life events in illness is not purely to understand social causation but also to influence intervention. Life events can be both positive and negative. Positive events have been shown to aid in recovery from disorder. Help-seeking is also an important aspect, with support from close others at the time of a life event crisis showing protective effects for both the onset and chronicity of a disorder. Befriending interventions, which provide support in dealing with events and ongoing difficulties, have been shown to have a significant effect on recovery from a disorder. Cognitive Behaviour Therapy reportedly has similar positive effects, albeit under broader social structural conditions that shape and constrain such interventions. Thus, life events continue to be key components in both the disease and recovery process within a stratified world where numerous factors impact on health and illness.

See also: *Social Class; Ageing and the Lifecourse; Geneticization*

REFERENCES

Bifulco, A., Bernazzani, O., Moran, P.M. and Ball, C. (2000) 'Lifetime stressors and recurrent depression: preliminary findings of the Adult Life Phase Interview (ALPHI)', *Social Psychiatry and Psychiatric Epidemiology*, 35: 264–75.

Bifulco, A. and Brown, G.W. (1996) 'Cognitive coping response to crises and onset of depression', *Social Psychiatry and Psychiatric Epidemiology*, 31: 163–72.

Brown, G.W. and Harris, T.O. (1978) *Social Origins of Depression: A Study of Psychiatric Disorder in Women*. London and New York: Tavistock.

Brown, G.W. and Harris, T.O. (1989) *Life Events and Illness*. New York: The Guilford Press.

Caspi, A., Hariri, A.R., Holmes, A., Uher, R. and Moffitt, T.E. (2010) 'Genetic sensitivity to the environment: the case of serotonin transporter gene (5-HTTT) and its implications for studying complex diseases and traits', *American Journal of Psychiatry*, 167 (5): 509–27.

Monroe, S.M. and Reid, M. (2008) 'Gene–environment interactions in depression research: genetic polymorphisms and life-stress procedures', *Psychological Science*, 19 (10): 947–56.

Risch, N., Herrell, R., Lehner, T., Liang, K.-Y., Eaves, L., Hoh, J., Griem, A., Kovacs, M., Ott, J. and Merikangas, K.R. (2009) 'Interaction between the serotonintransporter gene (5-HTTLPR), stressful life events, and risk of depression: a meta-analysis', *Journal of the American Medical Association*, 301 (23): 2462–71.

Roelfs, D.J., Shor, E., Davidson, K.W. and Schwartz, J.E. (2011) 'Losing life and livelihood: a systematic review and meta-analysis of unemployment and all-cause mortality', *Social Science & Medicine*, 72 (6): 840–54.

Uher, R. (2008) 'The case for gene–environment interactions in psychiatry', *Current Opinion in Psychiatry*, 21 (4): 318–21.

Antonia Bifulco

Neoliberal Globalization and Health Inequalities

> *Neoliberalism is a mode of political-economic organization characterized by the deregulation of markets, privatization, the removal of capital controls, cuts in social welfare and the abandonment of full employment policies, while globalization is a process of integration of national economies and societies into a world system through 'movements of goods and services, capital, technology and (to a lesser extent) labour' (Jenkins, 2004: 1).*

How has the increased integration of national economies and societies into the global market (globalization) affected health and health inequalities? Although globalization is often conceptualized as a multi-dimensional process that includes social, economic and political factors, it has mainly been driven by economics. In particular, globalization has been driven and shaped by policy reforms promoted by international financial institutions (IFIs) such as the International Monetary Fund (IMF), the World Bank, and more recently the World Trade Organization (WTO), and the governments of wealthier nations (and the economic interests they represent). The Bank and the Fund are often referred to as the Bretton Woods Institutions, after the location of the 1944 conference where they were established along with the General Agreement on Tariffs and Trade (GATT), the precursor of the WTO.

The end of the Second World War was followed by a period sometimes described as the golden era of capitalism, inspired by a Keynesian approach to development that incorporated government interventions, capital controls, fixed exchange rates, full employment policies, and the expansion of social protection. Keynesianism guided international economic integration until the 1970s, a decade that began with the abandonment of the convertibility of US dollars to gold in

1971 and ended with the rise to power of Margaret Thatcher in the UK and Ronald Reagan in the USA. Subsequently, and in response to the shifting political climate, the IFIs embraced a new model of development characterized by deregulation, privatization, the removal of capital controls, floating exchange rates, cuts in social welfare, and the abandonment of full employment policies. This new model of development is referred to as neoliberalism, and today represents the conventional wisdom in development economics. As chief World Bank economist (subsequently US Treasury Secretary and president of Harvard University) Lawrence Summers claimed: 'The laws of economics are like the laws of engineering. One set of laws work everywhere' (quoted by Ellman, 2000: 197). Although the 2008 global financial and economic crisis has led to some moderation in such claims, they still underpin most of the economic policy recommendations emanating from the Bretton Woods Institutions, rich country governments, and the corporate world. For this reason, we refer to neoliberal globalization.

One approach to examining neoliberal globalization's effects on health and health equity compares health outcomes in countries ranked according to the different degree by which they have embraced specific reforms, such as trade liberalization. Feachem (2001) argued that 'globalization is good for your health' because countries that integrated more fully into the global economy, especially through trade liberalization, grew faster and were better able to reduce poverty and so improve health. Evidence cited to support such claims included the positive association between trade openness and life expectancy and studies indicating that countries defined as 'globalizers', whose ratio of trade to Gross Domestic Product (GDP) increased after 1980, grew faster than 'non-globalizers'. However, these 'non-globalizers' were already more integrated into the global economy at the start of the study period than were many of the 'globalizers' at the end of that same period. Moreover, the data on long-term trends on poverty reduction after the 1980s do not support the neoliberal position. Even before the economic crisis of 2008, worldwide progress towards poverty reduction was modest during a quarter-century (1981–2005) in which the value of the world's economic product quadrupled. World Bank researchers estimated that 1.4 billion people, in the year 2005, were living in extreme poverty (defined as an income of $1.25/day or less, in 2005 dollars, adjusted for purchasing power parity). This represented a decline of 500 million since 1981, but on a worldwide basis that decline was accounted for entirely by China's fast growth. In the developing world outside China wherever people escaped extreme poverty, a comparable number fell into poverty somewhere else. Based on a higher poverty line of $2.50/day, the number of people living in poverty worldwide increased from 2.7 billion to 3.1 billion, with the reductions in China offset by substantial increases in India and sub-Saharan Africa (Chen and Ravallion, 2008). In other words, when the benefits of growth 'trickle down' at all, they do so slowly and unevenly.

Although worldwide average life expectancy has risen consistently since the 1950s, the overall improvement after the 1980s was much slower than that experienced between 1950 and 1980. A slower improvement in life expectancy mirrored an overall slowing of annual Gross National Product (GNP) growth per capita, from 2.6 per cent during the period 1960–1979 to 1.0 per cent between 1980 and 1998

(Cornia, 2001). After a sustained period of global health convergence between countries in the 1960s and 1970s, a pattern of divergence began in the 1980s (Moser et al., 2005), largely as a result of falling life expectancies in sub-Saharan Africa and Eastern Europe, and in spite of the large health improvements in East and South Asia. At the national level, financial deregulation, privatization and trade liberalization have been associated with higher poverty rates; poorer health outcomes after financial crises; and increased exposure to risk factors such as smoking and deteriorating diets. In fast-growing economies like those of China and Vietnam, the commodification of health care that has accompanied neoliberal domestic policies has increased its cost and reduced access for much of the population.

Starting circa 1980, the World Bank and IMF offered loans allowing developing countries to reschedule their external debts, but demanded in return a package of policies involving domestic marketization and a lowering of the barriers to imports and foreign investment. The effects of these 'structural adjustment' programmes provide an especially important body of evidence about the impact of neoliberal globalization on developing countries. Although the Bank has claimed that 'adjuster countries' generally succeed in improving health, education, and social welfare programmes compared to 'non-adjusters', the majority of studies show negative health effects from policy reforms comprising structural adjustment, which consistently increase economic inequality and insecurity. IMF programmes have also been found to be linked to poorer macroeconomic performance, lower public expenditure on health and education (as countries are told to use donor funds for paying down debt and building foreign exchange reserves), and a higher prevalence of diseases such as tuberculosis.

Neoliberal globalization has widened health inequalities between and within countries. On some measures in England and Wales, the health disparities between rich and poor are now wider than at any point since the 1920s (Thomas et al., 2010). Increasing economic inequality is among the most important candidate explanations. In spite of claims that globalization and neoliberal economic policies have reduced inequality, a thorough review by Wade (2004) found that on most of the inequality measures used in such studies, world income inequality has been rising during the past two to three decades. Wade also added that analyses indicating that income inequality has been falling were entirely influenced by China which, far from being an orthodox 'globalizer', initially adopted almost none of the neoliberal policies advocated by international institutions. A recent paper recalculating global wealth inequalities with updated data to 2009 showed that the richest decile of the world's people receive 57 per cent of global income, substantially more than the previously estimated 50 per cent allocation (Milanovic, 2009). According to a 2008 World Institute for Development Economics Research study, the richest 2 per cent of adults in the world own half of global household wealth while 50 per cent of the world's adults own just 1 per cent of global wealth (Davies et al., 2008). In the UK, the post-1997 Labour government conspicuously failed to halt the increase of inequality begun by the economic policies of the Thatcher era.

Although the interpretation of findings is still subject to methodological dispute, two recent systematic reviews agreed that more equal societies exhibit better *average* health outcomes than less equal societies (Lynch et al., 2005; Wilkinson and

Pickett, 2006). A recent cross-national analysis showed that income inequality explains about one-eighth of the cross-national variability in life expectancy in societies where the income per capita is comparable (Babones, 2008). The most commonly proposed mechanisms by which income inequality affects health are material deprivation (Lynch et al., 2005) and psychosocial factors (Marmot and Wilkinson, 2001). These lines of explanation are not mutually exclusive. Income inequality is related to health through poverty and limited social provisions: countries with high income inequality are often characterized by a higher prevalence of poverty, lower levels of education, and lower public investments in health and social protection. However, negative effects on health do not result only from poverty and a lack of material resources. High income inequality is also associated with multiple sources of stress, which has many adverse physiological effects, including mental illness and a tendency to engage in risk behaviours.

In summary, in the early post-Second World War era high-income societies found a compromise between the search for profit and the need to avoid exaggerated inequalities in economic and political power. Relatively decent wages, social security and full employment as policy objectives were viewed as necessary to offset market-driven inequities within national borders, although not among countries. Since the late 1970s, international economic integration and domestic neoliberal policies have been presented as the only feasible route to development and prosperity. The effects of these policies in terms of health and health inequalities have been disappointing, if not actively destructive. In 2008, more than thirty years of financial liberalization resulted in the worst global economic crisis since the Great Depression, increasing global unemployment by 34 million and pushing 50–100 million people into severe poverty (ILO-IMF, 2010). Today, working people around the world are being asked to foot the bill for a crisis caused by the financial sector. Policy responses are outside the scope of this entry, but it is worth noting the importance of reforms that prioritize human rights as a counterweight to the power of the global marketplace (Schrecker et al., 2010).

See also: *Material and Cultural Factors; Psychosocial Factors*

REFERENCES

Babones, S. (2008) 'Income inequality and population health: correlation and causality', *Social Science & Medicine*, 66: 1614–26.

Chen, S. and Ravallion, M. (2008) 'The Developing World Is Poorer Than We Thought, But No Less Successful in the Fight against Poverty'. *Policy Research Working Paper 4703*. Washington, DC: World Bank.

Cornia, A. (2001) 'Globalization and health: results and options', *Bulletin of the World Health Organization*, 79: 834–41.

Davies, J., Sandström, S., Shorrocks, A. and Wolff, E. (2008) 'The world distribution of household wealth', in J. Davies (ed.), *Personal Wealth from a Global Perspective*. Oxford: Oxford University Press.

Ellman, M. (2000) 'Transition economies', in H-J. Chang (ed.), *Rethinking Development Economics*. London: Anthem Press.

Feachem, R. (2001) 'Globalisation is good for your health, mostly', *BMJ*, 323: 504–6.

ILO-IMF (2010) *The Challenges of Growth, Employment and Social Cohesion.* Oslo: Joint International Labour Organization–International Monetary Fund Conference in Cooperation with the Office of the Prime Minister of Norway. Online: http://www.osloconference2010.org/discussionpaper.pdf

Jenkins, R. (2004) 'Globalization, production, employment and poverty: debates and evidence', *Journal of International Development,* 16: 1–12.

Lynch, G., Smith, G., Harper, S., Hillemeier, M., Ross, N., Kaplan, G. and Wolfson, M. (2005) 'Is income inequality a determinant of population health? Part 1: A systematic review', *Milbank Quarterly,* 82: 1074–80.

Marmot, M. and Wilkinson, R. (2001) 'Psychosocial and material pathways in the relation between income and health: a response to Lynch et al.', *BMJ,* 322: 1200.

Milanovic, B. (2009) 'Global inequality recalculated: the effect of new 2005 PPP estimates on global inequality', *Policy Research Working Paper 5061.* Washington, DC: World Bank.

Moser, K., Shkolnikov, V. and Leon, D. (2005) 'World mortality 1995–2000: divergence replaces convergence from the late 1980s', *Bulletin of the World Health Organization,* 83: 202–9.

Schrecker, T., Chapman, A., Labonté, R. and De Vogli, R. (2010) 'Advancing health equity in the global marketplace: how human rights can help', *Social Science & Medicine,* 71: 1520–6.

Thomas, B., Dorling, D. and Smith, G. (2010) 'Inequalities in premature mortality in Britain: observational study from 1921 to 2007', *BMJ,* 341: c3639.

Wade, R.H. (2004) 'Is globalisation reducing poverty and inequality?' *World Development,* 32: 567–89.

Wilkinson, R. and Pickett, K. (2006) 'Income inequality and population health: a review and explanation of the evidence', *Social Science & Medicine,* 62: 1768–78.

FURTHER READING

Birn, A-E., Pillay, L. and Holtz, T. (2009) *Textbook of International Health,* 3rd edn. Oxford: Oxford University Press.

Labonté, R., Schrecker, T., Packer, C. and Runnels, V. (2009) *Globalization and Health: Pathways, Evidence and Policy.* New York: Routledge (selected chapters are available at http://www.GKN-Routledge-book).

Roberto De Vogli, Ted Schrecker and Ronald Labonté

Ageing and the Lifecourse

Ageing in humans is a multi-dimensional process of accumulating physical, psychological and social changes across a person's life-span. The lifecourse is a sequence of significant social and biological life events that occur throughout a person's life-span.

Ageing is the process of growing older. While it is a universal biological process, among humans ageing also has important social and cultural dimensions. The term 'ageing' incorporates different concepts such as 'chronological ageing' (how old a person is measured in terms of time since birth), 'biological ageing' (the changes in a person's physical state that accompany chronological ageing), 'functional age' (defined on the basis of functional measures of daily living), and 'social ageing' (social expectations about how people should behave or appear as they grow older).

Ageing in humans thus refers to a multi-dimensional process of accumulating physical, psychological and social changes across a person's life-span, not just in later life. In general, ageing in early life is referred to as growth and development, while in later life it is commonly used to refer to life processes of decline and loss. However, there is considerable potential for physical, mental and social development even in later life, such as through adult learning activities.

As ageing is a multi-dimensional process, there are a number of ways of measuring it. At a basic level, chronological age is measured by units of time. Within biomedical sciences, biological age can be measured in terms of processes related to the ability for cells to divide. Functional age can be calculated on the basis of a lack of disease and disability as well as in terms of high cognitive, physical, psychological and social functioning.

'Social age' does not have such clear or established measures of ageing. There is a greater focus on qualitative descriptions of ageing. This makes measurement more contested because of the great variability between societies and cultures in the social markers of ageing. Some argue that 'being old' is a modern construct, which was previously conceptualized in terms of declining health, resources and autonomy (Johnson, 2005). Roles such as grandparenthood could be more important in terms of feeling or being perceived as 'old' than chronological age. The body, in terms of appearance or physiological capacity, is also a key marker of social ageing. For professional ballet dancers, the onset of professional old age is markedly early, somewhere in the mid- to late twenties, due to increasing difficulties with maintaining peak physiological abilities (Wainwright and Turner, 2006). For women in some cultures, perceptions of being old are strongly related to their fertility status. Rather than measuring social ageing, some sociologists have focused attention on the experiences of ageing, as exemplified in concepts like the 'mask of ageing' which explore the mismatch between an older person's external appearance and their inner self (Featherstone and Hepworth, 1991).

Despite such differences in the meanings of ageing and old age, there are some common and significant biological and social life events that occur throughout a person's life-span. These include: birth, growth, learning, education, puberty, adolescence, partnership or marriage, employment, separation, functional loss and death. An individual experiences social ageing through a sequence of these social and biological life events, collectively referred to as the lifecourse. Again, research interest in the lifecourse transcends any specific academic discipline, though biomedical approaches have tended to dominate, albeit with increasing attention being given to social factors (for example, the impact of poverty and inequality).

The study of the long-term effects on chronic disease risk of physical and social exposure during gestation, childhood, adolescence, young adulthood and later adult life has been referred to as a lifecourse approach to chronic disease epidemiology (Ben-Shlomo and Kuh, 2002). These studies investigate how biological, behavioural and psychosocial pathways operate across an individual's lifecourse, as well as across generations, to affect their health later on in life, especially in terms of the risk of chronic disease. This lifecourse perspective is now being extended beyond the study of aetiology of chronic disease to include the determinants of ageing.

There are two main conceptual models of how social and biological factors over the lifecourse affect chronic disease risk and ageing – the critical period model and the accumulation model (Ben-Shlomo and Kuh, 2002). *The critical period model* highlights the importance of a specific period of the lifecourse, during which exposure to risk results in lasting or lifelong effects on the structure or function of organs, tissues and body systems. This is also known as 'biological programming'. One of the examples of this model of the lifecourse is the 'fetal origins of adult disease' hypothesis (Barker, 1992). Poor growth in utero leads to a variety of chronic disorders such as cardiovascular disease, non-insulin dependent diabetes, and hypertension. This model argues that a critical period for later life, cardiovascular risk and successful ageing is during the stage of fetal development, when exposures to risk permanently alter anatomical structures and a variety of metabolic systems. Critical period models of ageing can also refer to periods of the lifecourse which emphasize successful social ageing processes such as the socialization of children or success in primary education.

In contrast to the critical period model, *the accumulation model* suggests that risk factors that damage health or impede successful ageing occur throughout the lifecourse and are not restricted to any particular period of time. These risk factors tend to accumulate gradually between birth and death. While such risk factors to health and successful ageing may be separate and independent of each other, most of the time they cluster together in socially patterned ways. For example, children living in disadvantaged social circumstances are more likely to have been exposed to passive smoking and other environmental pollutants, poor nutrition during growth and poor educational opportunities. In addition to the clustering of these risk factors in disadvantaged social groups, these factors may also increase the risk of poor health through probabilistic causal pathways or 'chains of risk'. For example, leaving school without any qualifications earlier on in the lifecourse increases the likelihood of unemployment, which in turn increases the risk of partnership dissolution, leading to poor psychosocial outcomes.

Some models of the lifecourse also divide old age into two stages: the Third Age, a period of creativity and personal fulfilment after retirement from work but before infirmity (Laslett, 1989); and the Fourth Age, a period characterized by illness, physical and mental decline, and death (Whittington, 2008). However, these concepts are highly specific to particular cohorts in some countries and, even within these cohorts, there is considerable heterogeneity in ageing experiences with many individuals never experiencing a Third Age. Others have criticized the concept of the Third Age in terms of its elitist values and lack of empirical evidence (Bury, 2000).

Population ageing is the process by which older individuals come to represent a larger proportion of the total population of a country or community. Population ageing is a process that started in more developed countries during the twentieth century, but is now apparent in most of the developing world as well. Increasing life expectancy in later life is one of the indicators of population ageing. The demographic determinants of population ageing follow a process known as the 'demographic transition' in which mortality and then fertility decline from higher to lower levels. While relatively low fertility was a consistent feature of many developed countries for much of the twentieth century, survival to older ages improved considerably during that period (Grundy, 1996). Not only are more people surviving to old age, but once they reach older ages, they also tend to live longer.

Such population ageing results in a gender imbalance as men on average do not live as long as women. The majority of the elderly population is female, especially amongst the oldest age groups. While women in most societies are more socioeconomically disadvantaged compared to men, older women in particular are more likely to have poorer health, have fewer socioeconomic resources, be widowed, and have less access to support from relatives, and thus are more reliant on state, welfare and charity services (Arber and Ginn, 1994).

There are a number of social theories about the consequences of ageing, both for individuals and for populations. *Disengagement theory* suggests that as people get older, they separate themselves or disengage from active roles in society relating to work and the family (Cumming et al., 1961). *Activity theory*, in contrast to the disengagement theory, suggests that activity in later life is the key to successful ageing. One example is the 'use it or lose it' hypothesis which suggests that effortful mental activity is required to prevent cognitive decline in older age groups (Coyle, 2003). *The selectivity theory* of ageing combines disengagement and activity theories by suggesting disengagement may benefit some older people, while activity may benefit others. *Continuity theory* suggests that older adults will try to maintain continuity in their lifestyle, activities, behaviours and relationships by adapting strategies that are connected to their past experiences (Atchley, 1989).

Population ageing is often framed as having a big impact on society through economic and political processes that putatively create burdens for 'society more generally'. According to such reasoning, which has increasing political salience amidst cuts to public welfare spending, the elderly are labelled economically inactive and deemed to have greater need for welfare provision (such as health care, social services and welfare benefits) than younger populations. Hence, even though older people have contributed and may continue to contribute to 'society' in many important ways (including economically vital activities that are not remunerated, such as unpaid childcare), there are common concerns about the economic costs of population ageing and whether the neoliberal state can afford to maintain and increase its welfare provision for an increasingly older population. However, as indicated above, this conceptualization of the elderly as dependent and 'costly' is problematic and can be questioned on numerous grounds. Indeed, economic 'dependency' among older people may itself be an artefact of government policy. Most states try to fulfil the economic objectives of low unemployment through the removal of large numbers of older individuals from the labour market (through early retirement policies), despite their ability to continue working (Townsend, 1981). Hence this group of post-retired individuals may not be dependent or 'costly' if they were allowed to continue working.

One of the causes and consequences of characterizing the elderly as dependent and costly is ageism. Negative *stereotyping* of and *discrimination* against individuals or groups because of their age is often indirect and implicit, as seen in a general lack of priority for older people's needs in health and social care (Roberts et al., 2002). Despite their growing numbers, older people often experience a kind of social and cultural invisibility. Certainly, in Britain, old age pensioners are more likely to be affected by poverty than paid workers (Ogg, 2005). And in a context of neoliberal globalization more generally, the potential for the marginalization of older populations by the state and market remains a significant threat to their well-being.

See also: *Social Class; Gender; Material and Cultural Factors; Life Events*

REFERENCES

Arber, S. and Ginn, J. (1994) 'Women and aging', *Reviews in Clinical Gerontology*, 4: 349–58.
Atchley, R.C. (1989) 'A continuity theory of normal aging', *The Gerontologist*, 29 (2): 183–90.
Barker, D.J.P. (1992) *Fetal and Infant Origins of Adult Disease*. London: BMJ Books.
Ben-Shlomo, Y. and Kuh, D. (2002) 'A life course approach to chronic disease epidemiology: conceptual models, empirical challenges and interdisciplinary perspectives', *International Journal of Epidemiology*, 31: 285–93.
Bury, M. (2000) 'Health, ageing and the lifecourse', in S.J. Williams, J. Gabe and M. Calnan (eds), *Health, Medicine and Society: Key Theories, Future Agendas*. London: Routledge.
Coyle, J.T. (2003) 'Use it or lose it: do effortful mental activities protect against dementia?', *New England Journal of Medicine*, 348 (25): 2489–90.
Cumming, E., Henry, W.E. and Damianopoulos, E. (1961) 'A formal statement of disengagement theory', in E. Cumming and W.E. Henry (eds), *Growing Old: The Process of Disengagement*. New York: Basic Books.
Featherstone, M. and Hepworth, M. (1991) 'The mask of ageing and the postmodern life course', in M. Featherstone, M. Hepworth and B.S. Turner (eds), *The Body: Social Process and Cultural Theory*. London: Sage.
Grundy, E. (1996) 'Population ageing in Europe', in D. Coleman (ed.), *Europe's Population in the 1990s*. New York: Oxford University Press.
Johnson, M. (2005) 'Ageing in the modern world', in *The Cambridge Handbook of Age and Ageing*. Cambridge and New York: Cambridge University Press.
Laslett, P. (1989) *A Fresh Map of Life: The Emergence of the Third Age*. London: Weidenfield and Nicolson.
Ogg, J. (2005) 'Social exclusion and insecurity among older Europeans: the influence of welfare regimes', *Ageing & Society*, 25: 69–90.
Roberts, E., Robinson, J. and Seymour, L. (2002) *Old Habits Die Hard: Tackling Age Discrimination in Health and Social Care*. London: King's Fund.
Townsend, P. (1981) 'The structured dependency of the elderly: a creation of social policy in the twentieth century', *Ageing & Society*, 1: 5–28.

Wainwright, S.P. and Turner, B.S. (2006) '"Just crumbling to bits"? An exploration of the body, ageing, injury and career in classical ballet dancers', *Sociology*, 40 (2): 237–55.

Whittington, F.J. (2008) 'The potential of retirement', *The Gerontologist*, 48 (3): 401–4.

Tarani Chandola

Social Capital

> Social capital is generally defined as the social resources that accrue to individuals by virtue of their membership of informal and formal social networks, and which may impact on their life chances and health.

Those who write about social capital do not always agree about how the concept might be defined. The construct involves components that are not always differentiated: the mechanisms that generate social capital; the types of resource that are made available; the outcome of possessing those resources; and the type of social network in which resources arise and are given material effect (Portes, 1998). Moreover, there is a distinction in the literature between those who describe social capital as a capacity of individuals to mobilize resources, and those who see it as a collective property or social good, for example, when researchers refer to the 'stock' of social capital in communities or society at large.

Regarding health, the main focus has been on social capital as a feature of communities and this has been used to explain the observed differences between the degree of income inequality in a given society and levels of mortality (Kawachi et al., 1997). The definition of social capital in these studies is taken from Putnam, a political scientist, who conceives of social capital as a public good or 'civic' property of communities that inheres in 'features of social organization such as networks, norms, and social trust that facilitate action and cooperation for mutual benefit' (1995: 67). In Putnam's concept of social capital, we see a clear lineage to Durkheim's classical sociological theory of social integration and social cohesion, which emphasizes the network of ties between individuals that function to bind individuals to society, providing them with a moral compass, regulatory norms and social supports to guide social action. Putnam's theory equates the 'stock' of social capital in a given community with levels of civic participation. This is measured by a number of indicators, including: participation in voluntary organizations; democratic engagement (captured by newspaper consumption and voting); and individuals' expressions of interpersonal and institutional trust. These are the relational aspects of social capital.

social capital

41

Social capital also takes different structural forms. Gitell and Vidal (1998) distinguish between what they term *bonding social capital* and what Putnam (1995) calls *bridging social capital*. The former refers to informal networks such as family ties where members who share the same beliefs are bound together through the norms of trust and reciprocity. This type of social capital functions as both a form of social control and social support. The latter form of social capital denotes the formal but looser network of ties between different social groups generally of the same social status that function to promote community and civic participation. Szreter and Woolcock (2004) further distinguish *linking social capital* as the ties that connect social groups across status and power differentials, for example, when people interact with formal institutions to access strategic resources. The manifest function of this type of social capital is to promote institutional trust. As Szreter and Woolcock (2004: 655) explain: 'especially in poor communities, it is the nature and extent (or lack thereof) of respectful and trusting ties to representatives of formal institutions – e.g. banks, law enforcement officers, social workers, health care providers – that has a major bearing on their welfare'. They also note that these further conceptual distinctions of the structure of social networks were prompted by Putnam's own observation that not all forms of network promote norms of trust that benefit the community as a whole.

Let us now consider the various explanations of how social capital, as a structural property of communities, may impact on health. According to Putnam (1995), it is voluntary association and the density of interactions (frequency and intensity) with and between networks of association that protect health. The overall stock of the network of ties that bind individuals to each other (and hence the collective) through relations of reciprocity and mutual trust are the very foundations of social support. Social support has a direct bearing on health by modulating the psychological impact of social stressors that compromise health. The civic component of social capital is claimed to have an indirect impact on population health. The more people are involved in social organizations and the greater the frequency of the interactions between social organizations across formal and informal networks, the more they are said to engage with political decisions that impact on health and to collectively demand better services (Kawachi et al., 1999).

The evidence in support of the direct and indirect impact of social capital is based on large-scale, population and health survey data. In the USA, Kawachi et al.'s (1999) findings demonstrate a strong statistical relationship between state levels of social capital and individuals' self-reported health when socio-economic status and individual risk factors are controlled for. However, such findings are not replicated in other research. In a similar but more extended study conducted in Canada, Veenstra's (2000) findings do not support either the direct or indirect social capital/health hypotheses. In this study the strongest statistical indicator for self-reported health is socio-economic status. In a more recent nation-wide study conducted in Norway, Dahl and Malmberg-Heimonen (2010) found that none of the social capital variables that they measured had any significant statistical association with longstanding illness. Also, contra Kawachi et al. (1999), they conclude that social capital does not mediate the impact of socio-economic position on health. Their study did, however, find that two indices of the social capital measure – namely 'neighbourhood satisfaction' and 'general trust' – were associated with self-reported health.

Another body of literature, which is considered to lend weight to the social capital thesis, is the social epidemiological studies of Wilkinson and colleagues (Wilkinson, 1996; Wilkinson and Pickett, 2009). This work is important because its analysis of the problem of health inequalities (and social problems more generally) clearly points to the necessity of equalizing income and wealth distribution. Wilkinson's seminal (1996) work tackles what increasingly appears as the intractable problem of health inequalities in affluent societies. Briefly, it demonstrates that there is a threshold beyond which the absolute wealth of a nation ceases to have any bearing on population-level health outcomes. Wealthy countries with the greatest health inequalities also have in common the greatest level of income inequality. These countries, such as the USA, are also marked by the lowest stocks of social capital compared to the Nordic countries. In countries such as Norway, Denmark and Sweden the social democratic welfare model underpinning social solidarity is based on income solidarity. Correspondingly, a greater proportion of wealth is redistributed from the richest to the poorest in society.

Wilkinson (1996) identifies income inequality as the major determinant of health inequalities, and argues that its impact on health is through a psychosocial pathway. In unequal societies people with fewer resources are alienated from the dominant social ethos, producing feelings of low self-worth, insecurity and anger. There are two dimensions to this theory. First, in wealthy societies, it is *relative* as opposed to *absolute* poverty that impinges on population health outcomes. Second, relative poverty (as a measure of income inequality) impacts on health *via* people's perceptions of being socially excluded from mainstream society; in other words, their health is affected by their psychosocial reaction to having less than others in the face of an expanding horizon of material, cultural, and social expectations. The stress and anxiety produced by such alienation have a direct bearing on health by affecting the body's immune system, and an indirect effect as feelings of alienation encourage unhealthy coping behaviours in the absence of supportive networks.

Area- and community-based studies (Cattell, 2001), along with reviews of international health survey data (Lynch et al., 2004), continue to point to the causal relationship between individual-level material resources (measured by socio-economic status) and population health outcomes. However, these studies also lend support to the importance of social capital as a contextual feature of communities, which can compound health outcomes, particularly for lower socio-economic groups living in areas where there is a spatial clustering of material disadvantage. In countries with weaker welfare states, Dahl and Malmberg-Heimonen (2010) accept that social capital (or rather the lack thereof) may play a more significant role in mediating between socio-economic position and health outcomes. These empirical studies illustrate an ongoing debate in sociology about which aspects of the social environment are most pertinent to health outcomes and the mechanisms by which these occur.

Putnam's (1995) theory, which equates the stock of social capital in a given society with levels of civic participation, has proved influential in policy discussions. His idea has supplanted the sociological understanding of social capital as a product of social relationships in the sense that benefits accrue to individuals and not to society as a whole (Portes, 1998). Hence, a key debate in the general sociological literature centres on whether social capital should be understood and operationalized as a *collective* or an *individual* resource (Portes, 1998). This reflects the debate in the health inequalities literature about whether the concept is best understood as a structural feature of network ties or as an outcome of broader economic and political structural relations. Whereas the former emphasizes social integration and social cohesion at the level of the community, the latter stresses the mechanisms by which different groups gain access to or are excluded from the resources that benefit health.

The broader social context is instructive when making sense of and evaluating these debates. Social capital attained its status in policy discourse at the same time as neoliberal policies were being pursued across traditional ideological political lines in the promotion of global capitalism and the demotion of the welfare state. Putnam's (1995) thesis on the apparent demise of 'community' and its causal relationship to a decline in interpersonal and institutional trust had immediate appeal for policy makers across the political divide in the USA where communitarian ideologies, which promote community self-government over state responsibility, prevail (Navarro, 2002). Critics of Putnam's thesis argue that he fails to address the structural causes of the demise of interpersonal and institutional trust; rather, he simply re-labels problems through a 'catch-all' and nebulous concept in which causes and effect are conflated (Portes, 1998). For critics like Navarro (2002), social capital is embraced by policy makers not because it points to real problems like social anomie but because the type of analysis that it promotes distracts attention from the kinds of decision made by the global corporate class and national political elites that alienate and disenfranchize citizens and adversely affect their life opportunities, health and well-being. Global neoliberal policies have been shown to increase social insecurity, widen economic inequalities and increase poverty in real terms, all of which will have a direct bearing on health outcomes, as well as deepening social anomie. In Wilkinson's more recent work with Pickett (2009), the emphasis of their analysis is squarely on the political economy of late capitalist society in determining the flow and distribution of material and political power in embedding inequality into the very fabric of societies.

Perhaps one fruitful way of combining both a materialist and social capital explanation of health inequalities – which retains a strong emphasis on structural and *structuring* relations that are not, at all times, reducible to material causes – can be found in Bourdieu's concept of social capital. Principally, Bourdieu (1977) distinguishes between the 'network of durable ties', or what Zierch (2005) refers to as the 'infrastructure' of social capital, and the 'resources' that different networks make available to individual members. Social capital, from this perspective, is an individual resource linked to an individual's socio-economic position, which determines the interplay between different types of capital – bodily, economic, social and cultural, and symbolic. Put simply, people will have access to different types of social networks depending on their social location, and the key distinction between networks is the value of the resources that social ties make available to individuals. In the context of health, some resources are more strategically important than others in determining health outcomes for individuals by giving them access to social support, strategic resources and influence. As Muntaner and Lynch (1999) note, descriptions of social capital as a collective good may well be masking class relations and the reproduction of social inequalities as processes that are central to explaining health inequalities. The future task of medical sociology, one might argue, is to critically and reflexively engage with concepts such as social capital in order to promote more refined theoretical understandings that may also inform public and policy debates.

See also: *Material and Cultural Factors; Neoliberal Globalization and Health Inequalities*

REFERENCES

Bourdieu, P. (1977) *Outline of a Theory of Practice*. Cambridge: Cambridge University Press.

Cattell, V. (2001) 'Poor people, poor places, and poor health: the mediating role of social networks and social capital', *Social Science & Medicine*, 52 (10): 1501–16.

Dahl, E. and Malmberg-Heimonen, I. (2010) 'Social inequality and health: the role of social capital', *Sociology of Health & Illness*, 32 (7): 1102–19.

Gitell, R. and Vidal, A. (1998) *Community Organizing: Building Social Capital as a Development Strategy*. Thousand Oaks, CA: Sage.

Kawachi, I., Kennedy, B.P. and Glass, R. (1999) 'Social capital and self-rated health: a contextual analysis', *American Journal of Public Health*, 89 (8): 1187–93.

Kawachi, I., Kennedy, B.P., Lochner, K. and Prothrow-Stith, D. (1997) 'Social capital, income inequality, and mortality', *American Journal of Public Health*, 87 (9): 1491–8.

Lynch, J., Davey-Smith, G., Harper, S., Hillemeier, M., Shaw, M., Ross, N., Kaplan, G.A. and Wolfson, M. (2004) 'Is income inequality a determinant of population health? Part 1: A systematic review', *The Milbank Quarterly*, 82 (1): 5–59.

Muntaner, C. and Lynch, J. (1999) 'Income inequality, social cohesion, and class relations: a critique of Wilkinson's neo-Durkheimian research program', *International Journal of Health Services*, 29 (1): 59–81.

Navarro, V. (2002) 'A critique of social capital', *International Journal of Health Services*, 32 (3): 423–32.

Portes, A. (1998) 'Social capital: its origins and applications in modern sociology', *Annual Review of Sociology*, 24 (1): 1–24.

Putnam, R. (1995) 'Bowling alone: America's declining social capital', *Journal of Democracy*, 6 (1): 65–78.

Szreter, S. and Woolcock, M. (2004) 'Health by association? Social capital, social theory, and the political economy of public health', *International Journal of Epidemiology*, 33 (4): 650–67.

Veenstra, G. (2000) 'Social capital, SES and health: an individual level analysis', *Social Science & Medicine* 50 (5): 619–29.

Wilkinson, R.G. (1996) *Unhealthy Societies: The Afflictions of Inequality*. London: Routledge.

Wilkinson, R.G. and Pickett, K. (2009) *The Spirit Level: Why More Equal Societies Almost Always Do Better*. London: Allen Lane.

Zierch, A.M. (2005) 'Health implications of access to social capital: findings from an Australian study', *Social Science & Medicine*, 61 (10): 2119–31.

social capital

Orla McDonnell

Part 2
Experience of Health and Illness

Medicalization

Medicalization describes a process by which non-medical problems become defined and treated as medical problems, usually in terms of illnesses or disorders.

Medicalization is now well established as a key sociological concept yet it is difficult to be specific about when it first entered the social scientific lexicon. It seems that the process was originally referred to by critics of the growing influence of psychiatry in the 1960s (although these critics did not use the term explicitly), and it increased in popularity in the 1970s when linked with the concept of social control. Since then medicalization has been applied to a variety of putative problems that (at times contentiously) came to be defined as medical, ranging from childbirth and the menopause through to alcoholism and homosexuality.

According to Conrad and Schneider (1980), medicalization can occur on three distinct levels: conceptually, when a medical vocabulary is used to define a problem; institutionally, when organizations adopt a medical approach to treating a problem in which they specialize; and at the level of doctor–patient interaction, when a problem is defined as medical and medical treatment occurs. As these distinctions illustrate, the process often involves physicians and their treatments directly. However, this is not necessarily so, as in the case of alcoholism where the medical profession may be only marginally involved or not involved at all.

Conrad and Schneider's typology can be mapped onto the distinction between macro, meso, and micro levels of analysis. Macro-level actors include medical researchers and journals, governments and national organizations and the meso level would include local organizations, while doctor–patient interaction concerns mainly micro-level actors. Halfmann (2011) argues that medicalization occurs at all three levels. Thus, medical discourses can be deployed at the meso level by the hospital manager and at the micro level by patients and doctors, as well as at the macro level. He also notes that medicalization at the micro level can involve clinical personnel other than doctors and non-medical actors such as teachers and counsellors. Furthermore, he recognizes that micro-level medicalization can occur through the identity construction of various actors, with doctors, for example, fulfilling cultural expectations to varying degrees about what 'being a doctor' involves.

Medicalization is often associated with the control of deviance and the ways in which deviant behaviours that were once defined as immoral, sinful or criminal have been given medical meanings. The process of medicalizing deviant behaviour is not straightforward, however, and can be seen as encompassing a five-stage sequential process (Conrad and Schneider, 1992). The first stage involves a behaviour being defined as deviant, usually before the emergence of modern medical definitions. For example, chronic drunkenness was held to be highly undesirable before any medical writer defined it as such. The second stage occurs when the medical conception of a deviant behaviour is announced in a professional medical journal. Descriptions of a new diagnosis (for example, hyperactivity) or the proposal of a medical aetiology for a type of deviant behaviour (for example, alcoholism) are used to redefine this as a medical problem. Next comes claims-making by medical and non-medical interest groups. This stage is crucial if a new deviance designation is to emerge. Medical claims-makers are not usually organized specifically to promote a new medical deviance category but involve a loose alliance of people with similar professional interests. The activities of non-medical claims-makers (for example, pharmaceutical companies or self-help groups) may be more overt and involve engaging in publicity campaigns or political lobbying. They will often align themselves with medical claims-makers and use these medical champions to lend scientific credibility to their claims. The fourth stage in the process involves the legitimation of a claim. This occurs when claims-makers launch an instrumental, as opposed to a merely rhetorical, challenge to the existing deviance designation. Finally, medicalization occurs when the medical deviance designation is institutionalized. This can happen when a deviance designation is codified within a medical classification system, or when a bureaucracy is created to provide institutionalized support for medicalization. The value of this theoretical model is that it suggests that attempts to conceptualize deviance as a medical problem are often hotly disputed and carry uncertain outcomes. Perhaps surprisingly, however, there has been little attempt to evaluate its usefulness or to try and develop it (but see Conrad and Jacobson, 2003).

The logic of this model suggests that the degree to which a condition is medicalized will vary. For some conditions medicalization may be total whereas for others competing definitions may exist and their medicalization will remain incomplete or even minimal. According to Conrad (1992), a number of factors may affect the degree of medicalization. These include the support of the medical profession, the availability of interventions or treatments, the existence of competing definitions, and the actions of groups challenging medical definitions. Nor should it be assumed that medicalization is only a one-way process. It is also possible for demedicalization to occur if a problem ceases to be defined in medical terms and medical treatments are no longer seen as an appropriate solution. Indeed, Halfmann (2011) argues that medicalization and demedicalization can occur simultaneously and that even when one of these processes seems to be dominant it is often incomplete.

The most frequently mentioned example of demedicalization is homosexuality in America which, until 1973, was defined by the American Psychiatric Association (APA) as an illness. After protests and picketing by the gay liberation movement and support from some sympathetic psychiatrists, the APA voted to declassify it as an illness, a decision that was later endorsed in the UK. As a result, homosexuality became more widely recognized as a lifestyle choice. With the onset of the AIDS epidemic in the 1980s, however, it became partially re-medicalized, although in a different form. Overall, the evidence to date is that medicalization is far more apparent than demedicalization but it remains important to see it as a two-way process.

While there is now some consensus about the nature of medicalization, there is no such agreement about its cause. Some have argued that the expansion of medical jurisdiction is primarily a consequence of the medical profession exercising its power to define and control what constitutes health and illness in order to extend its professional dominance. Others have considered medicalization to be the result of broader social processes to which doctors are simply responding. Thus, Illich (1976), for example, attributes medicalization to the increasing professionalization and bureaucratization of medical institutions associated with industrialization. For him the expansion of modern medicine has created a dependence on doctors and taken away people's ability to engage in self-care. Zola (1972), too, has argued that medicalization is rooted in the development of an increasingly complex technological and bureaucratic system and a reliance on experts.

More recently, Conrad (2007) has identified a shift in what is driving medicalization, with pharmaceutical and biotech companies, along with consumers, playing an increasingly important role. For Conrad, pharmaceutical companies have become the major players, promoting their products more aggressively to doctors as well as consumers. In the USA and New Zealand, drug companies can now advertise directly to the public through direct-to-consumer-advertising on television, thereby creating a market for their products by encouraging consumers to ask doctors to prescribe their particular drugs. Biotechnology companies are set to become increasingly important, with the prospect of genetic tests for specific diseases, thereby creating the new medicalized status of 'potentially ill', and biomedical enhancements for bodily characteristics and mental and social abilities. And consumers are said to have become major players as health and health care have become commodified. The body has become a site for varies types and degrees of 'makeover' with medicine as the vehicle, and patients have been transformed into consumers who are said to have become increasingly vocal about the kind of health care they want.

Many writers tend to conceive of medicalization in a negative way, focusing on how the phenomenon has resulted in a form of medical social control that serves particular interests in society. For Marxists, such medicalization is best seen as serving the interests of the ruling capitalist class. From this standpoint, the creation and manipulation of consumer dependence on medicine is merely one example of a more general dependence upon consumer goods propagated by that class. For feminists, the focus has tended to be on how a male-dominated medical profession has increasingly defined women's problems in medical terms and advocated medical interventions. Women's experience of childbirth has been a particular focus of attention. Here it has been suggested that doctors' use of obstetric techniques such as foetal monitoring machines, pain-killing drugs, induction and forceps without telling women patients why such techniques are necessary, or what the risks are, has resulted in their experiencing childbirth as alienating. Moreover, as it is usually male doctors who often control such technology, its coercive utilization is seen as reinforcing existing patriarchal social relations.

In contrast, others emphasize the real clinical and symbolic benefits of medicalization. Redefining a condition as appropriate for medical attention opens up opportunities for the alleviation of symptoms or a cure and also legitimates it, potentially reducing the stigma and censure that may be attached. In the case of chronic fatigue syndrome, for instance, it seems that patients may benefit from a diagnosis simply because it renders an otherwise incoherent and disruptive experience meaningful, and opens up possibilities for managing and living with the syndrome (Broom and Woodward, 1996). Similarly, those seen to have 'a drinking problem' may benefit from the definition of alcoholism as a disease, enabling them to counteract attributions of blame and moral weakness. Medicalization has also meant that they are now less likely to be prosecuted for being drunk in a public place and more likely to be medically treated in a potentially more humane way than would otherwise be the case.

The medicalization thesis has much to recommend it, including the creation of new understandings of the social processes involved in the development and response to medical diagnosis and treatment and the development of a critical framework for analyzing medicine, health and health care. However, a number of significant criticisms have also been levelled against it, especially its more negative variant. In particular, it has been criticized for portraying the individual patient and the lay public more generally as essentially passive and uncritical in the face of modern medicine's expanding jurisdiction. For example, Kohler Riessman (1989) in her discussion of women's experience of different conditions, ranging from childbirth to premenstrual syndrome, has drawn attention to the way in which women have at times actively participated in the medicalization process to meet their own needs and have not simply been the passive victims of a medical ascendancy. Williams and Calnan (1996) developed this critique further by drawing on arguments about 'risk society' and lay re-skilling. They suggest that in late modernity there is a far more critical relationship between medicine and the lay populace and that people's trust in medicine increasingly has to be won and maintained in the face of a growing public awareness of the risks as well as benefits of medicine and the limits of medical expertise. Ballard and Elston (2005) agree with this assessment and see the move to a late- or postmodern world as one where there is likely to be more contestation of medicalization and the possibility of its decline.

Others suggest that the concept has outlived its usefulness and propose that it should be replaced. Thus, Clarke et al. (2003) argue that medicalization should be re-conceptualized in terms of biomedicalization, as this better captures the transformations in the organization and practice of medicine since the 1980s. In particular, they assert that much more attention needs to be given to the role of techno-scientific innovations (for example, the computerization of patient medical records) and the increasingly technological and scientific nature of biomedicine (for example, the geneticization of biomedicine and drug design). However, Conrad (2007) argues that biomedicalization is too broad a concept, one which emphasizes a more extensive set of changes than is meant by medicalization and as such compromises its focus.

While many of the criticisms of medicalization are well made, it remains a useful multi-dimensional concept for sociologists of health and illness. There is, however, a need to go beyond the accumulation of different cases of medicalization in order to try and develop a more integrated theory of the process of medicalization, its causes and consequences, and to relate these to recent changes in medical organization and knowledge and the growing challenge to medical authority.

See also: *Risk; Geneticization; Medical Autonomy, Dominance and Decline; Consumerism*

REFERENCES

Ballard, K. and Elston, M.A. (2005) 'Medicalization: a multi-dimensional concept', *Social Theory & Health*, 3 (3): 228–41.

Broom, D.H. and Woodward, R. (1996) 'Medicalization reconsidered: toward a collaborative approach to care', *Sociology of Health & Illness*, 18: 357–78.

Clarke, A., Mamo, L., Fishman, J.R., Shim, J.K. and Fosket, J.R. (2003) 'Biomedicalization: technoscientific transformations of health, illness and biomedicine', *American Sociological Review*, 68: 161–94.

Conrad, P. (1992) 'Medicalization and social control', *Annual Review of Sociology*, 18: 209–32.

Conrad, P. (2007) *The Medicalization of Society*. Baltimore, MD: Johns Hopkins University Press.

Conrad, P. and Jacobson, H. (2003) 'Enhancing biology? Cosmetic surgery and breast augmentation', in S.J. Williams, L. Birke and G.A. Bendelow (eds), *Debating Biology: Sociological Reflections on Health, Medicine and Society*. London: Routledge.

Conrad, P. and Schneider, J.W. (1980) 'Looking at levels of medicalization: a comment on Strong's critique of the thesis of medical imperialism', *Social Science & Medicine*, 14A: 75–9.

Conrad, P. and Schneider, J.W. (1992) *Deviance and Medicalization: From Badness to Sickness*, 3rd edn. Philadelphia: Temple University Press.

Halfmann, D. (2011) 'Recognizing medicalization and demedicalization: discourses, practices and identities', *Health*, 16: 186–207.

Illich, I. (1976) *Medical Nemesis*. London: Calder and Boyars.

Kohler Riessman, C. (1989) 'Women and medicalization: a new perspective', in P. Brown (ed.), *Perspectives in Medical Sociology*. Belmont, CA: Wadsworth.

Williams, S. and Calnan, M. (1996) 'The "limits" of medicalisation? Modern medicine and the lay populace', *Social Science & Medicine*, 42: 1609–20.

Zola, I. (1972) 'Medicine as an institution of social control', *Sociological Review*, 20: 487–54.

Jonathan Gabe

Illness and Health-Related Behaviour

Illness behaviour refers to how people interpret and define their symptoms and their actions in coping with or accommodating these, whereas health-related behaviour, especially in biomedical research, typically refers to lifestyle 'choices' associated with an increased mortality risk.

Illness behaviour refers to people's experiences, definitions and interpretations of the symptoms of illness/disease/injury etc., and their interactions with various social networks as they try to cope with or accommodate these symptoms. Illness behaviour is a long-standing topic within medical sociology (see, for example, Zola, 1973). Health-related behaviour is also of interest to medical sociologists, albeit in a more critical manner. Such behaviours reportedly have a determinate influence on the major causes of mortality. Qualitative methods typically inform research on illness behaviour while quantitative methods tend to be used when researching health-related behaviour, though this distinction is not absolute (Young, 2004).

Before unpacking these concepts further, it is worth offering four caveats. First, according to Armstrong (2009), the focus on illness and health behaviours reflects post-Second World War concerns about 'the problem of behaviour' in the larger population, with their antecedents in moralized public health efforts to target child hygiene alongside biologists' reductionist foci on the individual. Accordingly, questions such as the following should be borne in mind: 'Whose morality?', 'What conception of the body is being formulated?' and 'Whose interests does this conception reflect and serve?' Second, past and present sociological writing on the illness behaviours of the poor and powerless in (state) funded research should not detract critical attention from the socially structured *illness-producing behaviours* of the rich and powerful. In his polemically-named Greedy Bastards Hypothesis (GBH), Scambler (2002) considers how the 'illness behaviours' of global capitalists may (unintentionally) amplify health inequalities. More specifically, he refers to the maldistribution of wealth and income, which, we should note, is taking a particularly perverse form following the 2008 financial crisis. Third, the reference to 'health' in the study of 'health-related behaviours' is arguably a misnomer: health is negatively defined in contrast to the positive meanings often ascribed to health and well-being in everyday life. The criticism levelled at the sociology of health and illness in the past decade, for its asymmetrical focus on illness (disease, pathology and suffering) to the relative neglect of health (as variously constructed) (Monaghan, 2001), could be extended to biomedical and interdisciplinary writings on health-related behaviours. Fourth, from an interpretivist sociological perspective, the term 'action' or 'conduct' is preferable to 'behaviour'. Although widely used in health studies, 'behaviour' connotes notions of stimulus and response that are outside of human interpretation, intentionality, projection and planning. In contrast, 'action' (social actions, interactions, conduct) implies meanings and definitions, the very 'stuff' of socially constructed 'life worlds'.

Despite such problems and limitations, sociological writings on 'illness behaviour' from the mid-twentieth century onwards provide a useful point of reference and building blocks for subsequent work on the illness experience. Following on from and also critiquing Parsons' structural functionalist writing in 1951 on illness as a form of behavioural deviance, sociologists have provided empirical and theoretically informed insights into the human world of sickness, pain and suffering alongside people's varied and contingent efforts to cope with and attenuate their symptoms with or without medical help. Medical sociologists have explored, for example, the 'lay referral system' or how people typically talk with others in their social networks before consulting medical professionals. The contingent nature of these networks vis-à-vis people's uptake of formal health care is documented in the literature amidst changing familial and other social relations (Rogers et al., 1999). An emphasis on social networks is also evidenced in Pescosolido's (1992) influential work, a 'social organization strategy framework', where illness behaviour is understood as a fundamentally social action. Indeed, for Pescosolido, the patterns and pathways to care cannot be understood without fully appreciating people's connections to diverse networks, and, in turn, institutions.

Young (2004) presents a selective review and synthesis of the social scientific literature on illness behaviour. Young explains that the 'illness behaviour' concept can be traced back to the 1920s, though its salience among sociologists was elaborated after Parsons in the 1950s. In addition to critically reviewing research on the economic, geographical, socio-demographic and psychosocial dimensions of illness behaviour and service (under) utilization in a global context, Young considers micro-sociological writings on medical consultations in Western nations. We are informed that these qualitative studies have, among other things, questioned the dominance of medical professionals in their 'dealings' with patients. Such studies challenged the earlier Parsonian emphasis on the asymmetrical and hierarchical relationship between the paternalistic doctor and supplicant patient. Increasing knowledge among patients, for instance, has been shown to reduce the power that clinicians exercise over the sick and the institutionalization of a more egalitarian, contractual and consultative type relationship. Such concerns, of course, are increasingly significant given the growing burden of chronic illness among ageing populations and the proliferation of information sources, exemplified by the internet and eHealth, that are also co-opted by formal health services. Arguably, under such conditions the sick role concept limits the analysis of illness behaviour given the complex interactions and interdependences that transcend the doctor–patient relationship, including the diverse 'social networks, institutions and government and world systems that comprise the broad view of the problem of illness behaviour' (Young, 2004: 10).

An exhaustive review of the literature on illness behaviour is beyond the scope of this entry, though some seminal and classic sociological literature should be flagged. Writings here include Mechanic and Volkart (1960), who, in the opening volume of the *Journal of Health and Human Behavior*, 'described the problem of patients' failure (sic) to consult with health services in terms of "illness behavior"' (Armstrong, 2009: 919). For Mechanic and Volkart, 'illness behaviour' included 'the ways in which given symptoms may be differentially perceived, evaluated, and acted (or not acted) upon by different kinds of persons' (1960: 87). Underscoring the responses of these 'different kinds of persons', they suggested that social factors (for example, education, religion and social class) shaped illness behaviour.

Subsequent sociological research substantiated these claims. Zola (1973) described how different ethnic groups in New York responded to illness, with social factors or 'triggers' ultimately resulting in the decision to consult (for example, sanctioning from another person or disruption to work roles). The import of social factors is illustrated by the contrasting orientations of Irish and Italian respondents to illness, with the former group presenting as more stoical and less expressive than the latter. Moving from ethnicity to the intersections of gender and class, Blaxter and Paterson (1982) explored Scottish working-class mothers' understandings and accommodation of health problems. Amidst demanding gendered role obligations, illness was deemed a normal part of daily life and women seldom accessed the sick role even when experiencing symptoms (for example, backache). This observation corresponds more generally with research on class-related understandings of health, with the working class typically expressing functional definitions that reflect the need to continue working in order to secure their hard-earned lives.

More recent observational studies explore *specific settings* that are embedded within global systems of exploitation. Bloor (2005) offers an interesting example. His ethnography of illness behaviour on a merchant cargo ship, owned by a multinational corporation, illustrates how 'globalization is possibly reducing the readiness of the workforce to mitigate health threats through medical consultation' (p. 776). Bloor explains that the seafarers' access to shipboard medical consultations was ostensibly 'free' and, from a medical perspective, often necessary amidst demanding, exhausting, and dangerous working conditions. Yet, in practice, medical consultations were virtually non-existent due to the seafarers' concerns about being deemed unfit for work, which could risk their own and their families' economic security. Under such conditions, 'workers "soldiered on" through illness, injury, and exhaustion in the service of economic efficiency' (p. 770).

Moving to 'health-related behaviour', public health and policy prioritize strategies that are intended to promote health maintenance through lifestyle changes. Despite the disappointing results of intervention studies and the limited role of lifestyle factors in explaining the social gradient in ill health, so-called 'health behaviours' are typically framed as changeable habits that are conducive to health, or key to reducing risk. Sociologists have engaged such concerns in relation to what is called 'the health role' (Frank, 1991), where the prevention of illness and maximization of productive capacity are prioritized. Supporting the health role, health professionals typically expect people to monitor/change their everyday behaviours as part of a 'responsible' and ultimately individualized qua entrepreneurial project of self-control or governance. This expectation is rearticulated via the increasingly popular notion of 'nudging' (seeking to change behaviour through 'unobtrusive influences'), though that concept has been criticized as vague, based on limited evidence, and potentially harmful (Bonnell et al., 2011).

While the idea of 'nudging' is problematic, medical sociologists would not necessarily dismiss the relevance of cultural/behavioural factors as explained in Part 1 of this book. Certainly, medical sociologists are interested in, for example, ethnic differences in health-related behaviours, including nutritional behaviour as a possible explanatory variable in health inequalities research (Riley Bahr, 2007). However, such research is tentative. Furthermore, while the promotion of health behaviours may appeal to various groups (for example, paternalistic governments seeking to 'nudge' populations and cut costs, individuals seeking to embody fashionable thinness), such calls cannot be taken at face value. Health behaviours, after all, are not 'freely chosen' in a social vacuum: choices are shaped and constrained by the inequitable material conditions of existence. Hence, when undertaking health studies it makes sense to emphasize life chances more so than lifestyles, which are always indebted to social structures such as class, gender, and ethnicity.

Reviewing and critiquing 'health behaviours' research is not limited to a structuralist type of analysis. Using post-structuralism, Armstrong (2009) explains how the idea of 'health-related behaviour' has proliferated in medicine over the past forty years. Whether the notion of health-related behaviour is entirely new is debatable, though Armstrong considers the genealogy of this concept using Foucauldian theory. His discussion on health-related behaviour is noteworthy when considering the *experience* of illness. After all, it is within the idiom of a widely recycled 'behavioural' discourse that (potentially) sick people risk being positioned as culpable for their actual or anticipated ills, rendering them open to various forms of opprobrium or stigma, meddlesome advice, and 'encouragement' (nudging), etc. Arguably, such positioning is the consequence of surveillance medicine where people are increasingly labelled 'diseased', 'ill', or 'at risk' of illness without necessarily feeling ill or accepting the biomedical definitions that constitute them as (potentially) sick. The maximization of self-responsibility is also noteworthy here in relation to what has been called 'the bio-citizen' (Rose, 1999). This concept is suggestive of new modes of subjectivity, with people charged with becoming 'active agent[s] in the maintenance of health . . . exercising a reflexive scrutiny of personal' conduct in the putative interests of the common good (Rose, 1999: 228).

The rise of molecular science and the marketing of pharmaceutical 'solutions' for myriad 'ills', ranging from obesity to mental health, gives added impetus to bio-citizenship where biological and social bodies are mutually implicated in health outcomes and risk. Genetic susceptibility emerges in this future-oriented vision, though medical science also authoritatively frames the major causes of death in behavioural terms. For Rose (2007: 9) this framing reproduces 'a culture of prevention and precaution', comprised of 'technologies of life' and the embodiment of 'responsibility, foresight and prudence'. Framing health outcomes in behavioural terms is thus far from innocent. Armstrong asserts that the dominant behavioural focus is individualizing, positioning social agents as 'autonomous' in their 'choice' of 'whether to act in response to illness (illness behaviour) or to maintain their health (health behaviour)' (2009: 919). The possible consequences of this biopolitical framing include the relative neglect of health care in favour of individual behaviours or, in line with marketization, 'consumer choices' that have a wider significance.

In sum, 'illness behaviour' and 'health-related behaviour' are common concepts within sociological and other health-related disciplines and discourses. While caveats are necessary and limitations exist in the research, important studies are identifiable. Classic interactionist research on illness behaviour, in particular, elucidates the meanings and experiences of diverse groups as they make sense of, and cope with, symptoms and health problems with or without medical assistance. Increasingly, in relation to an anticipatory medicine and bio-citizenship, the focus has also shifted towards so-called 'health-related behaviour' (for example, in the context of nutrition) and medical sociologists have vital contributions to make here. However, the task and promise of a critical sociology is to evaluate multi-dimensional and multi-disciplinary approaches to health and illness *behaviour*, including the assumption that this behaviour manifests itself in the materiality of the (im)prudent body.

See also: *Social Class; Material and Cultural Factors; Embodiment; Sick Role; Surveillance and Health Promotion*

REFERENCES

Armstrong, D. (2009) 'Origins of the problem of health-related behaviours: a genealogical study', *Social Studies of Science*, 39: 909–26.

Blaxter, M. and Paterson, E. (1982) *Mothers and Daughters: A Three Generation Study of Health Attitudes and Behaviour*. London: Heinemann Educational Books.

Bloor, M. (2005) 'Observations of shipboard illness behaviour: work discipline and the sick role in a residential work setting', *Qualitative Health Research*, 15 (6): 766–77.

Bonnell, C., McKee, M., Fletcher, A., Wilkinson, P. and Haines, A. (2011) 'One nudge forward, two steps back', *BMJ*, 342: d401.

Frank, A. (1991) 'From sick role to health role: deconstructing Parsons', in R. Robertson and B.S. Turner (eds), *Talcott Parsons*. London: Sage.

Mechanic, D. and Volkart, E.H. (1960) 'Illness behaviour and medical diagnoses', *Journal of Health and Human Behaviour*, 1: 86–94.

Monaghan, L.F. (2001) 'Looking good, feeling good: the embodied pleasures of vibrant physicality', *Sociology of Health & Illness*, 23 (3): 330–56.

Pescosolido, B. (1992) 'Beyond rational choice: the social dynamics of how people seek help', *American Journal of Sociology*, 97: 1096–138.

Riley Bahr, P. (2007) 'Race and nutrition: an investigation of Black–White differences in health-related nutritional behaviours', *Sociology of Health & Illness*, 29 (6): 831–56.

Rogers, A., Hassell, K. and Nicolaas, G. (1999) *Demanding Patients? Analysing the Use of Primary Care*. Buckingham: Open University Press.

Rose, N. (1999) *Powers of Freedom: Reframing Political Thought*. Cambridge, MA: Cambridge University Press.

Rose, N. (2007) 'Molecular biopolitics, somatic ethics and the spirit of biocapital', *Social Theory & Health*, 5: 3–29.

Scambler, G. (2002) *Health and Social Change: A Critical Theory*. Buckingham: Open University Press.

Young, J.T. (2004) 'Illness behaviour: a selective review and synthesis', *Sociology of Health & Illness*, 26 (1): 1–31.

Zola, K. (1973) 'Pathways to the doctor: from person to patient', *Social Science & Medicine*, 7: 677–89.

Lee F. Monaghan

Stigma

Stigma commonly refers to a negatively defined condition, attribute, trait or behaviour conferring 'deviant' status, which is socially, culturally, and historically variable. It is a political process related to macro-social issues such as power, discrimination, and the distribution of resources in society.

The term 'stigma' has a long lineage, predating the advent of the social sciences as we know them today. The Greeks, in fact, originated the term to refer to bodily signs, cut or burnt into the body, which were designed to expose the bearer as a slave, criminal, or social outcast. Stigma was thus a political phenomenon intimately related to citizenship and (the lack of) entitlement to community membership. Today, exclusionary practices are still enacted toward those who are stigmatized (Reidpath et al., 2005) though the term 'stigma' is applied more widely to any condition, attribute, trait, or behaviour that symbolically marks the bearer out as 'culturally unacceptable' or 'inferior' and has, as its subjective referent, the notion of shame or disgrace. Blame may also emerge, with the stigmatized being held culpable when illness, disease or injury is cast as (self-inflicted or perpetuated) deviance (Scambler, 2009).

Seminal work on stigma was undertaken within the interactionist tradition in sociology, which explores the structure of face-to-face encounters and issues pertaining to identity and selfhood. While recent sociological literature revisits and deepens such thinking in order to underscore the role of macro-social structures in stigma relations, and we will refer more to this work below, attention should first be drawn to Goffman's pioneering (1968) study, tellingly entitled *Stigma: Notes on the Management of Spoiled Identity*. As part and parcel of his own inimitable dramaturgical perspective on the vicissitudes of self-presentation in everyday life, Goffman's concern in this book is with the maintenance and integrity of the self, or perhaps more correctly in this case, the presentation of a discredited or discreditable self. Taking such a stance, in other words, provides a 'special application of the arts of impression management' (p. 155), revealing through its potential disruption, much about the taken-for-granted or tacit ways in which people organize their lives and everyday encounters.

Goffman identifies three distinct types of stigma, namely: (1) stigmas of the body (such as blemishes or deformities); (2) stigmas of character (the mentally ill or the criminal, for example); and (3) stigmas associated with social collectivities ('racial' or tribal), all of which he stresses are socially, culturally, and historically variable. Perhaps most significantly for this discussion, Goffman's social definition of stigma turns on the distinction he draws between 'virtual social identity' – normative expectations, that is to say, of what the person *ought* to be – and 'actual social identity' – the category or attributes the individual *actually* possesses (p. 12). The stigmatized, from this perspective, are those who possess a deeply discrediting *discrepancy* between their virtual and actual social identity *vis-à-vis* those 'normals' for whom no such discrepancy occurs. 'A stigma, then, is really a special kind of relationship between attribute and stereotype' (Goffman, 1968: 14); a meaning imposed on an attribute via negative images, stereotypes and attitudes that potentially discredits a member of a particular social category. This, in turn, maps onto another notable distinction which Goffman draws between the *discredited*, whose stigma is evident or 'known about', and the *discreditable*, whose situation is the precise opposite (p. 14). In the former case, the prime dramaturgical task is one of 'managing tension', while in the latter case, it is one of 'managing information'. '[T]o tell or not to tell', to reveal or conceal, that is the question (p. 57).

Goffman's treatment of these issues echoes labelling theory. Such theory eclipsed Parsonian perspectives on illness as social deviance in the 1960s, stressing how stigma springs from the definitional workings of society, rather than the inherent qualities of the attribute or behaviour itself. The basic idea here, building on the work of Lemert and espoused by writers such as Becker, Erikson and Kitsuse, is one of 'primary deviance' (the original infraction), societal reaction (a public/professional 'crisis'), and 'secondary deviance' (the person's response to the negative societal reaction). Such processes lead to a 'master-status' (which drowns out all other roles and sources of identity) that is extremely difficult to disavow or shake off. In short, stigma as a societal reaction 'spoils identity', a phenomenon generated in social situations and the contingencies they entail by virtue of unrealized norms, which impinge on the encounter in more or less pressing and predictable ways.

Goffman, however, in typical iconoclastic fashion, adds a further twist. His penchant for mentioning troubling truths about individuals is clearly evident when he notes that the blind, the deaf, the ex-mental patient, the prostitute, the ex-convict, and many others discussed in the pages of his book, are not the only ones who experience stigmatization. Norms of identity, Goffman comments, breed deviations along with conformity. Stigma management is a general phenomenon, a process that occurs wherever there are identity norms. Few people are totally without discrediting attributes. The reader is led, therefore, to realize that 'stigma involves not so much a set of concrete individuals who can be separated into two piles, the stigmatized and the normal, as a pervasive two-role social process in which every individual participates in both roles . . . The normal and stigmatized are not persons but rather perspectives' (pp. 163–4). This provides Goffman with the rationale for claiming that if people are to refer to the stigmatized individual as 'deviant', they might more profitably regard them as a 'normal deviant' (p. 155).

These ideas and arguments have translated more or less readily into sociological studies of the meaning and experience of illness, both mental and physical, over the years. The sociology of chronic illness, for example, has proved a particularly fertile terrain upon which to explore these insights, developing and refining them along the way. Scambler's (1989) research on epilepsy in Britain is worth briefly reiterating here, not least given its subsequent uptake, review and revision (Scambler, 2004, 2009). His (1989) hidden distress model contains a useful distinction between 'felt' and 'enacted' stigma. The former pertains to the fear of being discriminated against due to cultural 'unacceptability' or 'inferiority', whilst the latter, in contrast, refers to actual cases or enactments of discrimination. For Scambler's respondents, it was the fear of stigmatization which was most disruptive of their lives, rather than actual cases of enacted stigma, rendering information control particularly salient. Research on HIV-related stigma in India (Steward et al., 2008) echoes and builds on concepts formulated in Goffman-inspired studies of epilepsy. Thus, Steward et al. (2008) refer to internalized stigma, which, for 'normals', is associated with prejudice and possible distress among those who are stigmatized. However, Scambler (2004, 2009) has revisited and critiqued his own and other research on illness-related stigma and has posed challenges for the medical sociology community. In short, he has called for a more ambitious sociology of illness-related stigma which is attuned to macro-social structures. This re-framing of stigma is intended to complement and deepen interactionist analyses by going beyond them and asking the questions which Goffman (1968) did not address, such as the causal significance of class, gender, ethnicity, command and so on. Notions of blame also figure here, with critical attention being directed at how stigma is but one 'ingredient' of disadvantage in neoliberal societies comprising many faces of oppression (Scambler, 2009: 450).

This re-framing arises from an engagement with conflict theory and disability studies. Following an appreciation and critique of Goffman (1968), and his influence in medical sociology from the 1970s with regard to a 'personal tragedy' or 'deviance' model of stigma, Scambler (2009) flags the impact of 'a rival oppression paradigm' as advocated by disability theorists from the 1980s onwards. In particular, he notes how the social model of disability articulates issues prefigured within at least some medical sociology, and specifically, how 'quasi-liberated' individuals publicly proclaim their identity (for example, in relation to epilepsy) and seek to educate others in an attempt to challenge stigma. Taking a politicized approach, disability theorists focus their critical attention on the labellers, rather than the labelled, who discriminate against bodies that are marked as 'different' (inferior). While we would not dismiss the materiality of the body, what is deemed particularly pertinent here are the exclusionary effects of social oppression or 'disablism' which devalues 'impaired' bodies and engenders exploitation, marginalization, powerlessness, cultural imperialism, and violence (Young, 1990; cited in Scambler, 2009: 449). Arguing that we are now in a position to learn from this 'clash' of paradigms, and the disability theorists' emphasis on 'structured' social relations, Scambler makes a strong case for moving beyond 'Goffman-like, personal-tragedy exegeses'. In short, he stresses the need to address issues such as discrimination and power as exercised through social structures and various configurations that transcend the interaction order while remaining potentially consequential for individual identities, life chances, and health.

Reidpath et al. (2005) also seek to go beyond, without abandoning, the individual when discussing stigma, social value, and social exclusion. Their basic argument relates to social investment and how the stigmatized are marked as 'unworthy' amid finite resources and expectations of reciprocity. In short, the stigmatized risk being considered a drain on resources, or people who cannot socially reciprocate (for example, by working) risk stigmatization and exclusion given their perceived lack of social function or productivity. Under conditions of social devaluation and exclusion, these authors explain that stigma may adversely affect people's health in numerous ways, ranging from psychological stress and discrimination in health care settings (for example, as reported by women labelled 'morbidly obese') to disinvesting from the general social infrastructure (they cite the impact of racism in the USA, which affects ethnic minorities and, indirectly, ethnic majorities). Unlike Scambler (2009), Reidpath et al. (2005) do not critique notions of individual culpability for illness or neoliberal ideologies of personal responsibility, but they do draw attention to poverty and how stigma hinders social justice. Similar to Scambler (2009), they also consider strategies to reduce stigma. These include efforts to socially include people who are stigmatized and increase their perceived social value, described as 'worthiness for membership in the community – *i.e.* whether one merits social investment' (Reidpath et al., 2005: 472). However, the political impact of this strategy in reducing disadvantage, and the dyadic of shame and blame, might be limited in light of Scambler's (2009) critique of the class mechanisms, structures and ideologies which differentially determine social value.

In sum, sociological analyses of illness-related stigma are undertaken at various levels, ranging from the micro to the macro. They are also entering a new phase of development amid the dialogue and debate with contributors from within and outside of medical sociology (for example, disability theorists and other activists). Certainly, much still remains to be done, not only in terms of theory development and empirical research but also as regards stigma reduction and attempts to get critical sociological analyses publicly recognized and credited under the present social, cultural, economic, and political conditions. However, what is encouraging in more recent writings that seek to go beyond 'personal tragedy' types of analysis is an attempt to offer more politicized and ambitious conceptualizations that incorporate conflict as well as interactionist sociology (Scambler, 2009). Such writings usefully draw attention to the larger social structure and challenge the uncritical acceptance of the dominant societal or medicalized framings of stigma, which, we would stress, are consequential for health, well-being, and social justice.

See also: *Chronic Illness; Disability; Illness Narratives; Social Constructionism*

REFERENCES

Goffman, E. (1968) *Stigma: Notes on the Management of Spoiled Identity.* Harmondsworth: Pelican Books.
Reidpath, D.D., Chan, K.Y., Gifford, S.M. and Allotey, P. (2005) '"He hath the French pox": stigma, social value and social exclusion', *Sociology of Health & Illness*, 27 (4): 468–89.
Scambler, G. (1989) *Epilepsy.* London: Routledge.
Scambler, G. (2004) 'Re-framing stigma: felt and enacted stigma and challenges to the sociology of chronic and disabling conditions', *Social Theory & Health*, 2 (1): 29–46.
Scambler, G. (2009) 'Health-related stigma', *Sociology of Health & Illness*, 31 (3): 441–55.
Steward, W., Herek, G., Ramakrishna, J., Bharat, S., Chandy, S., Wrubel, J. and Ekstrand, M. (2008) 'HIV-related stigma: adapting a theoretical framework for use in India', *Social Science & Medicine*, 67 (8): 1225–35.

Lee F. Monaghan and Simon J. Williams

> Embodiment is a multi-dimensional process that cannot be reduced to biology or society, but instead involves the complex interplay of various modalities of our 'lived body' or bodily-being-in-the-world.

Medical sociology deals with corporeal concerns and, as such, the concept of embodiment has particular salience. Illness, disease, pain and suffering as well as health, comprising the embodied pleasures of 'vibrant physicality' (Monaghan, 2001), are inseparable from our 'lived bodies' as the site of meaning, experience and expression. While a philosophical concern with embodiment, as a challenge to Western dualism, can be traced to the rise of phenomenology in the twentieth century, particularly via Merleau-Ponty's (1962/1945) work, in recent years sociologists have further elaborated on this concept and deepened the realm of 'body studies'. For instance, recent revisions of seminal studies of the body and society (Turner, 2008) have underscored body politics and how our biological vulnerability could serve as a basis for human rights. Indeed, there seems to be a convergence in recent writing with regard to body ethics and the two-way, or dialectical, relationship between human embodiment and an inequitable social world. For instance, issues pertaining to the social patterning of health and illness *vis-à-vis* class, gender and ethnicity, as discussed earlier in this book, all impact on human bodies as socially located, lived and experienced.

While there are legitimate complaints about sociology's general neglect of the embodied dimensions of human existence – reflecting a puritan legacy and efforts to establish sociology as a discipline that is separate from the biological sciences – this neglect was never absolute, as explained by Shilling (2005), Turner (2008) and Williams and Bendelow (1998). Relations between sociology and biology moreover have at times been quite close (Fuller, 2006). Writings in embodied sociology have explained that the body has always had something of an 'absent presence' within the discipline and, by re-reading the classics in a corporeal light, the sociological imagination may be reworked so that it is more attentive to embodiment *and* the discipline's classical heritage. As these contemporary writings suggest, it is not solely or simply a question of the body as a product of society or society as a product of the body, but of bodies both as *shapers of* and *shaped by* the society and social relations of which they are a part. Embodiment, then, provides a crucial missing link between structure and agency or macro and micro social planes.

Recent theorizing, which attempts to consolidate the proliferation of body studies, is informative and paves the way for future research. Shilling (2005), when critically surveying classical and more recent writings on body matters, offers a compelling case for a 'corporeal realist' approach that sees bodies as the multi-dimensional medium for the constitution of society. By this, he means human bodies are the source, location and means of society – i.e. bodies have an independent causal role in the creation of society, they are a site on which the structures of society inscribe themselves and they are a means for positioning individuals within society in ways that may or may not foster human potentiality. Shilling explains that while these three dimensions may be separated for analytical purposes, they are, in actuality, 'co-existing moments' of a process that unfolds over time. Formulated as an explicitly critical approach, corporeal realism relates well to matters of health, illness, and medical practice. A more recent empirical study in embodied sociology offers comparable thinking on the medicalized and government-sponsored 'war on obesity' (Monaghan, 2008). The pervasive anti-obesity offensive is comprised of aggressive moralizing and the (unintended) reproduction of intolerance, body dissatisfaction and size discrimination that together spoil embodied identities.

Unsurprisingly, medical sociology has provided fertile terrain for the development of body studies and an embodied sociology that 'puts minds back into bodies, bodies back into society and society back into the body' (Williams and Bendelow, 1998: 3). The entry on embodiment in the first edition of *Key Concepts in Medical Sociology* included a reference to Kelly and Field (1996) who argued for sociological conceptualizations of chronic illness and the body to incorporate biological and social facts. Biology, in this respect, is sociologically significant because it may impinge directly on the self, provide signals for identity construction, and act as a limiting factor on social action for the sufferer. This, in turn, brings to the fore the experiential and expressive dimensions of embodiment, as illustrated in sociological writings on pain (Williams and Bendelow, 1998). Such writing has also foreshadowed more detailed sociological debates on biology and the relations between health, medicine and society (Williams et al., 2003), plus the relevance of 'body work' as a concept in studies of health and social care (Twigg et al., 2011). All of this fits well with Shilling's (2005) corporeal realist thinking – an approach that recognizes the materiality of real flesh-and-blood bodies in contrast to extreme social constructionist accounts.

Discussions of embodiment within medical sociology have tended to foreground issues such as suffering and pain and how such experiences 'problematize' our bodies in various ways. Pain calls into question our normal taken-for-granted relationship with the world and the embodied basis upon which this rests. The existentially charged and emotionally laden nature of such events – themselves inflected through factors such as class, gender, age and ethnicity – is all too apparent here, underlining the importance of biography, the self and identity alongside the materiality of the body. Attempts to reintegrate the body, self and society, in this respect, include the search for meaning through narratives – themselves embodied stories and stories of embodiment – together with various strategies and styles of adjustment. While biographical themes of disruption and negative meanings of pain as displeasure abound in such contexts, other more positive renderings of pain are nonetheless possible – pain as constructive, creative and productive, for example in relation to childbirth, or in more populist terms the 'no pain, no gain' mantra or motif exalted by exercise buffs. Here again we can glimpse the material and intentional, physical and emotional dimensions of mindful embodiment and their inextricable intertwining across culture, time, and place. We can also come to appreciate how the biological body is not so much lost sight of, but placed within a broader embodied, non-reductionist perspective that is grounded in our being-in-the-world.

As part of an embodied sociology which engages the corporeal meanings and experiences of 'health' as well as illness, we would also cite research that has sought to redress the almost exclusive focus on suffering, disease, illness, and 'pathological' bodies (as politically important as that may be). Thus, Monaghan (2001), as part of his concern to redress the asymmetry that characterizes the sociology of health and illness, offers ethnographic insights into gym culture, the embodied pleasures of body modification, and the sensuous experiences of lifting weights. Observing the tendency within medical sociology to focus on ill bodies, Monaghan (2001) maintains that the study of 'healthy' bodies requires an empha-sis and wider acknowledgement within the newer (embodied, non-dualistic) sociology of health and illness. This is necessary because the concrete corporeal manifestations of 'health' in everyday life – as the components of and precondi-tions for embodied social practice – may, paradoxically, erode bodily capital while simultaneously contributing to it. His research also considers illicit steroid use, a normalized practice among dedicated bodybuilders that may enhance the quasi-erotic sensations of exercise while also amplifying bodily risk (for example, drug side-effects, injury to muscles and tendons). That research also utilizes Watson's (2000) useful 'male body schema', which is attuned to different modalities of embodiment, including: the normative (body size, shape, weight, appearance), experiential (for example, the sense of well-being), pragmatic (relating to gen-dered role requirements in everyday life), and the visceral (the hidden biological processes that may be medically visualized or glimpsed during exercise).

Recent research on sleep, as another vital yet neglected corporeal matter (Williams and Crossley, 2008), has also made significant contributions to the soci-ology of health, ageing and gender of late. The meanings, methods, motives and management of sleep are socially patterned and variable across the lifecourse and are bound up with matters of health and illness, work-time and work-ethics, gen-der and ageing, family roles and responsibilities (Arber et al., 2007). Sleep then, as this suggests, is not simply a fascinating embodied topic in its own right, but a rich way of revisiting familiar sociological issues in a new and novel corporeal light. To the extent, moreover, that sleep, or the lack of it, is now rendered a matter of grow-ing public concern, and to the extent that sleepiness is being recast as an 'at risk' somatic state and a morally suspect or blameworthy corporeal condition – i.e. drowsiness as the new drunkenness – then sleep is very clearly a political or bio-political matter. It is intimately bound up with the governance of bodies in con-temporary society (Williams, 2011).

The focus on embodiment in health and illness has certain advantages. Besides redressing a 'cognitive bias' (Turner, 2008) in social theorizing, it helps bridge the structure–agency, micro–macro divide, opening up a great many black boxes in doing

embodiment

so. Freund (2006), for instance, following his work on the 'expressive' body and embodied ways of feeling (dis)empowered, points to the possible neurohormonal consequences of stress. The dramaturgical stresses and strains of role performance, he suggests – themselves an index of social hierarchies of power and status, domination and control – translate more or less readily into the health and illness of embodied agents and include neurophysiological perturbations of many different sorts, whether consciously experienced or not. These embodied processes are most consequential for people in subordinate positions, via the invalidating definitions of others and the threats to selfhood and ontological security these engender. This reveals yet another powerful pathway through which the negative effects of inequality take their toll.

The attention given to fleshy matters of lived embodiment, as these brief illustrations suggest, provides a more promising way forward than (strong) constructionist approaches in which the body is seen, solely or simply, in discursive terms. Both approaches, of course, have their merits, and attempts to reconcile them are now very much on the agenda. For some critics, nonetheless, the focus on embodied experience and expression draws attention away from other, more macro-oriented concerns and extra-corporeal sociological matters. This, however, as shown above, is not inevitable; indeed some of the most promising work is located precisely at this juncture. As the multi-dimensional medium for the constitution of society, the body is central to these debates and their attempted resolution. Other classic sociological themes, moreover, can themselves be re-read in this new and more embodied light, augmenting (rather than replacing) former (classic) concerns and insights along the way.

One particularly important issue to confront, within and beyond the sociology of health and illness, concerns whether or not we wish to advocate a sociology *of* the body, a sociology *of* embodiment, or an *embodied* sociology. A sociology of the body would reflect on the body as an object of sociological analysis. A sociology of embodiment, in contrast, would take the lived meanings and experiences of bodies seriously, in health as elsewhere. An embodied sociology, however, very much in keeping with our thinking, would go one step further, taking the embodiment of its practitioners, as well as those we seek to study, seriously (Williams and Bendelow, 1998). This, in turn, throws up questions concerning the relationship between reason and emotion, the role of emotions in social life, and the emotional underpinnings of sociology itself as a supposedly 'rational' or 'dispassionate' enterprise.

Whatever one's view of these embodied matters, the implications are clear. Sociology's own somewhat disembodied past is now being critically redressed, breathing new corporeal life into its classically rationalist bones.

See also: *Emotions; Chronic Illness; Disability; Illness Narratives*

REFERENCES

Arber, S., Hislop, J. and Williams, S.J. (2007) 'Editors' introduction: gender, sleep and the life course', *Sociological Research Online*, 12 (5): Online: http://www.socresonline.org.uk/12/5/3.html

Freund, P. (2006) 'Socially constructed embodiment: neurohormonal connections as resources for theorizing about health inequalities', *Social Theory & Health*, 4: 85–108.

Fuller, S. (2006) *The New Sociological Imagination*. London: Sage.

Kelly, M. and Field, D. (1996) 'Medical sociology, chronic illness and the body', *Sociology of Health & Illness*, 18 (2): 241–57.

Merleau-Ponty, M. (1962/1945) *The Phenomenology of Perception*. London: Routledge.

Monaghan, L.F. (2001) 'Looking good, feeling good: the embodied pleasures of vibrant physicality', *Sociology of Health & Illness*, 23 (3): 330–56.

Monaghan, L.F. (2008) *Men and the War on Obesity: A Sociological Study*. New York: Routledge.

Shilling, C. (2005) *The Body in Culture, Technology and Society*. London: Sage.

Turner, B.S. (2008) *The Body & Society*, 3rd edn. London: Sage.

Twigg, J., Wolkowitz, C., Lara Cohen, R. and Nettleton, S. (2011) 'Conceptualising body work in health and social care', *Sociology of Health & Illness*, 33 (2): 171–88.

Watson, J. (2000) *Male Bodies: Health, Culture and Identity*. Buckingham: Open University Press.

Williams, S.J. (2011) *The Politics of Sleep: Governing (Un)Consciousness in the Late Modern Age*. Basingstoke: Palgrave Macmillan.

Williams, S.J. and Bendelow, G. (1998) *The Lived Body: Sociological Themes, Embodied Issues*. London: Routledge.

Williams, S.J. and Crossley, N. (2008) 'Editors' introduction: sleeping bodies', *Body & Society*, 14 (4): 1–13.

Williams, S.J., Birke, L. and Bendelow, G.A. (eds) (2003) *Debating Biology: Sociological Reflections on Health, Medicine and Society*. London: Routledge.

Simon J. Williams and Lee F. Monaghan

Emotions

Often defined as the part of consciousness that involves bodily 'feeling', emotions provide the crucial link between the mind, body and society. Sociological theory and research on emotions is of particular relevance when understanding stress, mental health and chronic illness.

Traditionally, theories of emotion have been dominated by psychosocial approaches that emphasize the biological origins of instinctive survival mechanisms known as 'signal functioning'. This is popularly understood through examples such as 'fight or flight' reactions involving surges of adrenaline, which are interpreted as fear or anxiety. Although these accounts do provide an explanation of physical 'symptoms' – or feelings which are activated by cognitive awareness – they largely ignore, or under-emphasize, the importance of socio-cultural meanings and the structural divisions that frame emotional expression. Moreover, the biological 'hard-wired' nature of these models sees emotions as uncontrollable and beyond our individual control, hence the polarized positioning of rationality versus emotionality which is so deeply embedded throughout Western social thought.

Perhaps the most significant challenge to this dominant 'organismic' orthodoxy can be found in Hochschild's social theory of emotion (2003 [1983]). Hochschild stresses that although emotions have a biological substratum, they are socially shaped and managed. Restated, emotions may be subject to manipulation within a network of social relations, meanings and practices. This is in line with various social divisions such as class, gender, age, and sexuality. For example, the lower one's status is in the social hierarchy, the more one may have to conform to social expectations. Hochschild's concepts of *emotion management* and *emotion work* combine both internal subjective states and bodily displays in the development of *status shields*, which are the socially distributed resources that people have for protecting their sense of self in various social situations. This interactionist approach sees emotion through the notion of the 'mindful body' as the nexus of phenomenological experience and the body in its social context. Emotions, in this model, are the link not just between mind and body, but also between mind, body, and society.

Grief provides a clear example when discussing the sociological approach to emotions. Grief is a manifestation of emotional pain which is inseparable from its bodily experience, often described as 'agonising and gut churning'. Furthermore, the 'appropriate' management of grief varies according to socio-cultural context. Certainly, anthropologists have long recognized how displays of grief at funerals vary widely, in accord with culturally embedded social expectations and relations. Similarly, sociological explorations of sickness, madness, pain, disability and death make clear that these are human events which are literally 'seething with emotion' (Williams and Bendelow, 1996). The development of sophisticated interactionist concepts of emotion – which emphasize the contextual social shaping of their embodied expressivity (Freund, 1990) – is crucial for understanding the illness experience. As I will elaborate below, such thinking also has particular value for deconstructing the (much used, but rarely defined) concept of stress as well as other concerns.

Stress is cited as a major risk factor within illness aetiology, and 'stress-related illness' is one of the most commonly given reasons for work absenteeism (Wainwright and Calnan, 2002). However, within *the dominant medical orthodoxy* there is no actual diagnostic category, specialism or curriculum focus on stress. Within scientific discourse, stress has traditionally been theorized as being located in individual biology or the psyche, and through the elaboration of mechanistic and homeostatic models which invoke images of 'tension' and 'pressure'. Most models suggest that physiological, behavioural and psychological processes may directly influence health in specific ways, and adaptation models describe stress as an ongoing process of adaptation – alarm–resistance–exhaustion. Thus, temporary stress can cause a useful adaptation as long as the body can return to homeostasis. Chronic stress may prevent homeostasis and lead to ill health, possibly in the following sequence:

As understood within medical sociology, which takes a non-reductionist approach to the human body (Bendelow, 2009), biology is important, but social context and the complex intertwining of emotion and embodiment are also crucial *vis-à-vis* the experience/distribution/consequences of stress. Such concerns are underplayed in biomedical scientific discourse. In contrast, sociological understandings of health and illness help to illuminate the transaction between individuals and society, and take into consideration the individual's repertoire of coping resources and vulner-abilities. This is neatly captured in writings on the psychosocial determinants of health inequalities (Wilkinson and Pickett, 2009). Building upon the idea of health as capital across all the aspects that Bourdieu (1984) described – namely eco-nomic, social and cultural – it is possible to develop and refine sophisticated mod-els of stress. As detailed elsewhere (Bendelow, 2009), the sociology of emotion can draw upon a health capital model to explain how individuals with more resources and fewer vulnerabilities may be less likely to perceive a given set of circumstances as stress-provoking. And even when events are perceived as stressful, these indi-viduals seem better able to adjust and cope. Thus, intensely perceived stress may activate physiological, behavioural, and psychological and social processes that will place individuals at a heightened risk of suffering from health problems or illness behaviour. In this way, both responses to feeling stressed and to stressful situations are socially constructed: they are not purely individual 'biological' responses, but are strongly influenced by socio-economic, environmental and cultural factors.

Such considerations bring to light the limitations of Cartesian dualism – a long-standing hallmark of biomedicine which separates mind and body. Such dualism typically reduces individuals to 'body machines', thereby revealing the socially controlling propensities of biomedicine (Foucault, 1973). The traditional divide between physical and mental illness has also historically reinforced hierarchical divisions within medicine itself. This is because anything that is classified as a mental illness has been consistently stigmatized and marginalized, and psychiatry has always been low in the hierarchy of medical specialisms. Complicating this picture is the *biopsychosocial* model. This model has gained much popularity amongst physicians since the 1980s. Its multi-causal definition has allowed for a variety of perspectives to be taken into account in diagnosis and treatment, imply-ing a multi-disciplinary approach. However, it too can be criticized for not fully addressing mind/body dualism as the patient can still be compartmentalized, with the physician addressing biomedical symptoms and the psychologist/psychiatrist the psychosocial element. Although some specialist areas (for example, pain clin-ics, oncology, liaison psychiatry) are developing integrated theory and practice, it is still the case that traditional, biomedically orientated, healthcare professionals remain ill prepared to fully understand the connections between mental and physical health.

The recent shift towards inter-disciplinarity in many areas of healthcare prac-tice has resulted in *integrated* models becoming the preferred consensual term for

emotions

many practitioners and theorists. Integrated models are now permeating medical education and practice and serve to highlight further the outmoded relevance of mental/physical labels. Again, contextual factors are salient here, and, thus, so is embodied emotionality. In industrialized countries the patterning of disease and illness changed dramatically over the course of the twentieth century as mortality from infectious disease declined. These changes in life expectancy, while bestowing huge benefits in terms of living longer, resulted in far greater rates of morbidity and a huge expansion of illness categories which incorporated both physical and emotional components. Alongside illnesses associated with older age, changes in epidemiological patterning include the increasing incidence of chronic illnesses which require management across the lifecourse (for example, asthma).

Many chronic conditions are manifested through medically unexplained symptoms (MUS), which can compound the emotional difficulties encountered by people with illnesses. This acronym, MUS, signifies illnesses or syndromes which cannot be defined in terms of organic pathology and are thus seen as abnormal and lowly placed in the medicalized 'illness hierarchy' (Nettleton et al., 2004). Likewise the term 'contested conditions' is used to signify illnesses that have a controversial scientific status (for example, Chronic Fatigue Syndrome, Repetitive Strain Injury). Here, patients experience distressing physical symptoms such as impaired mobility or coordination, intermittent paralysis, fitting, pain and fatigue. Once again, however, there is usually an absence of physical signs, clinical explanations, or medical diagnoses.

Chronic pain is a classic example of the dilemma of modern medicine. Medicine promises to treat or alleviate pain, but what actually constitutes pain can be defined in many ways. Medical practice concentrates on the sensory aspects of pain, employing the acute/chronic differentiation which does not necessarily take into account the emotional aspects of pain. Yet as well as being a medical 'problem', the experience of pain is so much wider, lying at 'the intersection of bodies, minds and cultures' (Morris, 1991: 1) and not just confined to our anatomy and physiology. The limitations of the medical model become especially highlighted when the acute/chronic differentiation is evoked, and it is universally acknowledged that one of the most complex and difficult types of pain to treat is *idiopathic* pain – that is, pain for which there is no established physical pathology – often termed *chronic pain syndrome*.

To help redress such limitations within biomedicine, emotions need to be taken seriously in all their multi-dimensional complexity, along with insights from those disciplines that study emotions. Social science, in particular the sociological literature on chronic illness, offers a framework for understanding the emotional experiences and consequences of chronic pain by focusing on the *person* rather than the pain per se. Concepts such as biographical disruption, narrative reconstruction and illness adjustment (Bury, 1991) are particularly valuable, and the theoretical and methodological explosion of interest in illness narratives has helped to convey the highly emotional and phenomenological experience of illness, pain and suffering (Kleinman, 1988). The development of narrative medicine and medical humanities has also highlighted the importance of embodied knowledge and lay expertise.

'Expert patients' have since gained much currency in medical as well as social science research (Greenhalgh, 2009).

This throws up issues relating to what is called self-management. Using models from the recovery movement in mental health, self-management for chronic illnesses is gaining momentum as a high-profile policy initiative, having been introduced within the UK in the last decade. Self-management is a reflexive holistic approach which is seen to combine an individual's emotional literacy and lay expertise in order to develop autonomy and self-determination in health maintenance and illness prevention. Much in the way that *sexual health* has become an umbrella category for service provision which encompasses emotional, cultural and lifestyle factors as well as medical aspects, the term *emotional health* is gaining popularity amongst both practitioners and the lay public (Bendelow, 2009). However, scepticism is needed to ensure it is not simply a strategy to shift the responsibility for health entirely onto the individual and relocate the economic burden associated with chronic illness from the welfare state and public health services to 'private consumers' of health care.

In conclusion, addressing the role of emotions in health and illness – as with an embodied approach to sociology more generally – helps to challenge the dualistic legacies within Western philosophy and biomedicine. These theoretical and methodological insights also enable the development of integrated and holistic models of health, medicine, and illness. In turn, this process enables more sophisticated understandings of the relationship between social structure and health. It also furnishes insights into the socially constructed aspects of diagnosis and the phenomenological experience of chronic illness, stress, and pain.

See also: *Embodiment; Illness Narratives; Emotional Labour*

REFERENCES

Bendelow, G. (2009) *Health, Emotion and the Body*. Cambridge: Polity Press.

Bourdieu, P. (1984) *Distinction: A Social Critique of the Judgement of Taste*. London: Routledge.

Bury, M. (1991) 'The sociology of chronic illness: a review of research and prospects', *Sociology of Health & Illness*, 13 (4): 451–68.

Foucault, M. (1973) *The Birth of the Clinic*. London: Tavistock.

Freund, P. (1990) 'The expressive body: a common ground for the sociology of emotions and health and illness', *Sociology of Health & Illness*, 12 (4): 452–77.

Greenhalgh, T. (2009) 'Patient and public involvement in chronic illness: beyond the expert patient', *BMJ*, 338: b49.

Hochschild, A. (2003 [1983]) *The Managed Heart: The Commercialization of Human Feeling*. Berkeley: University of California Press.

Kleinman, A. (1988) *The Illness Narratives: Suffering, Healing and the Human Condition*. New York: Basic Books.

Morris, D. (1991) *The Culture of Pain*. Berkeley and London: University of California Press.

Nettleton, S., O'Malley, L., Watt, I. and Duffy, P. (2004) 'Enigmatic illness: narratives of patients who live with medically unexplained symptoms', *Social Theory and Health*, 2 (1): 47–67.

Wainwright, D. and Calnan, M. (2002) *Work Stress: The Making of a Modern Epidemic*. Buckingham: Open University Press.

Wilkinson, R. and Pickett, K. (2009) *The Spirit Level: Why More Equal Societies Do Better*. London: Penguin.

Williams, S.J. and Bendelow, G. (1996) 'Emotions, health and illness: the "missing link" in medical sociology?', in J. Gabe and N. James (eds), *Health and the Sociology of Emotions*. Oxford: Blackwell.

Gillian Bendelow

Chronic Illness

> *Chronic illness commonly refers to those forms of long-term health disorders that interfere with social interaction and role performance. It is often disruptive of people's lives, though responses can and do vary depending on context.*

Medical sociologists have long been interested in studying illness experience and especially chronic illness. The public health and demographic reasons for this are not hard to find. In the last half of the twentieth century, most developed countries (and now many developing nations) have experienced a 'demographic transition'. A decline in mortality at all ages, but especially in infancy and early adulthood, has led to an increase in average life expectancy from birth and (in the presence of low fertility rates) an ageing population. Today the majority of men and women expect to live into old age. As deaths from infections have declined and as a greater proportion of the population comprises the elderly, those disorders associated with adult and later life have grown in prominence. Many of these are chronic disorders, such as arthritis, stroke, dementia, Parkinson's disease, and some forms of heart disease and cancer.

Sociological interest in chronic illness has, in part, stemmed from the limitations of medical treatment for chronic disorders. While some forms of treatment are very effective, such as hip replacement and cataract surgery, many disorders can only be treated palliatively, to relieve pain and to help physical functioning. The long-term implications of chronic illness inevitably bring social and psychological factors to the fore and many physicians have looked to wider forms of collaboration with medical sociologists in order to understand the issues as they are experienced and managed by lay people. A perusal of a key medical sociology journal, *Sociology of Health & Illness*, makes clear that these issues are many and varied; for instance, real and anticipated stigma or the uncertainty and fear associated with the diagnosis of a chronic condition (Lawton, 2003; Williams, 2000).

Sociological interest in chronic illness stemmed from key work carried out in the 1960s and 1970s, especially in the USA. Initially, research focused on the

experience of health and illness

social patterning of chronic illness and whether this differed from life-threatening conditions that produced high mortality. Conover (1973) reviewed and re-analysed data that had been the subject of a debate between two sociologists, Kadushin and Mechanic, and concluded that the occurrence of chronic illness was, indeed, related to social class and poverty. Critically, while such a finding suggests that more should have been written on the political economy of chronic illness, most sociological research has been micro-interactionist in approach. Indeed, much research has explored the meanings and consequences of chronic illness, and the steps taken to mitigate the effects of chronic conditions as experienced by sufferers themselves in a micro-social context (for example, in relation to family, friends and carers).

In contrast to the 'systems' perspective formulated in Parsons' writing on 'the sick role', sociological research on chronic illness has largely focused on people's experiences within their contexts of everyday life. While Lawton (2003) reviews some of this literature, focusing specifically on articles published in *Sociology of Health & Illness* during the previous 25 years, there are important antecedents. Perhaps the most significant publication in the 1970s, in this regard, was Strauss and Glaser's book, *Chronic Illness and the Quality of Life* (1975). Although Strauss and Glaser began by noting the health care implications of chronic illness, and especially the need for professionals to widen their horizons from their preoccupation with acute conditions, the main thrust of the chapters in their book was strongly interactionist in tone. From this viewpoint, chronic illness is not just a given biological entity, patterned by social conditions, but is itself a 'negotiated reality'. Chronic illness and its outcomes are shaped by the decisions, tactics and organization of 'work' carried out by patients and others, over the 'trajectory' of the illness. The contingent nature of this process is part of a general view of society, which is seen to be the product of interaction and negotiation.

In Britain, Bury (1982) developed this position to argue that chronic illness might be conceptualized as a form of 'biographical disruption' or critical situation. This concept is worth focusing on since, as observed by Williams (2000: 45), it has been an 'abiding theme within the sociology of chronic illness since the early 1980s'. In Bury's (1982) research on rheumatoid arthritis, the impact of serious and persisting symptoms on everyday life was seen to threaten sufferers' taken-for-granted world. Modern medical categories, the medical understanding of disease and the treatment it could offer might be appropriated by patients, and employed in legitimating and explaining their altered condition to family and friends. At the same time, the diagnosis and its implications for the future might confirm the fact that the individual was suffering from a progressively disabling condition from which there was no escape. In the absence of a medical cure, the individual would have to negotiate and manage their altered state with whatever support they could muster.

In a later paper, Bury (1991) distinguished between three dimensions of this process. First, he argued that *coping* referred to the cognitive processes employed by the chronically ill to sustain a sense of self-worth and to come to terms with both an altered situation and an altered body. Second, he held that the term *strategy* referred to the actions and processes involved in the management of the condition and its impact on interaction and life chances. The strategic management of the disorder and its effects required decisions about how to mobilize resources and how to balance demands on others and remain independent. Third, he stated that chronic illness involved the adoption of a particular *style* of living, or different *styles of adjustment*. Lifestyle for the chronically ill would often mean deciding how much should be disclosed or disguised about the condition, how far the person should 'come out', and in what way, in interacting with others. For some groups, withdrawal from all but essential interaction has been observed. For others 'normalization' has meant integrating the disorder into an altered and public identity. Biographical disruption may not, therefore, be the only outcome. Depending on outlook and circumstance, biographical reinforcement may also be possible.

Much research and debate has been published in recent years on the variable meanings and consequences of chronic illness and people's different, context-dependent, ways of trying to cope. Here lay perspectives and voices are given due weight, rather than remaining hidden behind closed doors and eclipsed by a bio-medical remit that has traditionally emphasized cure over care, and acute over chronic illness. Interestingly, contrary findings have emerged during empirical research, serving to complicate the picture as well as confirm aspects of Bury's (1991) later writings, such as the significance of people's expectations. Substantive issues and themes include, for example, the stage of the life-course within which chronic illness occurs and thus whether or not that illness is disruptive or is in fact anticipated (Pound et al., 1998). As the aforementioned researchers demonstrate in the case of stroke among elderly respondents in the East End of London, age may mediate chronic illness so that it is considered 'not that bad'. Such an observation also makes sense when placed within its socio-economic context. London East Enders living in poverty did not have high expectations of good health, especially as they aged and bore witness to continued or worsening hardship in their hard-earned lives. It is in this shared context of adversity that a stroke, relatively speaking, was not 'that bad'.

Given such evidence, the biographical disruption concept has been subject to a theoretical reappraisal. Following his own incursions into sociological debates on the body in research on chronic illness and disability, Williams (2000) has sought to develop an approach that is 'fit' for the twenty-first century where a diversity of experiences characterize chronic illness. Here he poses such questions as: 'Does a focus on "disruption" mask as much as it reveals?' And: 'Can equal weight be accorded both to chronic illness's role in the creation of biographical disruption and biographical disruption's role in the creation of chronic illness?' (2000: 41). After defending the biographical disruption concept against postmodernist and disability theorists' critiques, where bodies and pain are dissolved into discourse and social oppression, Williams (2000) makes several interesting points. For example, he maintains that the common focus on disruption remains adult-centric, obscuring the realities of chronic illness among children who may have congenital conditions and where illness has always been part of the embodied self, and thus where 'continuity rather than change remains the guiding principle' (p. 50). Williams also connects with research on people's circumscribed expectations of health and illness amidst a 'normal crisis', highlighting the largely under-researched implications of other social divisions that interact with age and class, such as ethnicity and gender, and people's varied experiences of chronic illness. Another key issue, which is consonant with earlier yet underdeveloped research on the social distribution of chronic illness, concerns the possible aetiology of chronic illness. Here Williams raises the possibility, implicit in much of the research on illness narratives, that biographical disruption may cause chronic illness, with embodied narratives perhaps providing an emotionally rich 'radical critique' of the status quo (for example, in relation to workplace exploitation, gendered role requirements and oppressive regimes in former Soviet-occupied Eastern Europe). In that respect, Williams locates chronic illness and 'personal troubles' within the larger realm of public issues and global social structure, 'itself a defining hallmark of the sociological imagination' (p. 54).

Finally, it is worth noting a recurrent tension in much of these discussions on chronic illness. This concerns discrepancies between a 'problems' or 'personal tragedy' perspective, in which the difficulties people face are documented and brought into view, and one in which chronic illness can be approached in a positive, if not always an overtly political, light. Calls to move beyond a largely 'reformist' position on the one hand, and a 'radical' position on the other – positions attributed respectively to medical sociologists and disability activists – have been complicated by an emphasis on a postmodern culture of illness and disability. Charmaz (2000), for example, suggests that sociology needs to go further than document the 'patient's perspective' and the normalization processes that 'contain' the effects of illness and disability on everyday life, important though these are. Significantly, she goes on to say that 'chronic illness can mean embarking on an odyssey . . . to integrate the self on a different level . . . facing such losses moves them [the chronically ill] towards transcending loss' (p. 287). As with other sociological writers, especially in North America, the dividing lines between chronic illness, disability and health appear to become blurred in such arguments. Here a form of 'biographical reinvention' may be seen, whether among disability activists, patients' groups or others, in what Frank (1997) calls the 'remission society', a society where large numbers of people may be experiencing or recovering from a variety of bodily ills. What in the earlier literature was seen to be a process of stabilization and normalization by the chronically ill now becomes a ceaseless and nomadic journey with no clear end point (see Williams, 2001, for a critique). The links between body, self and society, in this viewpoint, are not simply the outcome of interactional difficulties or 'social oppression', but constitute a shifting terrain, on which individuals and groups attempt to construct new identities and new realities.

There is a need for medical sociology to examine empirically the salience of such thinking, as well as the more political stance of some disability researchers, by conducting studies among representative samples of the chronically ill and disabled. Without this, both medical sociology and disability studies may be caught up in forms of rhetoric that will be difficult to evaluate. The testing of many of the ideas that have grown in recent years (see, for example, Sanders et al., 2002; Sanderson et al., 2011) would seem to be the most urgent task facing medical sociology in relation to chronic illness and disability.

See also: *Medicalization; Disability; Illness Narratives; Social Movements and Health*

REFERENCES

Bury, M. (1982) 'Chronic illness as biographical disruption', *Sociology of Health & Illness*, 4 (2): 167–82.

Bury, M. (1991) 'The sociology of chronic illness: a review of research and prospects', *Sociology of Health & Illness*, 13 (4): 451–68.

Charmaz, K. (2000) 'Experiencing chronic illness', in G.L. Albrecht, R. Fitzpatrick and S.C. Scrimshaw (eds), *The Handbook of Social Studies in Health and Medicine*. London: Sage.

Conover, P. (1973) 'Social class and chronic illness', *International Journal of Health Services*, 3 (3): 357–68.

Frank, A. (1997) *The Wounded Story Teller: Body, Illness and Ethics*. Chicago: University of Chicago Press.

Lawton, J. (2003) 'Lay experience of health and illness: past research and future agendas', in *Sociology of Health & Illness*, 25 (3): 23–40.

Pound, P., Gompertz, P. and Ebrahim, E. (1998) 'Illness in the context of older age: the case of stroke', *Sociology of Health & Illness*, 20 (4): 489–506.

Sanders, C., Donovan, J. and Dieppe, P. (2002) 'The significance and consequence of having painful joints in older age: co-existing accounts of normal and disrupted biographies', *Sociology of Health & Illness*, 24 (2): 227–53.

Sanderson, T., Calnan, M., Morris, M., Richards, P. and Hewlett, S. (2011) 'Shifting normalities: interactions of changing conceptions of a normal life and the normalisation of symptoms in rheumatoid arthritis', *Sociology of Health & Illness*, 33 (4): 616–33.

Strauss, A. and Glaser, B. (1975) *Chronic Illness and the Quality of Life*. St Louis, MO: Mosby.

Williams, G. (2001) 'Theorizing disability', in G.L Albrecht, K.D. Seelman and M. Bury (eds), *Handbook of Disability Studies*. London: Sage.

Williams, S.J. (2000) 'Chronic illness as biographical disruption or biographical disruption as chronic illness? Reflections on a core concept', *Sociology of Health & Illness*, 22 (1): 40–67.

Mike Bury and Lee F. Monaghan

Disability

> Disability is a complex and much debated issue pertaining to impaired bodies, social structures and processes. From a politicized perspective, disability should not be seen as a purely medical problem since many of the problems faced by disabled people arise as the result of the way that society is organized.

Disability cannot be considered a universal category rooted in an impaired biological body. Indeed, what is considered a disability is culturally variable. Martha's

Vineyard in Massachusetts, USA, is a famous example, where hereditary deafness was commonplace and normalized for almost two centuries until the early twentieth century (Groce, 1985). The picture is also complicated because disabled people can have impairments that are stable or progressive, and these can range from mild to severe, constant or episodic, and the impairment itself can be culturally produced. Even so, definitions are adopted within the international policy literature in order to operationalize disability, gauge its prevalence alongside associated problems, and ultimately seek to protect human rights. In the preamble to the UN *Convention on the Rights of Persons with Disabilities* (UNCRPD, 2006), disability is described as 'an evolving concept [that] results from the interaction between persons with impairments and attitudinal and environmental barriers that hinder their full and effective participation in society on an equal basis with others'.

The World Health Survey estimates that around 15 per cent of the world's population (just over one billion people) have some form of disability and of these between 110 million and 190 million have significant difficulties in functioning (WHO, 2011a). Included in this latter group are people who have quadriplegia, paraplegia, severe depression or blindness. The prevalence and seriousness of disability have been increasing, largely due to demographic factors with people suffering more from chronic illnesses that are associated with older age, though that is only part of the picture. The World Health Organization (WHO, 2008) estimates that 95 million (5.1 per cent of) children under the age of 14 have some form of impairment, of whom thirteen million (0.7 per cent) are defined as having a 'severe disability'.

Disabled people form the world's largest minority group. Reflecting macro socio-economic inequalities, 80 per cent of disabled people live in the Global South. Disability and poverty are closely linked and the World Bank estimates that around 20 per cent of the world's poorest people are disabled. Not only are poor people more likely to become disabled, as a consequence of their material conditions of existence, but also disabled people face barriers to education, employment and public services which can further impoverish them. In addition, disabled people tend to be seen within their own communities as being among the most disadvantaged (Braithwaite and Mont, 2009). Disabled people generally have less access to health care services and therefore experience unmet health care needs. Of course, disabled people do not constitute a homogeneous group and the disadvantage experienced by them intersects with other equality issues. Disabled women, for example, might be multiply disadvantaged. Such women risk discrimination in terms of inequitable gender arrangements and oppressive disablist attitudes, which can combine and serve to reinforce each other (WHO, 2011b). One might consider the intersections of other divisions here as well, such as age, ethnicity, sexuality and location (incorporating issues ranging from local community service provision to the broader distribution of resources between and within nations).

Socially constructed barriers that disable bodies have been conceptualized as a form of violence: 'The violence of disablism' (Goodley and Runswick-Cole, 2011) incorporates various dimensions: psychoemotional, systemic, cultural, and actual physical assaults. As explained by Goodley and Runswick-Cole, disabled children might be vulnerable under certain social conditions that are commonplace in Western capitalism. For instance, the highly individualistic and competitive neo-liberal values that children are enculturated into at school reinforce and amplify (ableist) divisions. However, without trivializing disturbing observations such as those reported in the aforementioned study, the last thirty years have, at least in the Global North, seen changes to the way disabled people are positioned in policy discourse and other contexts. For instance, 45 countries have passed anti-discrimination and other disability-specific laws. Disabled people are now far more likely to live in their local community rather than be confined to long-stay institutions or other segregated provision. These changes also mean greater consideration is now being given to environmental, attitudinal and institutional barriers than to the body per se. This re-framing was the result of a conceptual shift from a 'medical model' to the 'social model' of disability (Oliver, 1990).

The social model of disability is closely associated with disability studies. This model emerged from the ideas of disabled activists in affluent Western nations who were dissatisfied with the way that they were treated by society and the services they received. The ideas were later given academic credibility by disabled academics who were similarly disillusioned with the way that sociology in general, and medical sociology in particular, defined and researched disability. Social and cultural theories of disability, as Goodley and Runswick-Cole (2011) observe, have been heavily influenced by Parsons' structural functionalism with its 1950s conservative bent. Drawing on ideas from the emerging new social movements that developed in the 1960s and 1970s around ethnicity, sexuality and gender, groups of radical disabled people converged to form a distinct political movement. They demanded that disability be viewed as separate from medicine and campaigned against a perceived over-medicalization of disabled people's lives. This rejection of medicalization was accompanied by concerns around the individualization of disability, coupled with a focus on disability as a problem of welfare and the putative burden disabled people place on society.

The basic tenet of the social model of disability was laid out in a document published by the Union of the Physically Impaired Against Segregation, titled *The Fundamental Principles of Disability* (UPIAS, 1976). This document argued that disability was the result of society and the way it was organized and not the result of physical impairment. Disability, it stated, was socially produced. The analysis broadly followed that of early second-wave feminism: just as gender was seen as being socially constructed in contrast to the biological sex of the female and male body, so too was disability, the social, contrasted with impairment, the biological. UPIAS maintained that disabled people were an oppressed social group, constituting a minority similar to other minority groups, and that all disabled people shared a common experience. Advocates of the social model of disability directly challenged what was later termed 'the personal tragedy theory of disability' (Oliver, 1990: 2), which they felt dominated writings on disability at the time.

The (1976) UPIAS document is unashamedly aimed at activists and this demand for equality is still present in much of disability studies today. While straw person arguments are easily made in these debates, it is the activists' political focus on equality that perhaps most clearly separates disability studies from medical sociology (notably, micro-interactionist or phenomenological types of analysis). By redefining disability as an equality issue and shifting the focus from the individual's impairment to how society is organized, together with the discrimination and prejudice experienced by disabled people, proponents of the social model aim for the large-scale transformation of society. In the case of disability, it was felt that medical sociology had largely abandoned its discipline's traditional focus on the social, instead placing its emphasis on individual responses to living with a chronic condition or impairment. Unlike, for example, social constructionist studies of gender or ethnicity that interrogated definitional practices (such as the effects of sexist or racist stereotypes on people's life chances), disability activists felt that much of sociology – by linking chronic illness with disadvantage – had failed to explore the social creation of disability.

Oliver's influential monograph, *The Politics of Disablement* (1990), provides perhaps the clearest theoretical understanding of this approach to disability. Oliver draws on classical sociological theories, such as that offered by Marx, in order to provide a materialist analysis that affords primacy to power relations and places the cause of disability firmly in societal structures. These ideas are replicated in more recent texts (for example, Barnes and Mercer, 2010). Through adopting a materialist understanding of disablement, Oliver (1990) links the oppression that disabled people face to the material and ideological forces associated with capitalism. Disability is not, according to Oliver, 'defined or culturally produced solely in terms of its relationship to the mode of production' (p. 22); it is also culturally produced through the relationship between the mode of production and the central values of society. Capitalist society encouraged an ideology of individualism, which, coupled with medicalization and the development of rehabilitation, brought about profound changes in the way people with impairments were seen and treated. As a consequence of new work practices and an ideology of 'able-bodiedness', disabled people could no longer meet the demands placed on them as part of a workforce and so became excluded (p. 47). It is argued that the concept of 'disability' emerged under these conditions to control people's access to a state-sponsored welfare system. In effect, disability became medicalized, with the medical profession emerging as the definer and controller of disabled people on behalf of the state.

Although the analysis provided by the social model of disability has enabled disabled people to challenge their social exclusion, and the model remains influential, it is not without its critics from within disability studies and beyond. Those from outside of disability studies point to its failure to address impairment. Instead, they argue that a focus on the subjective experience of living with an impaired body should form the basis of any study of disability (Bury, 1996). Disabled feminists such as Thomas (1999, 2007), whilst broadly supporting the social model of disability's emphasis on barriers, point to the inadequate way that the model covers gender alongside the personal and experiential elements associated with disability. Similar arguments have been made around ethnicity and sexuality (Shakespeare, 2006).

Thomas (1999, 2007) asserts that the social model has been over-simplified by activists and as a consequence some of its claims have been unintentionally misunderstood. She maintains that in the *Fundamental Principles* (UPIAS, 1976) disability is described as being imposed 'on top of our impairments' and that the UPIAS definition does not claim that *all* restrictions of activity are socially caused. She adds that disability and impairment are both important, and they should both be the focus of attention. Thomas also argues for the development of a concept that she has called *impairment effects*. Impairment effects are the restrictions experienced by disabled people that are directly attributable to their impairment. While this is a potentially useful development it is, as Thomas herself explains, often very difficult to distinguish between impairments, impairment effects, and disability (2007: 137). For example, where people have a mental health problem it may be hard to determine where impairment effects end and disablement begins.

When critiquing the social model, Shakespeare (2006) argues that disability should be seen as neither purely medical nor purely social; it requires a balanced approach. Disabled people are, of course, discriminated against but they may also have health conditions that require medical and rehabilitation interventions. Disability, he argues, is a complex and multilayered phenomenon which cannot be reduced to either the social or the medical (see also WHO, 2011b).

There is clearly much to debate around disability, both in terms of how it is defined and in terms of who defines it. Disability activists, in conjunction with disability studies, have produced not just an intellectual challenge to the way that disability is understood and theorized – they have also established a new paradigm around disability. Such thinking has also directly challenged medical sociology. Both approaches have been at loggerheads but recent writings in medical sociology (for example, Scambler and Scambler, 2010) and disability studies (Thomas, 2007) suggest that there is some room for rapprochement and for a new, more constructive, relationship to emerge. Accordingly, there is an indication here that future work in medical sociology would benefit from a more politicized perspective that incorporates personal and experiential concerns with material or social structural factors.

See also: *Medicalization; Chronic Illness; Social Movements and Health*

REFERENCES

Barnes, C. and Mercer, G. (2010) *Exploring Disability*. London: Polity.

Braithwaite J. and Mont, D. (2009) 'Disability and poverty: a survey of World Bank poverty assessments and implications', *ALTER – European Journal of Disability Research/Revue Européenne de Recherche sur le Handicap*, 3: 219–32.

Bury, M. (1996) 'Defining and researching disability: challenges and responses', in C. Barnes and G. Mercer (eds), *Exploring the Divide: Illness and Disability*. Leeds: Disability Press.

Goodley, D. and Runswick-Cole, K. (2011) 'The violence of disablism', *Sociology of Health & Illness*, 33 (4): 602–17.

Groce, N.E. (1985) *Everyone Here Spoke Sign Language: Hereditary Deafness on Martha's Vineyard*. Cambridge, MA: Harvard University Press.

Oliver, M. (1990) *The Politics of Disablement*. Basingstoke: Macmillan.

Scambler, S. and Scambler, G. (eds) (2010) *New Directions in the Sociology of Chronic and Disabling Conditions: Assaults on the Lifeworld*. Basingstoke: Palgrave Macmillan.

Shakespeare, T. (2006) *Disability Rights and Wrongs*. Oxon: Routledge.

Thomas, C. (1999) *Female Forms: Experiencing and Understanding Disability*. Buckingham: Open University Press.

Thomas, C. (2007) *Sociologies of Disability and Illness: Contested Ideas in Disability Studies and Medical Sociology*. Basingstoke: Palgrave Macmillan.

UNCRPD (2006) *United Nations Convention on the Rights of Persons with Disabilities*. Online: http://www.un.org/disabilities/default.asp?id=260) (accessed 15 August 2011).

UPIAS (1976) *The Fundamental Principles of Disability*. Union of the Physically Impaired Against Segregation. Online: http://www.leeds.ac.uk/disabilitystudies/archiveuk/UPIAS/UPIAS.pdf

WHO (2008) *Global Burden of Disease*. Geneva: World Health Organization. Online: http://www.who.int/healthinfo/global_burden_disease/2004_report_update/en/index.html (accessed 12 June 2011).

WHO (2011a) *Disability and Health Fact Sheet Number 352*. Geneva: World Health Organization. Online: http://www.who.int/mediacentre/factsheets/fs352/en/ (accessed 13 June 2011).

WHO (2011b) *World Report on Disability*. Geneva: World Health Organization. Online: http://www.who.int/disabilities/world_report/2011/en/index.html (accessed 12 June 2011).

Nicholas Watson

Illness Narratives

Illness narratives refer to the story-telling and accounting practices that occur in the face of illness. Narrative analysis seeks to understand the 'plot' of the account given and its social and motivational dimensions.

Human cultures are reproduced through myths and narratives, that is, in the construction and telling of stories. Narratives provide the opportunity for using metaphors and other linguistic devices to convey and produce shared meanings and construct social identities, especially in difficult or threatening circumstances. Narratives have considerable relevance in the experiential world of illness, pain, suffering, vulnerability, and uncertainty.

Those interested in illness narratives typically seek to understand and analyse the meanings produced in one cultural setting and communicate this knowledge to an audience in another setting, often in the hope of informing policy and practice. The idea that patients' narratives can inform clinical practice has gained ground in the USA, the UK and other countries. At a time when 'evidence-based' practice has become the watchword in many medical systems, analysts have argued that the 'patient's view' is likely to be downplayed in favour of scientifically based and statistically oriented 'evidence'. However, attending to illness narratives may be just as important as evidence-based guidelines, especially in general practice which entails close contact with patients' everyday lives and the meanings attached to symptoms. Attending to such meanings is framed as 'narrative-based medicine' and is intended to help clinicians make better decisions (Greenhalgh and Hurwitz, 1999).

Sociologists and anthropologists interested in illness narratives have adopted a somewhat wider perspective, to include the multi-layered character of illness narratives, as well as their possible practical usage. Perhaps the best-known advocate of this approach is Kleinman (1988), an anthropologist and clinician who asserts that listening to and interpreting the illness experience is an art form that is often obscured during biomedical training. Dealing with clinical practice first, Kleinman argues that illness narratives are important for two reasons. Despite the scepticism which Kleinman believes many practitioners hold concerning illness narratives, patients with chronic disorders need to have a 'witness to suffering' and to their existential fears. Paying attention to illness narratives is also important in assisting in the practical management of such disorders. It is for these reasons that patients turn to doctors, even when they know that medical treatment may be limited.

Kleinman goes on to show that illness narratives also have many other functions, outside of the clinical situation. Most importantly, illness narratives help to deal with the altered situation and sometimes fundamental disruption which illness can create. In essence, illness narratives can help to address and fashion responses to the questions: Why me? Why now? And, 'What can be done? – the question of order and control' (Kleinman, 1988: 29). These are questions which the medical model often finds difficult to answer, especially, again, in chronic illness where many disorders have unknown aetiologies and are difficult to treat. Illness narratives thus construct meaning at a number of levels. Through an example of an elderly businessman with chronic heart disease Kleinman outlines a type of palimpsest, where each layer of meaning is written over another (1988: 32). So what begins with the 'internal' reality of the illness soon connects with other areas of the man's life, including serious alcohol problems, and the long-standing effects of having had a brutal father. On top of this, the man indicates, through his narrative, the need to work out both his own experience of loss and his relationship with his children, who openly wish him to go into a nursing home. In such accounts, Kleinman suggests, it is possible to see that narratives are more than a 'reporting' of illness (whether to practitioners or others), but are efforts to integrate or reintegrate individuals into their social worlds. There is in many such cases a 'narrative reconstruction' occurring, in which disturbance and suffering are brought under some form of meaningful control.

Illness narratives inevitably take particular forms as well as having specific contents. Each narrative will be fashioned by individuals in unique ways and to some extent in unique circumstances. Yet the sociological study of illness, especially chronic illness, has shown that narratives may involve one of a limited number of formal properties. These forms may, so to speak, exist prior to the construction or the telling of the story. They are 'accessed' through membership of a culture, where common understandings allow, indeed constrain, meanings to be fashioned in specific ways. The forms that illness narratives take will also be shaped by underlying psychological needs and motivations concerning the presentation of the self to others in particular contexts (for example, in an interview setting).

Bury (2001) has outlined three forms of illness narratives that subsume some aspects of schemes developed by other authors. The first of these, 'contingent narratives', are descriptions of the events surrounding the onset and early course of a disorder. They may deal with 'life events' such as bereavement or loss (particularly of a younger member of a family), or the 'external' circumstances of difficult or stressful work situations. They may also deal with the assimilation of medical explanations for the disorder and how these seem to tie in with the life experiences of the individuals concerned. Contingent narratives deal with proximate causes and proximate effects. They often outline the steps taken to deal with the illness and the strategies being employed to manage its effects. Such narratives tend to be practical and descriptive in nature, dealing with events as they unfold and the immediate impact these have on the relationship between the self and others.

In dealing with 'biographical reconstruction', individuals will often feel the need (not always consciously) to present themselves as culturally competent. In doing so they may employ 'moral narratives', the second form discussed by Bury. This moves the account a person may give from the descriptive to the evaluative. Narratives, in this sense, help not only to order experience but also to express the 'dynamic relations' between the self and others. Moral narratives may include social apologia in which the person tries to close the gap between their previous self-image and what they perceive or experience as failures in self-presentation or role performance, resulting from the effects of the illness. Moral narratives may also be a means to portray the self as active and socially engaged. Bury points out, however, that narratives may often be ambiguous; some may be ways of presenting the self as virtuous in comparison with others, whether sufferers or not. By praising oneself, one criticizes others. How the listener meets such claims to virtue is, of course, a different matter.

This brings us to Bury's third narrative form – what he calls 'core narratives'. These include 'genres of expression' through which the narrator 'emplots' herself in a more or less dramatic fashion. Such narratives may be epic or heroic, tragic, comic or didactic (Bury, 2001: 278). Research on chronic illness has, once again, furnished many examples of these illness narratives. Bury quotes Kelly and Dickinson's (1997) study of colitis where, even in the face of radical surgery, or perhaps because of it, some respondents present themselves as quietly heroic and sometimes with a dark humour. These authors note that the trope of courageously 'fighting' the illness has become a frequent invocation in public as well as private accounts.

Core narratives may also convey the underlying trajectory of the illness and the feelings associated with it. In this case, Robinson's (1990) study of multiple sclerosis illustrates how illness narratives may convey stable, progressive or regressive qualities. Robinson summarizes his analysis by saying that: 'a progressive narrative moves towards the personally valued goals, a regressive narrative away from such goals, and a stable narrative evaluatively sustains . . . the valued goals' (p. 1176). Progressive narratives, in particular, convey a positive and more engaging response by the individual. Such narratives also chime with a postmodern culture surrounding illness, one where 'restitution' and the search for a more positive identity through suffering may be found (Frank, 1995).

The analysis of illness narratives may be seen as part of the broadly interpretative wing of sociology. Clearly, the eliciting and recording of patients' narratives requires the employment of qualitative methods, especially extended interviews and life histories. Narrative analysis differs from other qualitative methods, however, in its stress on the need to examine long sequences of text and whole accounts rather than breaking the text up, as in thematic analysis. Whole narratives across a sample of respondents can then be compared for their similarities and differences. Though such narratives may take on the properties of one of the forms discussed here, it is likely, of course, that they will combine more than one element.

The concept of illness narratives has been important in eliciting key dimensions of the illness experience and its various meanings. In particular, it has suggested that the form of talk may constrain as well as facilitate expression in significant ways, revealing key elements in a given culture. The study of illness narratives has also shown important variations in people's responses to illness and has helped various audiences to understand the reasons why this should be the case. In particular, illness narratives have shown how the presentation of self in the face of illness frequently involves claims to moral as well as social competence.

However, as writers such as Riessman (1993: 2) have pointed out, the employment of interpretive methods in analysing illness narratives involves tackling 'the inevitable gap between the experience . . . and any communication about it'. This cautions against sociological approaches to illness narratives which regard them as a move in reclaiming illness from a dominant medical model as well as a 'colonial' medical practice. For example, illness narratives are, according to Frank, 'stories that are their own truth'. Frameworks of analysis are, from this viewpoint, merely devices to 'heighten attention' to these truths (Frank, 1995: 24). While, in one sense, it must be the case that individuals have a unique insight into their own experience, Riessman's (1993) methodological considerations suggest the need to proceed with care.

If illness narratives are treated as a 'revealed truth', then all claims take on equal weight. Yet the gap between experience and communication discussed by Riessman leads the researcher to ask the question, 'why was the story told that way?' (1993: 2). This question may reveal, in the analysis, contradictions and ambiguities in expression and in the relationship between the accounting procedures and the motivations for presenting matters in one way and not another. Motivational elements suggest that in sociology, and in clinical practice, illness narratives need to be interpreted and not taken as given. The ethic of the sociologist must be governed by the recognition that the teller 'has the first word on which the interpretation depends' (Riessman, 1993: 52), but at the same time that illness narratives are 'always edited versions of reality, not impartial or objective descriptions of it' (Riessman, 1990: 1197).

Such concerns have continued in recent years and been debated among key names in the medical sociology community. Thomas (2010), in reflecting upon the literature, offers a useful summary of and contribution to debates between Atkinson, Frank, Kleinman and others where '[m]atters of theoretical perspective, methodology, ethics, and personal politics are found to be at stake' (p. 647). She unpicks various claims and counter-claims when explicating Atkinson's critique of Frank, for instance, who is taken to task for romantically 'privileging' illness narratives as a source of authenticity – arguing that these are 'special' or 'valid' accounts about people's illness experiences. Where Atkinson argues for an analytic approach to narratives as 'speech acts', Frank and those with postmodern leanings are more inclined towards a mix of politics and advocacy in their interpretations.

Thomas (2010) locates claims and counter-claims about illness narrative research in a wider sociological context. What underpins the crux of the debate, according to Thomas, is the type of sociology (implicitly) being practised. She uses Burawoy's influential schema on sociology's division of labour to make sense of this. Some sociologists may be more interested in producing public knowledge for extra-academic audiences (patient advocacy groups, for example) rather than analytic accounts for their peers. Reflecting these tensions between professional and public sociologies, alongside the interplay of critical and policy lines of analysis, Thomas has sympathy with both sides of the debate. Thus, she endorses aspects of Atkinson's reasoning; notably, the importance of systematic research and formal analysis over sentimentality and romanticism. Various points raised by Frank and Kleinman are also credited where ethics and personal standpoint have dialogic significance and what she sees as 'emancipatory' potential for communities of ill people. Thomas arrives at such a position with reference to her personal experiences and in-depth research on illness narratives among people with cancer and their informal carers. She writes: 'I believe that qualitative social scientific research of the type referred to here can, if carefully disseminated, assist in making cancer and palliative care services more responsive to the needs and interests of patients, carers, and other service users' (Thomas, 2010: 657).

Whatever the reader's position might be in these debates, it is evident from Thomas (2010) and others that the concept of illness narratives continues to stimulate sociological research and discussion. In sum, such literature makes clear that medical sociologists must respectfully engage the rich and complex stories recounted by people, while also being reflexive about their own aims when interpreting and analysing illness narratives for different audiences.

See also: *Chronic Illness; Disability; Medical Model*

REFERENCES

Bury, M. (2001) 'Illness narratives, fact or fiction?', *Sociology of Health & Illness*, 23 (1): 263–85.
Frank, A. (1995) *The Wounded Storyteller: Body, Illness, and Ethics.* Chicago: University of Chicago Press.
Greenhalgh, T. and Hurwitz, B. (1999) 'Why study narrative?', *British Medical Journal*, 318: 48–50.
Kelly, M. and Dickinson, H. (1997) 'The narrative self in autobiographical accounts of illness', *The Sociological Review*, 45 (2): 254–78.

Kleinman, A. (1988) *The Illness Narratives: Suffering, Healing and the Human Condition*. New York: Basic Books.

Riessman, C.K. (1990) 'Strategic use of narratives in the presentation of self and illness: a research note', *Social Science & Medicine*, 30 (11): 1195–2000.

Riessman, C.K. (1993) *Narrative Analysis*. Newbury Park, CA: Sage.

Robinson, I. (1990) 'Personal narratives, social careers and medical course: analyzing life trajectories in autobiographies of people with multiple sclerosis', *Social Science & Medicine*, 30 (11): 1173–86.

Thomas, C. (2010) 'Negotiating the contested terrain of narrative methods in illness contexts', *Sociology of Health & Illness*, 32 (4): 647–60.

Mike Bury and Lee F. Monaghan

Risk

> *Risk involves exposure to a given danger or hazard.*

The language of risk is now frequently used in both popular and expert discourse, especially when it comes to discussing health issues. This has not always been the case. In pre-Renaissance times the dominant popular discourse was that of 'fate' – in which personal misfortune and disaster were explained in terms of chance, personal destiny, and the will of the gods. In this period dangers such as floods and epidemics were perceived as natural events rather than as man-made and the idea of human fault or responsibility was not considered. With the emergence of modernity in the seventeenth century, a new materialistic and deterministic discourse was established, premised on the belief that the social and natural world followed causal laws. From this standpoint risks were the products of such determinism and the vagaries of nature. Subsequently risk was scientized as a result of the growing influence of mathematical explanations relating to probability. During the nineteenth century it became possible to measure the risk of an event by calculating its statistical probability, thereby taming chance. Risk also came to be located in human beings as well as in nature and unintended outcomes were acknowledged as being a possible consequence of human action. According to Lupton (1999), modernist notions of risk also recognized that risk could be either 'good' or 'bad', involving gain or loss, and could thus be seen in neutral terms. Since the nineteenth century, however, the meaning of risk has been transformed and it has now mainly come to be seen as involving only negative outcomes. Risk now typically means danger, and the greater the risk the greater the danger. Against this dominant discourse there has nonetheless developed a counter discourse which

experience of health and illness

sees risk-taking more positively as involving emotionally charged dangerous activities which give pleasure, for example sky-diving or bungee-jumping, described by Lyng (1990) as 'edgework'.

Traditionally research on risk has been the preserve of the risk industry, drawing primarily on disciplines such as engineering, toxicology, biostatistics, and actuarial science. Assessing public health risks has also become a major issue for epidemiologists who aim to calculate the 'relative risk' or numerical odds of a population developing an illness when exposed to a risk factor, compared with a similar population that has not suffered such exposure. It is on the basis of these risk assessments that governments have conducted health education campaigns, for example about AIDS, to warn the public about the dangers of 'risky behaviour'. It is expected that the provision of information about such risky behaviours will lead to their reduction.

Since the 1990s a concerted effort has been made to develop social analyses of risk. In what follows a variety of such analyses will be discussed starting with the cultural approach, inspired by the anthropologist Mary Douglas. Douglas was one of the first to draw attention to the need for an analysis that challenged the status of risk as an objective measure, as argued by members of the risk industry. Instead she took a weak constructionist view, like many others after her, and considered that objective hazards were inevitably mediated by cultural processes and could only be known in relation to these processes. She was interested in why some dangers were selected as risks while others were not and how risk acted as a symbolic boundary between groups. For her what was of significance was that groups of people would identify different risk attributes and even types of risk as a result of their particular form of social organization and interaction in the wider culture. In her view the way in which such collectivities responded to risk was functional for the maintenance of their form of social organization. The argument was formalized in an analytic scheme that has come to be known as grid/group analysis. For Douglas the degree of collectivism found in groups and the degree of internal difference within groups impacted on perceptions of risk. Collectivism, whether strong or weak, was defined in terms of 'group', while the degree of difference is defined in terms of 'grid'. By linking grid and group, Douglas, along with her colleague Wildavsky (1982), identified four distinct world views which justified different ways of behaving towards a hazard. These were named hierarchist (high grid/high group), egalitarian (low grid/high group), fatalist (high grid/low group) and individualist (low grid/low group). Hierarchists, for example, were considered to be well-integrated (group axis) and to accept externally imposed risk assessments by experts (grid axis) while egalitarians, although being well-integrated too, tended to challenge the experts' assessments on the grounds that these experts' calculations threatened their group's way of life (grid axis). Douglas also believed that when people felt they were at risk, they tended to blame outsiders rather than focus on the dangers from within their own community. In the health field, grid/group analysis has been applied to studying differences in response to hazards in contexts ranging from hospitals to transport. While the approach has been criticized for being too static and for failing to explain how organizations and individuals can change their perception of risk over time, it nonetheless offers a way of exploring how conflicts over risk can be understood in terms of plural constructions of meaning that are culturally framed.

Other more sociological work on risk perception has adopted an interpretivist approach and generally concentrated on two broad areas: (1) perceptions of risk and risk behaviour, and (2) the relationship between lay and expert knowledge of risk. The first of these has emphasized the role of contextual factors in risk perception. For example, Clarke and Korotchenko (2009) examined the risk perceptions and behaviour of older women with regard to sun tanning. They found that these women measured and responded to risk based on their personal priorities and prior experience of negative health associated with sun tanning. While most of the women associated a suntanned appearance with notions of health and beauty, those who sunbathed downplayed the health risks and emphasized the health benefits, especially the absorption of Vitamin D. They also distanced themselves from those they felt most at risk from sun tanning, namely those who used tanning beds. In contrast, women who no longer sunbathed justified their behaviour in terms of previous health problems associated with tanning such as sunstroke, sun damage, and skin cancer.

Others have focused on the relationship between lay and expert perceptions of risk. For instance, Armstrong and Murphy (2008) have explored the extent to which lay understandings of cervical cancer risk incorporate medical professional understandings. They found that women's engagement with such expert understandings was complex. Where expert-defined risk factors were incorporated, they were transformed and woven into a coherent whole within the context of the women's prior understandings, experiences, and contextual factors. However, this process was hampered because of incomplete medical information about the link between behavioural risk factors such as sexual behaviour and smoking and cervical cancer.

In addition to this interpretivist work on group risk perceptions and behaviour, there have also been more macro-level studies about the role of social institutions and structures in the framing of risk. One key institution involved in shaping risk perception is the mass media, as discussed by Tulloch and Zinn (2011). They reviewed the literature on media and health risks and showed how the media would reproduce and amplify expert risk assessment yet also create limited opportunities for counter definitions to emerge. They also noted how the media frame health risks so that audiences may see such risks in one particular way and not another, and how audiences may act as critical consumers, questioning the media messages in terms of their own values. How the media framed health risks about obesity and the role of scientists in this process illustrated the importance of the media as an institution. Holland et al. (2011) analysed how the Australian press represented a scientific report on the long-term consequences of 'Australia's expanding waistline' for cardiovascular disease. The press framed the report as showing that Australia was the fattest nation in the world, overtaking the Americans. This was prompted by comments by the lead author when publicizing the report. However, the coverage failed to note that the scientific report itself did not include any international comparisons and was only based on data from middle-aged Australians. As Holland et al. stress, there was a lack of critical commentary on the report and a failure to test the obesity claims of its lead author.

As a result, preconceptions of the putative 'problem' were reinforced at the expense of findings about 'potential solutions' (or other crucial concerns, such as the ethics of obesity discourse and the unintended consequences of declaring a war on obesity).

The relationship between lay and expert knowledge has also been explored more broadly by social theorists in the context of declining trust in expert authority in late modern society. Giddens (1990), for example, has suggested that the judgements of experts are now under increasing scrutiny and are either accepted or rejected by lay people who are making 'pragmatic calculations' about the risks involved. In these circumstances, the most cherished beliefs underpinning expert systems are open to revision and alteration, thereby challenging a dominant source of authoritative interpretation. The degree to which people feel alienated from or at least ambivalent towards experts also relates to the German sociologist Beck's (1992, 2009) argument that we now live in a 'risk society' that is increasingly vulnerable to major socio-technical disruption and a growing global interdependency. Social and economic developments have created global hazards, ranging from nuclear accidents to ecological disasters, for which there is no adequate aftercare. These structural features highlight the need for trust in expert authority at a time when greater reflexivity and awareness of the indeterminate status of knowledge about risk combine to undermine it. One of the main criticisms of this 'reflexive modernization' thesis is that it is based on broad generalizations of structural and organizational processes that lack any grounding in the actual processes and experiences of institutional and everyday life. Nonetheless, this approach has been enormously influential and has provided valuable insights into the structural and political aspects of risk.

While the risk society, like the other approaches outlined above, has adopted a weak constructionist position about risk, accepting that risk is an objective hazard that is mediated through social and cultural processes, there is one approach that takes a strong constructionist position – that concerned with risk and governmentality. From this standpoint there is no such thing as an objective risk; rather risks are solely a product of discourses, strategies, practices and institutions around phenomena that turn them into risks (Lupton, 1999). This Foucauldian-inspired perspective is particularly interested in the way in which risk operates in relation to the political ethos of advanced liberalism. The latter conceptualizes individuals as rational agents who should take responsibility to protect themselves from risks rather than rely on the state to protect them. Rather than assume that individuals pre-exist as rational consumers, Foucauldians argue that they have to be configured as such through governmental practices. The approach can be illustrated by Harvey's (2010) study of commercially produced documents related to direct consumer genetic testing services for diet-related disease. She focuses on how genetic susceptibility testing is positioned as a health care resource by these commercial providers. She argues that the documents configure individuals as being empowered to choose health by using the testing service and that this will facilitate their journey towards a healthy selfhood. Configured in this way, users of the service become 'good citizens' of an advanced liberal democracy, increasing their own vital capital and contributing to the prosperity of all.

In sum, the social analysis of risk now incorporates a variety of approaches, ranging from Douglas's grid/group analysis through interpretivist and structural approaches to Foucauldian analyses of risk and governmentality. While there has been some debate about the continuing value of risk as a framework for analysis (Green, 2009), the approaches reviewed here suggest that each of them still has something to offer in helping us make sense of the meaning and nature of risk as a dominant feature of late modern society.

See also: *Lay Knowledge; Consumerism; Citizenship and Health*

REFERENCES

Armstrong, N. and Murphy, E. (2008) 'Weaving meaning? An exploration of the interplay between lay and professional understandings of cervical cancer risk', *Social Science & Medicine*, 67: 1074–82.

Beck, U. (1992) *Risk Society*. London: Sage.

Beck, U. (2009) *World at Risk*. Cambridge: Polity Press.

Clarke, L.H. and Korotchenko, A. (2009) 'Older women and suntanning: the negotiation of health and appearance risks', *Sociology of Health & Illness*, 31: 748–61.

Douglas, M. and Wildavsky, A. (1982) *Risk and Culture: An Essay on the Selection of Technological and Environmental Dangers*. Berkeley: University of California Press.

Giddens, A. (1990) *The Consequences of Modernity*. Cambridge: Polity Press.

Green, J. (2009) 'Is it time for the sociology of health to abandon "risk?"' *Health, Risk and Society*, 11: 493–508.

Harvey, A. (2010) 'Genetic risks and healthy choices: creating citizen-consumers of genetic services through empowerment and facilitation', *Sociology of Health & Illness*, 32: 365–81.

Holland, K.E., Warwick Blood, R., Thomas, S.I., Lewis, S., Komesaroff, P.A. and Castle, D.J. (2011) '"Our girth is plain to see": an analysis of newspaper coverage of "Australia's future fat bomb"', *Health, Risk and Society*, 13: 31–46.

Lupton, D. (1999) *Risk*. London: Routledge.

Lyng, S. (1990) 'Edgework: a social psychological analysis of voluntary risk taking', *American Journal of Sociology*, 95: 851–86.

Tulloch, J. and Zinn, J.O. (2011) 'Risk, health and the media', *Health, Risk and Society*, 13: 1–16.

Jonathan Gabe

The Sick Role

Intended as an ideal type, the sick role refers to the set of rights and obligations surrounding illness that could shape the behaviour of doctors and patients.

The concept of 'the sick role' was originally formulated over half a century ago in the work of American sociologist Talcott Parsons (1951). While Parsons recognized that health and illness have a biological basis, his account contributed to the early development of medical sociology by underscoring the sociological implications of illness and medical practice. For Parsons, 'the sick role' was central to this account, encapsulating in an 'ideal typical' or analytical sense those rights and obligations that surround illness when normal roles are relinquished or suspended. The concept emerged from the 'moral economy' (Varul, 2010) of mid-twentieth century US society, with notions of productivity and medical authority informing Parsons' schema in ways that belie certain assumptions (for example, in relation to middle-class values, gendered norms, and ascribed social values). He thus offered a socio-historical account of the normative expectations surrounding illness, sanctioned by physicians and defined as unmotivated deviance or the incapacity to perform valued social roles. For Parsons, the sick role had a nominal focus on the behaviour of a rational, income-generating masculine employee within a gendered division of labour, where paid work and doctors' judgements were privileged. Despite much social change, such values have not been entirely erased, and the sick role concept retains ongoing relevance for sociologists interested in the social aspects of the body, health, illness and medicine in late modern capitalist societies (Shilling, 2002; Varul, 2010; Williams, 2005). After describing the main thrust of Parsons' (1951) formulation, we will refer to more recent writing when critically considering the enduring relevance of and attention given to this concept.

The sick role concept first appeared in Parsons' description of 'The case of modern medical practice' in *The Social System* (1951). Adopting a functionalist approach that has antecedents in Durkheimian sociology, Parsons regarded the role of medical care as meeting certain 'prerequisites' that underpin the functioning of all social systems, especially modern ones. Within this theoretical framework, 'health' is crucial for the functioning of the social system, meaning that if the population's general health is 'too low' and 'the incidence of illness' 'too high' then this is 'dysfunctional' for society (p. 430). Accordingly, the key social function of medical practice is to help maintain an 'optimal' level of health in society.

While there are two different models of illness in Parsons' work (Gerhardt, 1989), the more complex and interesting model treats illness as deviance, and the sick role as a mechanism of social control. Illness constitutes 'deviance' in a dynamic work-oriented society because it disrupts everyday role requirements and obligations; correspondingly, in order to regulate this, doctors act as gate-keepers to the sick role. The sick role is important because it allows individuals temporary exemption from their ordinary role obligations, and provides the mechanism for returning people to health and therefore to normal role performance. Of course, in providing such exemption, the sick role may become an attractive alternative to everyday pressures, providing a way of 'evading social responsibilities' (Parsons, 1951: 431) and offering 'secondary gain'. Hence, the sick role is a 'contingent' one so that malingering, or motivated avoidance of role responsibilities, does not become too easy or 'dysfunctional' from a system viewpoint. In all modern societies, absence from work due to ill health is heavily regulated, often requiring medical certification. In short, medical practice is part of society's social control apparatus.

Parsons identifies two sets of four, mutually reinforcing, dimensions to the sick role; four for the performance of the doctor's role and four for the performance of the patient's. Together they constitute the necessary elements for a functional 'sick role'.

Doctors, like patients, have two obligations and two rights. First, Parsons (1951) argues that doctors have the obligation to be technically competent and meet 'selection criteria' separate from other elements of the person's social status (p. 434). In other words, the appointment of doctors and their practice should be based on technical expertise and not on their personal or social background. Second, the practitioner should be 'affectively neutral', tackling the medical problem in an 'objective way'. The doctor should thus have the welfare of the patient at heart and not personal or commercial considerations – 'the "profit motive" is supposed to be drastically excluded from the medical world' (p. 435). Parsons was keen, in this respect, to contrast medicine in the USA with the world of business (Bury, 1997: 84). Doctors should be 'collectivity oriented' and serve the community.

In return for meeting these obligations, two rights flow. First, doctors are treated by society as professional practitioners, with a degree of independence and self-regulation. This flows from the exercise of 'functional specificity' and 'universalism' so that doctors are expected to be expert in specific areas and utilize a body of knowledge that has universal application. The exercise of these skills allows doctors to claim a degree of freedom from the organizational and commercial constraints in which they work. Second, doctors are allowed access to tabooed areas such as the sick person's body. This access may involve physical examination or, more dramatically, surgery (Parsons, 1951: 451–2).

The exercise of this set of obligations and rights on the part of the doctor provides the basis for the patient entering the sick role. If the patient felt, for example, that the doctor was technically incompetent, was acting because of personal feelings, or was crossing boundaries in tabooed areas such as access to the body, then the sick role would be likely to break down immediately. Indeed, many recent high-profile controversies and scandals in countries such as the UK have involved just such elements, indicating the degree to which the sick role concept is an analytical abstraction that may not describe actual behaviour in the empirical world.

In the presence of effective and safe medical practice, however, it is anticipated that patients can enter the sick role with some degree of confidence. For those entering this role, Parsons identifies two rights and two obligations. The first right, noted above, is exemption from normal role responsibilities. This has to be legitimated, often by a doctor in the last analysis, thereby protecting the patient against the charge of 'malingering' (Parsons, 1951: 437). Second, the individual has the right not to be held responsible for their sickness. These rights are conditional on two obligations. First, the person must demonstrate a motivation to get well. Second, they must seek technically competent medical help and also cooperate with the clinician, producing a 'complementary role structure'. In this way, the 'secondary gain' of the sick role is limited, and the return to health is maintained as a primary goal.

The sick role concept has been criticized. It raises many questions, especially concerning its relevance to the wide range of illness states and forms of medical practice that exist in modern societies. Among other things, Freidson (1970) discussed how stigmatized illnesses may be treated as illegitimate with implications for the person's ability to access the rights and privileges of the sick role – an issue that resurfaces in more recent writings that engage the politics of stigma in neoliberal modernity. Also, empirically, it has long been recognized that not all forms of illness lead to the adoption of the sick role (Bloor and Horobin, 1975). In many cases, being 'legitimately ill' does not need the sanctioning of a doctor, and much self-treatment and self-help are employed in dealing with illness. Gallagher (1976) also identifies various problems. For example, in Parsons' scheme the sick role is essentially temporary; it is assumed the role will be occupied for a period leading to recovery and the resumption of normal roles. Yet, this is often contradicted by chronic illness, which, by definition, is long term and enduring. Gallagher also challenges what he takes to be Parsons' overly 'medico-centric' view of illness, the sick role and medical practice. In particular, Gallagher notes that while Parsons underscores the centrality of doctors (especially hospital doctors) in healthcare organizations, other healthcare workers (including family practitioners) as well as lay support and family structures are equally important (Gallagher, 1976: 213). Moreover, Parsons' claims about the need for an optimal level of health in the social system were contradicted by the low priority given by the medical profession to prevention at that time, where 'training and orientation [were] attuned to illness rather than toward the maintenance of health' (Gallagher, 1976: 215). The growth of primary care and health promotion marks some change in emphasis today, though – in contrast to Parsons' functionalist account – there are issues here concerning the degree to which 'health' (incorporating pervasive discourses of risk) is a politically expedient rationale for neoliberal governmentality and the (unintended) blaming and shaming of people for their (re)current or future ill health. Reflecting on the increased significance of chronic illness and the emphasis given to lifestyle health promotion, Varul (2010) also highlights the problematic status of the sick role concept in the contemporary era. At the same time, Varul acknowledges how the concept sheds light on normative expectations and the moral economy of health and illness.

In arriving at an evaluation of the sick role concept, it could be argued that not all criticisms can be taken at face value and the concept remains relevant for medical sociology. For example, despite Gallagher's (1976) telling points about the sick role's *temporary* character, the situation is often more complex than he allows. In a defence of his argument, Parsons (1978: 28) pointed out that even in the case of chronic disorders, such as diabetes, the physician has an obligation 'to reinforce the patient's motivation to minimize the curtailment of his [or her] capacities' and he recognized that a 'fulltime' occupancy of the sick role does not apply to all forms of illness, especially chronic illness. Also, while Parsons may be too prone to present the sick role as a means of providing an asymmetrical but complementary role structure (playing down its potential for conflict), when it is placed in his full discussion of health and medicine it does address issues of abiding concern. As Gerhardt (1979) notes, these range from the psychodynamic aspects of illness and treatment, to the structural issues of illness and incapacity, and thus to issues of social control and power. For Gerhardt, the sick role is part of a 'structural' view of illness, locating individual needs in the wider society, though, of course, how one conceptualizes the mechanisms and dynamics of society begs further questions, especially in an age of neoliberal globalization, hyper-commodification, pervasive body work, and ideologies of individual responsibility. Young (2004), when discussing illness behaviour, offers comparable thinking, noting there is much outside of the doctor–patient relationship that matters, including government and world systems.

While Parsons' (1951) sick role concept has its limitations, twenty-first century sociology repeatedly returns to this idea (Shilling, 2002; Varul, 2010; Williams, 2005). For instance, Varul (2010) draws from Parsons when discussing the precarious position of the chronically ill in terms of being governed by and consumers of medicine. Here Varul considers issues of reciprocity and recognition, their consequences within a broader moral economy, and thus – more experientially – the anxiety of not socially fitting in as a fully contributing (recognized) member of capitalist society. Highlighting both the negative and positive uptake of Parsons' (1951) concept, Shilling (2002) discusses how the productivity ethos that is central to the sick role concept underpins much health-seeking, except this is now enjoined with consumerism, a proliferation of body projects, and the search for pleasure. Correspondingly, rather than Parsons' (1951) concept being anachronistic, Shilling (2002: 622) explains that it has enduring significance within, and may be extended to make sense of, the cultural context of health consumption and 'pro-active, "vigilant" approaches towards the healthy body' in 'information rich' societies. The cultural (middle-class) value placed upon instrumentalism is flagged in this reading and Parsons (1951) is credited for locating illness, health and medical practice within the normative context of Western society rather than acting as an 'apologist for capitalism' (Shilling, 2002: 624). While Williams (2005: 140) claims Shilling (2002) is perhaps too quick to prioritize the 'information rich consumer of health' over the 'sick role', he similarly endorses the Parsonian legacy for medical sociology and contemporary debates on issues ranging from trust and emotion to the limits of expertise. It is for reasons such as this that the sick role concept has continued salience for sociologists interested not only in sickness, but also in the social dimensions of health, embodiment, and other abiding themes.

See also: *Illness and Health-Related Behaviour; Stigma; Practitioner–Client Relationships; Medical Model*

REFERENCES

Bloor, M. and Horobin, G. (1975) 'Conflict and conflict resolution in doctor–patient relationships', in C. Cox and A. Mead (eds), *A Sociology of Medical Practice*. London: Collier-Macmillan.

Bury, M. (1997) *Health and Illness in a Changing Society*. London: Routledge.

Freidson, E. (1970) *Profession of Medicine: A Study of the Sociology of Applied Knowledge*. New York: Harper & Row.

Gallagher, E. (1976) 'Lines of reconstruction and extension in the Parsonian sociology of illness', *Social Science & Medicine*, 10: 207–18.

Gerhardt, U. (1979) 'The Parsonian paradigm and the identity of medical sociology', *The Sociological Review*, 27 (2): 229–51.

Gerhardt, U. (1989) *Ideas About Illness: An Intellectual and Political History of Medical Sociology*. Basingstoke: Macmillan.

Parsons, T. (1951) *The Social System*. London: Routledge and Kegan Paul.

Parsons, T. (1978) *Action Theory and the Human Condition*. New York: The Free Press.

Shilling, C. (2002) 'Culture, the sick role and the consumption of health', *British Journal of Sociology*, 53 (4): 621–38.

Varul, M. (2010) 'Talcott Parsons, the sick role and chronic illness', *Body & Society*, 16 (2): 72–94.

Williams, S.J. (2005) 'Parsons revisited: from the sick role to … ?' *Health*, 9 (2): 123–44.

Young, J.T. (2004) 'Illness behaviour: a selective review and synthesis', *Sociology of Health & Illness*, 26 (1): 1–31.

Mike Bury and Lee F. Monaghan

Practitioner–Client Relationships

The practitioner–client relationship encompasses the ways in which health care workers and lay people interact during health-related consultations and activities. This relationship can be affected by the context of the consultation, the nature of the communication that takes place, and broader factors such as policies, protocols, and the use of technologies.

Health care today is more diverse than ever, and this diversity encompasses not just the range of personnel who deliver care, but also the settings in which they do so, the tools they employ, the tasks they accomplish, and the dilemmas they confront. There is a long history of addressing these relationships from a sociological perspective, focusing initially on the doctor–patient encounter in primary care.

The study of doctor–patient relationships has its beginnings with Henderson's (1935) description of interactions between physicians and patients as processes of mutual feedback, where each is constantly affecting the behaviour of the other. Two decades later, these observations influenced Parsons, who understood medicine as a way of practising social control. Sickness was seen by Parsons as a form of deviance, albeit unmotivated, and as such it had to be managed at a societal level to prevent or minimize the social disruption it could cause. This meant that interactions between doctors and patients were mediated by normative role expectations shared by all members of a society: that being sick was an undesirable state; that patients would want to get well; and that they would both seek medical help when appropriate and comply with the resulting recommendations. For such an interaction to be successful, participants must adopt the appropriate role expectations of doctor and patient and bring these to the interaction. From this viewpoint, the relationship operates as a consensus model, in that the uncontested or paternalistic authority of the doctor is seen as unproblematic or legitimate on the basis that s/he will always act in the best interests of the patient. How these interests are in fact to be established falls outside of the scope of the model.

Subsequent work by Szasz and Hollender (1956) proposed three distinct types of doctor–patient relationship: activity–passivity (likened to a parent/infant relationship); guidance–cooperation (likened to a parent/adolescent relationship, where authority is still unequally distributed); and mutual participation (seen as adult to adult). They noted, however, that these relationships were fluid and could change over time, or were dependent upon the nature of a specific illness. Szasz and Hollender argued that doctors had traditionally limited their concern to bodily matters rather than relationships with patients, and this criticism was echoed in Balint's (1957) advocacy of a psychodynamically informed approach to medical consultations that would elicit and address the patient's problems as well as diagnose and treat the illness. These two works had a pervasive influence on the sociological study of doctor–patient relationships for much of the rest of the twentieth century. The attainment of a mutual and collaborative approach has come to dominate recent policy, and since the 1960s doctor–patient relationships have often been found wanting by researchers, and have become the object of various reform efforts.

One consequence of this is that researchers have often treated doctor–patient interaction as a site where doctors exercise power over patients, as demonstrated by the lack of mutuality or collaboration in evidence in consultations analysed from a variety of perspectives (see, for example, Byrne and Long, 1976; Waitzkin, 1991). At the same time, other sociologists have attempted to explain this failure to achieve mutuality, with Freidson (1970) detailing the inherent differences doctors and patients bring to the relationship (such as the fact that for the doctor this may be a 'typical' case whereas for the patient it is specific and personal) as an inevitable source of conflict. Freidson argues that it is the function of the doctor to apply general knowledge to a particular patient, whereas patients will seek to retain an acknowledgement of their particularity, and hence an element of control over their future. This mismatch of perspectives results in conflict which can only be overcome by the doctor obtaining the patient's trust.

Despite work suggesting that some conflict within the doctor–patient relationship is inevitable, the perceived inadequacy of prevailing practice has led to an emphasis on an alternative model of doctor–patient relationships. This negotiated model emphasizes both doctor and patient as active, and what is commonly referred to as 'shared decision making' is increasingly held up as best practice. However, what counts as shared decision making is often poorly defined and hence difficult to assess. On a more fundamental level, its desirability and achievability have also been questioned, on the basis that the competence gap between doctor and patient exists necessarily, and as a result some patients will prefer that this competence is used by the doctor to direct treatment choices.

At the same time, some sociologists have taken a rather different approach to what is generally identified as the problem of medical dominance. Researchers working from a conversation analytic viewpoint have demonstrated how an asymmetry of interaction is not automatically derivable from institutional processes, but is instead constituted by both doctor and patient (see, for example, Maynard, 1991). In part, this is a way of handling the interactional difficulties the encounter presents, since part of what might be read as interactional dominance arises from the fact it is the patient's condition that is under review and the doctor who is expected to propose some solution (ten Have, 1991). As a result, patients actively choose to listen to doctors and to take advantage of the latter's greater knowledge and expertise. From this point of view, such apparent dominance may not always be problematic.

One final perspective on this is provided by Frank et al. (2010) who suggest we will make little progress in researching how treatment decisions might best be shared between practitioners and patients until we recognize that this is a distributed process. In other words, we need to acknowledge that it moves beyond the doctor–patient dyad and can be affected by multiple other mediators beyond client participation, including policies, protocols, and the use of technologies. For example, it is often argued that in a consumerist era patients have become more autonomous, assisted by resources such as the internet. At the same time, Bury (1997) suggests there has been an erosion of hierarchical relationships in late modern cultures, and a corresponding trend in the reduction of professionals' power. Such a shift is reflected in the Department of Health's 'Expert Patient' initiative in England, aimed at adults in England living with a chronic disease and putting the emphasis on user-led self-management programmes. The advent of organizations such as the UK's National Institute for Clinical Excellence, which places limits on the treatments that can be offered for particular conditions, alongside the introduction of clinical governance, has also had an impact. Unless we widen our research lens to take this distribution into account, we can only ever achieve a partial picture, and any recommendations for practice made as a result will not necessarily be realistic or desirable.

So far, and despite the title of this entry, we have only considered the doctor–patient relationship. Historically there has been some significant work, particularly in the USA, on other practitioner–client relationships, such as Coser (1963) on nurses. However, it is only in the past 10 or 15 years that we have seen a significant increase in the number of sociological studies that consider settings and activities beyond the doctor–patient consultation. As well as nursing, these include: health visiting, physiotherapy, homeopathy, pharmacy, the use of health-related helplines, etc. (see Pilnick et al., 2010). As Pilnick et al. (2010) note, whereas doctor–patient consultations in primary care may be fundamentally concerned with issues of diagnosis and treatment, other sites of practitioner–client interaction have very different concerns. For example, visits may be therapeutic in nature (for example, in physiotherapy), administrative (for example, admitting a patient to hospital), or related to teaching or training (for example, supervising a junior surgeon during an operation). This diversity of settings and activities raises a different set of issues, and we cannot assume models, principles or policies developed based on doctor–patient interaction in primary care can be transplanted wholesale. This problem is illustrated by a range of studies that demonstrate how 'blanket' recommendations for best practice can be problematic in the face of local contingencies. For example, comparative research by Perakyla et al. (2007) illustrates how the relevancy of various forms of patient or client participation has to be judged against the overall goal of the encounter, and how even within a single setting, practitioners will come across clients with different levels of knowledge, expertise, and commitment. Such research suggests that in order to better understand practitioner–client relationships in the twenty-first century, we need to go beyond the restriction of traditional models rooted in doctor–patient encounters, and move towards an analysis which recognizes the breadth and diversity that the term encompasses.

See also: *The Sick Role; eHealth; Trust in Medicine; Consumerism*

REFERENCES

Balint, M. (1957) *The Doctor, His Patient and The Illness*. London: Pitman.

Bury, M. (1997) *Health and Illness in a Changing Society*. London: Routledge.

Byrne, P. and Long, B. (1976) *Doctors Talking to Patients: A Study of the Verbal Behaviours of Doctors in the Consultation*. London: Her Majesty's Stationery Office.

Coser, R.L. (1963) 'Alienation and the social structure: case analysis of a hospital', in E. Friedson (ed.), *The Hospital in Modern Society*. New York: The Free Press.

Frank, A.W., Corman, M.K., Gish, J.A. and Lawton, P. (2010) 'Healer–patient interaction: new mediations in clinical relationships', in I. Bourgeault, R. Dingwall and R. de Vries (eds), *The SAGE Handbook of Qualitative Methods in Health Research*. London: Sage.

Freidson, E. (1970) *Profession of Medicine: A Study of the Sociology of Applied Knowledge*. Chicago: University of Chicago Press.

Have, P. ten (1991) 'Talk and institution: a reconsideration of the "asymmetry" of doctor–patient interaction', in D. Boden and D. Zimmerman (eds), *Talk and Social Structure: Studies in Ethnomethodology and Conversation Analysis*. Cambridge: Polity Press.

Henderson, L.J. (1935) 'Physician and patient and a social system', *New England Journal of Medicine*, 212: 448–95.

Maynard, D. (1991) 'Interaction and asymmetry in clinical discourse', *American Journal of Sociology*, 97: 448–95.

Perakyla, A., Ruusuvuori, J. and Lindfors, P. (2007) 'What is patient participation? Reflections arising from the study of general practice, homeopathy and psychoanalysis', in S. Collins, N. Britten, J. Ruusuvuori and A. Thompson (eds), *Patient Participation in Healthcare Consultations: Qualitative Perspectives*. Maidenhead: Open University Press.

Pilnick, A., Hindmarsh, J. and Gill, V.T. (eds) (2010) *Communication in Healthcare Settings: Policy, Participation and New Technologies*. Oxford: Wiley-Blackwell.

Szasz, T.S. and Hollender, M.H. (1956) 'A contribution to the philosophy of medicine: the basic models of the doctor–patient relationship', *Archives of Internal Medicine*, 97: 589–92.

Waitzkin, H. (1991) *The Politics of Medical Encounters*. New Haven, CT: Yale University Press.

Alison Pilnick

> *Quality of life refers to an individual's sense of social, emotional and physical well-being which influences the extent to which she or he can achieve personal satisfaction with their life circumstances.*

The term 'quality of life' has been used in many contexts. It first came into common parlance in the USA at the end of the Second World War to refer to the possession of material goods – for example, a car, telephone, or washing machine – which made life 'better'. Following the social movements of the 1960s (for example, civil rights, second wave feminism, youth counterculture and the New Left), material 'standard of living' was more clearly distinguished from the experience of personal freedom, autonomy and fulfilment. Hence, quality of life eventually came to signify the experience of 'a good life' in contrast to mere material success. At the same time, despite increasing economic prosperity, concern that groups in the population continued to experience poverty and limited opportunities led to the development of objective social indicators as alternatives to traditional economic measures such as Gross National Product (GNP) per capita. Statistics on divorce, crime rates, housing standards and environmental pollution, amongst others, were used as a form of social monitoring to show changes in quality of life at a societal level and to serve as a basis for policy interventions.

The increasing concern with quality of life in social research was soon matched by an interest in quality of life in a health context. By the 1970s, measures of quality of life began to supplement traditional clinical measures in the evaluation of health care interventions, particularly in relation to cancer, psychiatry and rheumatology. In this context, focusing on quality of life represented a broadening of the aims of health care from a traditional emphasis on survival and 'quantity of life' to include the impact of health problems on personal well-being and life satisfaction. As more people experienced the limitations imposed by chronic illness and disability, pondered the benefits of technologies which prolonged life in a diminished condition and struggled with the escalating costs of health care, quality of life became an increasingly important measure of the outcomes of health care interventions (Albrecht and Fitzpatrick, 1994).

Despite its widespread use, quality of life has remained a vague and abstract concept. It has been viewed as the extent to which: basic human needs have been satisfied; satisfaction or dissatisfaction has been felt with various aspects of life; and pleasure and satisfaction are considered to characterize human existence. From a phenomenological perspective, quality of life is seen as reflecting the gap between the hopes and expectations an individual holds and his or her present experience. Other definitions have variously emphasized the capacity of an individual to realize his or her life plans; the ability of an individual to manage life as he or she evaluates it; or the ability of an individual to lead a 'normal' life. A particularly influential definition within social gerontology identifies two objective conditions – general health and functional status, and socio-economic status – and two subjective evaluations – life satisfaction and self-esteem – as being at the core of quality of life (Bowling, 2005).

Within the health field, interest has focused on health-related quality of life (HRQL), a term which refers to a loosely related body of work on functional ability, health status, and subjective well-being. The conceptual framework for this work derives largely from the World Health Organization's definition of health which points to the need to take physical, mental and social well-being into account in assessing the health of individuals and populations. The concept itself, however, is not well developed theoretically and debate continues over the specification of the domains which comprise HRQL. Some present it as characterized by resilience, health perception, physical function, symptoms and duration of life, while others employ related concepts like health status, cognitive function, emotional state, social function, role performance and subjective well-being in order to define and assess HRQL.

Although HRQL has been investigated using qualitative methods, most of the efforts in this field have focused on the development of quantitative measurement instruments (Bowling, 2005). While some early measures were designed to be used by clinicians to obtain 'objective' assessments of physical or mental functioning, more recent measures have been designed to obtain the patient's subjective assessments and to reflect lay perceptions of the impact of illness on their lives. Generic instruments – for example, the SF-36, the WHOQOL-BREF and the EQ-5D – have been designed for use with any population group and to provide a broadly based assessment. Disease-specific instruments have also been developed to provide greater sensitivity in measuring aspects of symptoms and functioning relevant to particular conditions. A concern sometimes expressed about these instruments, which aim to obtain standard information from all patients, is that they impose on individuals an external value system which may not reflect their own values. In an attempt to address this, individualized measures have also been developed, which ask people to specify for themselves the domains of life that are most affected by their condition and the degree of disruption they experience. Such measures are more sensitive to differences between individuals or population groups with regard to the significance of illness and its effects on day-to-day life, but are also more difficult to interpret and analyse.

Measures of HRQL can be used in a variety of ways, from screening for and monitoring psychosocial problems in individual patients, to assessing perceived health problems in population surveys (Fitzpatrick et al., 1992). They are most commonly used, however, in clinical trials and evaluation research where they can provide subjective, patient-based assessments for evaluating the effects of health care interventions. In this context, they have been invaluable in drawing attention to outcomes which may be missed by more traditional clinical measures, in highlighting differences in assessments between patients and clinicians, and in demonstrating the limitations and deleterious side-effects of medical interventions. For example, in an early influential study, Croog et al. (1986) carried out a randomized control trial among 625 male patients with moderate hypertension to determine the effects of three commonly used drugs which acted in different ways to control blood pressure. Patients were randomly assigned to one of three groups, and a different drug was given to each group. After six months, patients in all three groups had similar levels of blood pressure control. However, clear differences were found between the groups in a range of measures of quality of life, including general well-being, physical symptoms and sexual dysfunction, cognitive function, work performance, and satisfaction with life. These findings demonstrated that anti-hypertensive drugs had an effect on wider aspects of patients' lives and that these effects could be reliably measured.

Quality of life measures are now routinely used in evaluation research and clinical trials to assess the outcomes of health care interventions. An interesting development from this has been the use of HRQL instruments in clinical practice to follow up patients and assess the quality of service they receive. For example, since 2009 patients in England having any of four common types of surgery (hip replacement, knee replacement, hernia repair, and varicose vein procedures) have been asked to complete a questionnaire on their health status before their treatment and six months afterwards. The results of these patient-reported outcome measures (PROMs) can then be used by health service providers in a number of ways, for example to identify the best performing hospitals and clinicians or to monitor progress in improvements in care against national objectives (Cole, 2009).

Measures of quality of life have also been used by doctors as an adjunct to the clinical interview to improve their management of patients. For example, in a study designed to evaluate the impact of the routine and repeated use of HRQL measures in a medical oncology clinic, Velikova et al. (2004) reported that physicians who received feedback from the measures found it useful and explicitly referred to it in the majority of consultations. Patients in turn showed clinically meaningful improvements in their quality of life. However, while these findings were promising, the practice is not yet extensive and evidence of its impact has so far been limited and inconclusive.

More controversially, quality of life measures are also used by health economists to provide a single index of the benefits of medical interventions, the quality adjusted life year (QALY). QALYs are a measure of life extension gained by a specific medical treatment adjusted by a 'utility' weight that reflects the relative value of the health status attained. For example, a year with the side-effects of anti-hypertensive treatment has been judged to be equivalent to 0.98 of a year with full health. Calculations of costs per QALY gained can then be made for different health care interventions. Perhaps not surprisingly, there has been much scepticism about the meaningfulness of QALYs and great unease about using them in making complex choices in resource allocation (Nord et al., 2009). Despite these criticisms, measures of quality of life are now a standard element in the decisions made by the UK's National Institute for Health and Clinical Excellence (NICE) about priorities for the public funding of health care interventions.

In an effort to develop a theoretical foundation for HRQL research, Wilson and Cleary (1995) have outlined a model which attempts to link traditional clinical measures with measures of health-related quality of life and measures of quality of life defined in broader terms. The model proposes causal linkages between five types of health care outcome, which move from the cell to the individual to the interaction of the individual as a member of society. At each subsequent level, concepts are increasingly integrated and increasingly difficult to define and measure, and the factors influencing them are increasingly complex and outside the control of the health care system.

According to Wilson and Cleary's model, *biological and physiological measures* assess the function of cells and organs and are usually undertaken by clinicians. *Symptom reports* shift the focus to the individual and depend on subjective assessments. *Measures of functional status* assess the individual's ability to perform particular tasks and are influenced by symptom experience and other factors in the individual (for example, personality, motivation) and the social environment (for example, income, housing, social support). *General health perceptions* are the global perceptions that individuals hold about their health and take account of the weights or values that they attach to various symptoms or functional impairments. Finally, *overall quality of life* is a measure of life satisfaction that represents a synthesis of a wide range of experiences and feelings that people have, including health-related quality of life, but also other salient life circumstances such as economic, political and spiritual factors.

This model highlights the complex factors that influence quality of life and which may at times produce what appear to be counter-intuitive or paradoxical assessments. For example, in a study of individuals with moderate to severe disabilities, Albrecht and Devlieger (1999) found that more than half reported a good to excellent quality of life despite experiencing severe difficulties performing daily tasks, being socially isolated, and having limited incomes and benefits. Such findings point to how the range of social and psychological processes involved in accommodating to illness or disability can produce changes in the internal standards for appraising current health status, or a redefinition of the notions of what constitutes a good quality of life, which may in turn influence perceptions of quality of life that are independent of an 'objective' health status or functional ability. Albrecht and Devlieger describe this process in terms of a balance theory, where the experience of well-being and life satisfaction derives from the individual's ability to reconstitute a balance between body, mind and spirit and build a harmonious relationship with their social environment. The use of HRQL measures in longitudinal research has increased interest in the cognitive mechanisms underlying this process, known as 'response shift' (Barclay-Goddard et al., 2009). Response shift reflects the dynamic nature of quality of life and may be regarded as either a confounding factor in assessing the outcomes of an intervention or, when medicine has little to offer, as the aim of clinical care itself (as in palliative care).

In summary, health-related quality of life represents an attempt to treat health as multi-dimensional, social and subjective in ways that sociologists have long advocated. Because much of its development has been in the context of applied policy considerations, theoretical and conceptual developments have been neglected. The emphasis has also been on quantitative assessment which misses out the rich descriptions of patients' experiences provided by more qualitative approaches. Nevertheless, factoring in quality of life in assessing the outcomes of medical care has served to draw attention to the broader impact of illness and health care on patients' daily lives and to provide a framework for incorporating a wider range of social and psychological factors in considerations of health and health care.

See also: *Chronic Illness; Disability; Evaluation*

REFERENCES

Albrecht, G. and Devlieger, P. (1999) 'The disability paradox: high quality of life against all odds', *Social Science & Medicine*, 48: 977–88.

Albrecht, G. and Fitzpatrick, R. (1994) 'A sociological perspective on health related quality of life research', in G. Albrecht and R. Fitzpatrick (eds), *Advances in Medical Sociology*, Volume 5. Greenwich, CT: JAI Press Inc.

Barclay-Goddard, R., Epstein, J. and Mayo, N. (2009) 'Response shift: a brief overview and proposed research priorities', *Quality of Life Research*, 18: 335–46.

Bowling, A. (2005) *Measuring Health: A Review of Quality of Life Measurement Scales*, 3rd edn. Buckingham: Open University Press.

Cole, A. (2009) 'New outcome measures are to be introduced in four types of surgery', *British Medical Journal*, 338: b648.

Croog, S., Levine, S., Testa, M., Brown, B., Bulpitt, C., Jenkins, C., Lerman, G. and Williams, G. (1986) 'The effects of antihypertensive therapy on the quality of life', *The New England Journal of Medicine*, 314: 1657–64.

Fitzpatrick, R., Fletcher, A., Gore, S., Jones, D., Spiegelhalter, D. and Cox, D. (1992) 'Quality of life measures in health care, I: applications and issues in assessment', *British Medical Journal*, 305: 1074–7.

Nord, E., Daniels, N. and Kamlet, M. (2009) 'QALYs: some challenges', *Value in Health*, 12 (supplement 1): S10–S15.

Velikova, G., Booth, L., Smith, A., Brown, P., Lynch, P., Brown, J. and Selby, P. (2004) 'Measuring quality of life in routine oncology practice improves communication and patient well-being: a randomised controlled trial', *Journal of Clinical Oncology*, 22 (4): 714–24.

Wilson, I. and Cleary, P. (1995) 'Linking clinical variables with health-related quality of life: a conceptual model of patient outcomes', *Journal of the American Medical Association*, 273: 59–65.

quality of life

Mary Boulton

> *Awareness contexts most commonly refer to those social processes surrounding death and dying or, more specifically, who knows what in relation to a person who is approaching death. The concept refers to the information, knowledge and cognition embodied within shifting types of awareness and the complex interplay of emotions.*

In the human world, death and dying are not simply natural or biological events. Death and dying, as with bereavement, are social processes imbued with meanings and emotions. Knowledge of these multi-dimensional processes is furthered through disciplines such as history, psychology, sociology, and anthropology (Walter, 2008). For example, historical work on death in Europe has proven influential across disciplines (Ariès, 1974, 1983). Anthropologists also document death rituals in traditional societies, while sociologists further our understanding of death as a social process in 'late modern' societies. In such societies dying is typically protracted given various factors, such as higher levels of mortality from chronic diseases, increasingly sophisticated biomedical technologies that allow medical staff to intervene in death, and shifting definitions of when a person is medically and legally categorized as dead. This picture, in turn, raises various issues such as awareness of death and dying and people's emergent experiences during social interaction.

Walter (2008) explains that the sociology of death has antecedents in Durkheim's classic writings on aboriginal religious rites and symbolism. However, it is interactionist sociology from the 1960s that is perhaps more widely recognized, discussed and engaged with by medical sociologists interested in death and dying (e.g. Timmermans, 1994; Mamo, 1999). Within this literature, the best known sociological concept is 'awareness contexts'. This idea forms part of a family of concepts that sensitize us to the social processes surrounding death and dying (for example, dying trajectories, sentimental order and social loss). However, other classic and contemporary writings should also be acknowledged. For example, Elias (1985) considers the loneliness of dying in modernity with reference to historical 'civilizing processes', while Lawton's (2000) ethnography explores, among other things, the concept of 'dirty dying' and the sequestration of certain categories of dying patient in a contemporary UK hospice.

Turning to classic interactionist sociology, Glaser and Strauss (1965) developed the concept of 'awareness contexts' when undertaking qualitative research among dying patients, their families and medical staff in hospitals in San Francisco. Formulated at a time when doctors largely withheld information of impending death from patients, awareness context theory is grounded in data and incorporates different people's perspectives, or who knows what, in relation to a dying patient. Considered as 'one of the bedrock examples of the grounded theory approach' (Timmermans, 1994: 323), the idea of awareness contexts has stood

experience of health and illness

the test of time, though it has been modified in recent years. This has happened amidst structural change and a greater sensitivity to how the often devastating news of an impending death is managed in the emotionally laden context of a terminal illness.

Glaser and Strauss's (1965) theory 'focuses on knowledge and the management of knowledge in social interactions in the context of dying' (Mamo, 1999: 14). Glaser and Strauss (1965) state that it is possible to identify up to 36 types of awareness context though they focus on four dominant situations: closed, open, suspect, and mutual pretence awareness.

Closed awareness denotes a situation where dying patients do not know about their impending death, even though everybody else does. This situation is contrasted with open awareness – which is more usual today, as exemplified in the hospice setting – where patients are informed by medical staff that their death is imminent. The two other dominant types of awareness context explored by Glaser and Strauss, which fall in between closed and open awareness, are suspicion awareness and mutual pretence awareness. With the former, patients suspect that other people know they are dying and they attempt to confirm or invalidate that suspicion. The other context occurs when each interactant defines a patient as dying but each also pretends that the other has not done so. Attuned to open-ended social processes, this theoretical formulation is anything but static. Rather, Glaser and Strauss state that types of awareness context are contingent and one type of context can, and often does, develop into another type as people interact and continually (re)define their respective situations. Correspondingly, Glaser and Strauss explore various facets of awareness and associated interactional work undertaken in each situation, such as people's tactics and counter-tactics, how changes in the awareness context are engineered by different parties, and the consequences of these dynamics for hospital staff, patients and relatives. In that respect, they propose that their study not only has theoretical relevance but also practical value by illuminating the social-psychological dimensions of terminal care.

In recent years the theory of awareness contexts has been revisited, extended and critiqued (Timmermans, 1994; Mamo, 1999). Timmermans' and Mamo's work, outlined below, connects the authors' own private troubles to the public issue of death and dying. Mamo (1999) also critiques Timmermans (1994) with a *more sustained* focus on the sociology of emotions.

Timmermans (1994) offers an introspective ethnographic account, based on his 'intense, personal experience' (p. 323) of his mother's stroke and subsequent death in a Belgian hospital. He had recently initiated a study of terminally ill patients and medical staff, but his personal experience transformed how he came to understand death and dying. Using grounded theory, he seeks to offer an account that fits the empirical data and is attentive to some of Glaser and Strauss's (1965) omissions. Timmermans (1994) maintains that the impact of emotions on types of awareness was omitted from the original theorization and that this should be redressed at a time when it is standard medical practice in the USA and Western Europe to inform terminally ill patients that death is imminent. Unlike Glaser and Strauss (1965), Timmermans (1994) underscores this point by prioritizing the patient's and family members' definition of the situation rather than focusing on the transfer of information from the medical staff to patients. He sees this as necessary at a time when 'more information does not necessarily result in open awareness' and, in challenging the original theory of awareness contexts, 'there seems to be something else necessary, apart from an increase in information, to create open awareness' (p. 325).

This 'something else' refers to how patients and relatives emotionally cope with terminal information. On this basis, Timmermans differentiates between three types of open awareness: (1) suspended open awareness, (2) uncertain open awareness, and (3) active open awareness. The first refers to how 'the patient or kin ignores or disbelieves the message communicated by the physician', the second denotes how family and patients dismiss 'the bad parts' of the prognosis but hope 'for the best outcome', while in the third context the interactants 'accept the impending death and prepare for it' (1994: 322).

As with Glaser and Strauss (1965), Timmermans (1994) agrees that awareness contexts are dynamic: people could shift between types of open awareness, ranging from death being seen as a taboo subject to an active preparation for death. Furthermore, Timmermans stresses that the disclosure of a terminal illness constitutes an emotional crisis; hence, it is necessary to modify what is meant by 'knowing' with reference to how patients and families cope with the changed situation brought about by news of a terminal illness. He adds that 'the most important implication of this modified theory of awareness contexts is that there is not one optimal or appropriate emotional response to a terminal diagnosis' (p. 335). Timmermans concludes that theory construction is open-ended and as such he invites others to contribute their experiences.

This invitation is taken up by Mamo (1999). She similarly revisits Glaser and Strauss (1965) using introspective ethnography; specifically, her experience of her mother-in-law's protracted death over a five-month period in the USA. Although Mamo (1999) describes Glaser and Strauss's work as ground-breaking, and emotions are acknowledged in their writing (for example, 'the sentimental order' of the ward), she critiques their implicit emphasis on physical and intellectual work, rather than on emotion work in a social context. Mamo adds that while Timmermans (1994) states that his 'revision reclaims the emotional power of terminal illness from the viewpoint of patients and relatives' (p. 322), he does not go far enough. Mamo (1999) contends that greater significance should be given to emotions, emotion management and the confluence of emotions and awareness in the context of dying. This argument is also extended to biomedicine which is similarly seen to be lacking in its consideration of emotions.

Critically reflecting on how rationalized knowledge is prioritized within modern biomedicine (for example, via technological applications and 'scientific' criteria), Mamo (1999: 14) asserts that 'the subjective and emotional' dimensions of death and dying are largely rendered 'invisible'. Mamo is not 'against' medicine per se. Rather, she proposes that her expanded 'approach will transcend the artificial dualisms of biomedicine, and enable the construction of a theory where emotions, suffering, hope, and uncertainty co-mingle with the "rational work" of biomedicine' (p. 14). In short, she seeks to incorporate the messy lived realities and relational experiences of death and dying, drawing on her experiences and the sociology of emotions to facilitate rich description and analysis. In furthering her work she uses the classic interactional studies of Goffman on self-presentation, and Hochschild on 'emotion work and feeling rules', where social actors 'evoke, manipulate, or customise particular emotions' according to what is deemed 'appropriate' in particular settings (Mamo, 1999: 19).

For Mamo (1999: 19), emotions are an 'embodied experience – occurring as an unconscious surge as well as conscious 'work''. Accordingly, she connects her 'cognitive processes' with her 'inside' experiences of coping emotionally with a loved one's terminal illness. In so doing, she modifies existing theory so that medical sociologists as well as clinicians could fully recognize that 'emotions and cognitions are intertwined' (p. 21). Here Mamo maintains that emotional surges and associated work (for example, holding back tears when seeking to maintain closed awareness) 'interacted with information and awareness in such a way that transformed the shape of awareness' (p. 21). She explains that 'pure cognitive processing' of information was unstable in the situation she experienced, instead shifting to incorporate, either simultaneously or separately, 'emotional management' amidst 'surges of emotions of devastation, loss, disbelief and numbness among others' (p. 22). She adds: 'The lived experience was not defined by information, it was defined by competing and interacting processes of emotion and cognition' (p. 22). She also asks several questions ignored by existing theories. These questions relate to how multiple social actors experience myriad emotions between themselves and within themselves over time. She states that the idea of a 'common awareness context' does not capture such complexity and that 'emotions are often beyond "voice" or words and cannot be easily explained' (p. 23).

In summary, Mamo (1999) proposes a modification rather than a rejection of awareness context theory. She identifies strengths in Timmermans' (1994) research, notably, his reference to emotional crisis. Building on this, she underscores the degree to which medical knowledge and information cannot be separated from their embodied, emotional, and thus shifting, social contexts. Her main conclusion is that the sociology of emotions should be combined with the sociology of health and illness. This would allow 'new' understandings to emerge, which could more adequately connect people, bodies and society.

Finally, recent sociological discussions on death and dying continue to extend our critical knowledge. Walter (2012) offers a noteworthy contribution that challenges existing research and theory. He does not explicitly engage in debates on awareness contexts (as outlined above) but he does link 'the death awareness movement' to professional power. The exercise of power, we are informed, renders this movement something of a 'mixed blessing', as 'the compassionate palliative care doctor gazes not only into my body but also into my very soul' (p. 128). Walter makes this point within a larger discussion on how sociological research on contemporary death practices obscures international differences as globalization interacts with localized conditions (glocalization). Unfortunately, existing studies are typically confined to the nation state so that the differences between countries tend to be ignored or remain under-theorized. Despite similar social structural conditions (for example, urbanization, rationalization, the dominance of professions and levels of technology), the management of death varies within the Western world. Such differences, according to Walter, are explicable in terms of cultural, historical and organizational factors. Hence, the challenge facing medical sociology is to explore these complicating factors, with the nation understood as an important variable in addition to 'more conventional' concerns such as class, gender and ethnicity.

See also: *Embodiment; Emotions; Illness Narratives; Emotional Labour*

REFERENCES

Ariès, P. (1974) *Western Attitudes Toward Death: From the Middle Ages to the Present*. London: Marion Boyars.

Ariès, P. (1983) *The Hour of Our Death*. London: Penguin.

Elias, N. (1985) *The Loneliness of the Dying*. Oxford: Blackwell.

Glaser, B. and Strauss, A. (1965) *Awareness of Dying*. Chicago, IL: Aldine.

Lawton, J. (2000) *The Dying Process: Patients' Experiences of Palliative Care*. London: Routledge.

Mamo, L. (1999) 'Death and dying: confluences of emotion and awareness', *Sociology of Health & Illness*, 21 (1): 13–36.

Timmermans, S. (1994) 'Dying of awareness: the theory of awareness contexts revisited', *Sociology of Health & Illness*, 16 (3): 322–39.

Walter, T. (2008) 'The sociology of death', *Sociology Compass*, 2 (1): 317–36.

Walter, T. (2012) 'Why different countries manage death differently: a comparative analysis of modern urban societies', *British Journal of Sociology*, 63 (1): 123–45.

ADDITIONAL RESOURCE

Virtual Special Edition on Death, edited by Clive Seale. *Sociology of Health & Illness*. Online: http://www.blackwellpublishing.com/shil_enhanced/virtual1.asp

Lee F. Monaghan

Part 3
Health, Knowledge and Practice

> *The medical model refers to the conception of disease established in the late nineteenth and early twentieth centuries, based on an anatomo-pathological view of the individual body.*

The concept of the medical model is frequently used by sociologists and others as a shorthand way of describing the dominant approach to disease in Western medicine. In the nineteenth century, this approach, based on a pathological anatomy of the body, broke away from earlier conceptions to establish the idea of specific diseases with specific causes. Earlier, disease in Western societies had been largely based on humoral theories and on exhaustive descriptions of symptoms. Thomas Sydenham, the seventeenth-century English physician, for example, would have no truck with dissection and the emerging field of anatomy, declaring: 'as for anatomy, my butcher can dissect a joint full and well; now young man, all that is stuff; you must go to the bedside, it is there alone you can learn disease' (cited by Porter, 1997: 229). Scepticism about scientific and laboratory-based medicine was common in the early modern period and in some contexts persists to this day.

However, by the mid-nineteenth century various alternative models of disease, including those based on observation and 'bedside medicine' (Jewson, 1976), were made to give way to a view that located disease in specific organs. Indeed, in 1800, Bichat had argued that the pathological processes giving rise to disease might not even be located in an organ, but in a specific tissue. By the 1880s bacteriology had begun to show that specific micro-organisms were responsible for specific diseases; for example, the tubercle bacillus for tuberculosis and the vibrio cholerae for cholera. Predictably, these findings were resisted by many physicians who were wedded to the idea that disease clearly involved the whole person and must be systemic in origin and character.

By contrast, the new model of disease contained three dimensions: (1) that a specific aetiology could be found underlying specific diseases; (2) that diseases caused lesions in the body which altered its anatomy and physiology; and (3) that these two processes, in turn, gave rise to symptoms. Though successes in applying this new approach were not immediate, by the end of the nineteenth century the antitoxin for diphtheria was showing dramatic results and the adoption of antisepsis was beginning to make hospital care and especially surgery safer. The development of antibiotics, especially following the identification by Fleming of penicillin in 1928, and its final introduction in 1941 (Porter, 1997: 457), showed that the medical model of disease could produce lasting and beneficial results.

The impact of the new medical model on the doctor–patient relationship was equally profound. As the conception of disease focused on processes inside the body, the task of the doctor was to elicit information about the signs and symptoms

of the disease and then locate these in the new nosology. Thus, the ability to diagnose became highly prized and was based on test results and judgements about deviations from 'the normal', rather than on observations of departures from the patient's 'natural state' (Lawrence, 1994: 45). From the patient's viewpoint, the task now was to pay attention to signs and symptoms and present them to the doctor at the appropriate time. As disease was seen to reside in the individual body, it could best be diagnosed and treated in a one-to-one situation by the clinician. Doctors were increasingly oriented towards individual 'presentation', rather than tackling the complexities and heterogeneity of the patient's familial, social or moral worlds. The medical model can be seen, therefore, as reinforcing individualism as a dimension of modern experience.

The growing allegiance of doctors to the medical model in the late nineteenth and especially early twentieth centuries is also partly explained by the association of the new approach to disease with social and sometimes political reform. Even in the early nineteenth century, as novels such as George Eliot's *Middlemarch* made clear, the reforming medical man, increasingly under the influence of the medical model, was part of the changing fabric of (in this case) English society. The medical model did not simply develop in a particular historical context: it was an important constitutive part of society's changing character. The progress in medicine was but one of a range of practices linked to changing cultural and social structures.

Lawrence (1994) argues that, by 1920, the idea of disease as individual pathology had become almost entirely dominant, pushing other theories and approaches aside. This underpinned and legitimated the development of a 'bounded' medical profession which increasingly exercised jurisdiction over medical matters (Lawrence, 1994: 77). State regulation of medicine and a ceding of quasi-judicial powers to the profession, for example, its ability to register or de-register ('strike off') practitioners, gave it enormous powers of autonomy and control. Senior hospital doctors, in particular, and those organized in the various Royal Colleges had, and arguably still have, particular access to these levers of power.

Not surprisingly, therefore, the development of the medical model has not always been met with unqualified acceptance, even by those doctors sympathetic to a scientific medicine. There are some within the profession, especially those in specialties such as public health and psychiatry, and in general practice, who have argued against the complete subsuming of medical practice under the aegis of the medical model.

The 1960s and 1970s saw a number of critiques emerge from within medicine. Thomas Szasz, a medically trained psychoanalyst, and R.D. Laing, an ex-army psychiatrist, among many others, issued broad critiques of the application of the medical model to mental illness. In addition, the 1970s saw strong reactions by leading epidemiologists in public health to what they perceived as the overreliance on (unevaluated) curative medicine by the public, and too great an influence on the part of the medical establishment. McKeown (1976), for example, examined the historical role of medicine and showed that for many if not all infections, mortality had fallen substantially before the medical model had uncovered their causes or, indeed, fashioned any preventative or curative responses. McKeown

demonstrated that public health measures and better living standards were responsible for improvements in health in the nineteenth and twentieth centuries. Part of the problem with the 'mechanistic' medical model's focus on 'engineering' interventions at the individual level was that the broader determinants of health were overlooked.

In medical sociology, early theorizing about health and medicine regarded medicine as socially functional. Parsons (1951) held medicine and the medical model of disease to be rational, counteracting the 'needs dispositions' of the ill. By addressing the individual's problems in medical terms, the tendency towards deviance, represented by illness states, could be safely channelled, pending the return of the individual to their former roles.

However, by the 1970s, medical sociologists were also becoming highly critical of the medical model and its application by the medical profession. Freidson (1970), in particular, set out a full-blown critique of the profession and, quite unlike Parsons, sought to challenge the apparent objectivity of the medical model. The belief in illness as an objective entity, Freidson argued, stemmed from the perception of 'viruses and molecules . . . [as a] physical reality independent of time, space and changing moral evaluation' (1970: 208). But, Freidson insisted, 'biological deviance or disease is defined socially and is surrounded by social acts that condition it' (p. 209). The failure of medicine to recognize this situation meant that far from acting as a socially functional institution, it left the patient in a passive position, with lay constructions given little or no credence. The 'clash of perspectives' between the patient's world and that of the doctor led to an underlying conflict: 'Given the viewpoints of the two worlds, lay and professional, in interaction, they can never be wholly synonymous' (p. 321).

As can be seen from the above, Freidson's argument rested on a distinction between illness (the experience of the patient) and disease (the conception of the doctor). While the application of the medical model of biological disease could vary depending on the cultural context, Freidson was more concerned to contrast the different perspectives of patients and doctors than follow through a detailed critique of the 'social construction' of disease.

It has perhaps been Foucault's critique of the medical model that has taken this question much further. In a number of writings on 'bio-power', Foucault set out what he took to be the social significance of the pathological anatomy view of disease. In his book, *The Birth of the Clinic*, Foucault (1976) centres his argument on Bichat and his dictum to 'open up a few corpses'. The significance of this move was, as noted earlier, to locate disease in what Foucault terms the 'volumes and spaces' of the body. This individuating and internalizing of disease, for Foucault, was the hallmark of the 'new' medical model. The growing dominance of this model, together with the associated growth in power and influence of the medical profession, demonstrated for him the intimate relationship between knowledge and power.

Like Freidson, medicine's monopoly over disease and illness, for Foucault, stemmed from the power to name and locate disease in the individual. Bringing the individual under 'the gaze' of medical perception was part of a growing tendency by modernity to rely on the 'discursive practices' of experts in effecting

social order. These practices divided populations according to their 'disciplinary' codes. In fact, in Foucault's work the term 'discipline' had a double meaning: the 'discipline' of medicine at one and the same time located the individual in a scientific schema, and, on the other, added to the tendency to create 'docile bodies' by regulating them in specific ways. The growth of medicine, psychology and the human sciences in general, no less than the growth of the clinic and hospital (like the school and the prison), was the institutional expression of 'disciplinary power' shaping and reshaping modern life.

The point of Foucault's critique was that the enormous growth in the power of medicine and the medical conception of disease was neither inevitable nor irreversible. He stated: 'this order of the solid, visible body is only one way – in all likelihood neither the first, nor the most fundamental – in which one spacialises disease' (Foucault, 1976: 3). The message is clear: things could have been otherwise, and therefore can be otherwise in the future. The apparent objectivity of the body and the permanence of the medical model are open to question and change.

These critical views of the medical model have done much to challenge the power of the medical profession and to fuel some of the challenges to 'medical dominance' now found in public as well as academic circles. However, despite the persuasiveness of these critiques, there are limitations which suggest that the medical model is more complex than envisaged. Two must suffice here.

First, the idea that the medical model is neither the first nor likely the last way of conceptualizing disease may be literally true, but paradoxically it understates the transformations that the medical model and other features of modernity have created. While alternative ways of conceptualizing disease and illness may emerge (health promotion, public health and the myriad of 'alternative practices' have all grown in recent years), the medical model shows little sign of disappearing. Developments in pharmacology, genetics and the neurosciences suggest that the power of medical knowledge and of the profession has grown in scope and reach, however problematic this sometimes appears. Indeed, recent work by sociologists on the 'new genetics' (Atkinson et al., 2009), and on normality and pathology in modern biomedicine (Rose, 2009), pays testament to the continuing development of scientific and medical thought, as well as their continuing cultural significance.

Second, the changing pattern of disease in Western countries, and especially the decline in infections, has meant that many areas of medical practice have moved away from a complete reliance on a narrow, 'mechanistic' view of the body or of illness, if indeed they ever accepted it fully. Many of those working with the chronically ill, for example, are as concerned with the physical, social and psychological functioning of the individual and with the pattern of informal care as they are with diagnosis or medical treatments. While a condition such as dementia is the focus for large-scale investments in laboratory research, medical practitioners continue to be concerned with the observable effects of the condition for individuals and their families. From this viewpoint, the medical model may never have been quite as fundamental to the everyday practice of medicine as Foucault and others believed.

scientific knowledge is determined by the distinct properties of its objects of study in the natural world. In structuralist accounts, this classical view of scientific knowledge is often assumed or left unquestioned and the point is to show how representations of reality are distorted in line with particular ideological interests reflecting the way power is played out according to pervasive social structures. Conversely, SSK takes a relativist, constructionist approach to the study of science. In highlighting the relative character of scientific knowledge, it reveals the social processes that are involved in the production of knowledge. In other words, the constructionist approach engages with the *content* of scientific knowledge as an empirical object of sociological investigation rather than taking social structures based on established interests and power as its analytical starting point. Whereas structuralists take a stance on the validity of knowledge claims, largely in relation to the predetermined structures that shape knowledge and the social implications of knowledge, constructionists are agnostic on this point. This agnosticism stems from the principle of 'methodological relativism', which is adopted as a strategy of objectivity in SSK. The basic theoretical precept guiding this approach is that since scientific knowledge is socially produced then it should be studied empirically like all other forms of knowledge. In short, it should be studied as sets of beliefs and conventions that are bound up with the context of knowledge production itself (Bloor, 1970). However, for those who can see common ground between structuralist and constructionist positions, in following Bury (1986), the agnostic stance taken by SSK towards the truth or falsity of knowledge claims limits constructionism as a form of sociological critique.

Empirical studies in SSK focus on scientific controversies and argue that such disputes reveal the social processes that are at play in determining a scientific consensus about the validity of competing claims. Nicolson and McLaughlin (1988) provide such an account in their case study of a medico-scientific dispute between vascular and immunological theories about the pathogenesis of multiple sclerosis (MS). In following the principle of methodological relativism, the authors give equal explanatory weight to the rival theories in the dispute. They show how experts put their own competing constructions on the reality of MS depending on their different professional traditions. Their study demonstrates how new knowledge is filtered through existing beliefs and theories, which affords experts a considerable degree of flexibility in interpreting the same body of evidence to support their rival propositions. As Nicolson and McLaughlin (1988: 235) put it: 'we understand the unknown in the light of what we already know – which, of course, in turn has its roots in training and in prior socialisation'. They argue that the immunological account of MS continues to hold sway over its rival because there is a stronger cognitive fit between this model and the clinical expertise involved in the management of the disease. Furthermore, the mode of treatment suggested by this model is in keeping with conventional drug treatment, which can more readily be accommodated within existing clinical practice than the alternative therapy developed on the basis of vascular theory. They argue that enrolling support for an unorthodox therapeutic approach depends on the relative power of its supporters, irrespective of the evidence. In this weaker version of constructionism we can see common ground with a structuralist approach when the local contingencies associated with knowledge production are further contextualized in relation to the broader political, cultural and economic structures in society.

The main debate about constructionism centres on its relativist claims about knowledge. For example, the implication of a constructionist approach for medical knowledge is that it has no objective basis in the properties of the 'things' that medical practitioners claim to know about. Logically, this argument also applies to sociological knowledge. Hence, for Bury (1986, 1987) and Williams (2001), the same propositions that constructionists apply to scientific knowledge may be used to undermine the very basis on which sociology engages with medical knowledge. To be sure, the naïve constructivist epistemology associated with postmodernist theories seems absurd to medical sociologists who wish, for example, to engage with medicine on the basis of the relevance of social structures and power relations as independent realities that impact on health and can be changed by human actions. A weaker version of constructionism, which is core to much sociological thinking, accepts epistemological relativism (rejecting the naïve realism of positivism) while also accepting ontological realism (rejecting naïve constructionism). In responding to Bury's (1986) critique of constructionism as applied to medical knowledge, Nicolson and McLaughlin (1987) insist that constructionist theory is realist in the ontological sense that it neither denies the physical reality of disease nor treats the objects of medico-scientific knowledge as mere artefacts. In characterizing the SSK version of constructionism as 'constructionist realism', Nicolson and McLaughlin (1988: 251) argue that 'knowledge may be regarded not as a unique representation or mirror of external reality, but as an instrument by which we may operate with that reality'. For these authors, the explanatory power of constructionism demonstrates that the contrasting perspectives and evaluations of medical knowledge are underdetermined by the properties of an external physical reality, while overdetermined by social processes.

In its different theoretical variants, sociology correctly emphasizes how knowledge about biology is socially constructed. However, for some sociologists (Williams, 2001; Shilling, 2005), constructionism has gone too far towards social determinism in countering biological determinism. This renders sociology blind to the external forces of nature that act dialectically with the making of human reality, both in terms of the limits and possibilities as well as the impact of human action. This critique is targeted at stronger forms of social constructionism influenced by the work of Michel Foucault and, in particular, postmodernist theories in which both the body and disease are treated wholly as discursive entities. Indeed, most sociologists recognize that ontological relativism is an unfeasible proposition for the enterprise of sociology. While constructionism has many meanings and the approaches associated with it are equally divergent, the concept continues to be debated. On the one hand, constructionism is accused of undermining sociological realism by placing too strong an emphasis on interpretative practices or local social contingencies, while underplaying the role that pervasive social structures play in the formation of knowledge and the accomplishment of reality. On the other hand, it is accused of challenging natural realism by embracing a relativist epistemology that cuts the ground from under science itself. Moreover, a relativist epistemology, when applied to constructionism itself, undermines it as a form of sociological critique. While these debates continue, most sociologists seek some common ground between constructionist and structuralist approaches, and theoretical choice is more likely to be determined by the focus of analysis and the degree of contextualization demanded of any explanatory approach.

See also: *Medicalization; Medical Model; Geneticization; Surveillance and Health Promotion*

REFERENCES

Berger, P.L. and Luckmann, T. (1967) *The Social Construction of Reality: A Treatise in the Sociology of Knowledge*. New York: Anchor Books.

Bloor, D. (1970) *Knowledge and Social Imagery*. London: Routledge and Kegan Paul.

Bury, M.R. (1986) 'Social constructionism and the development of medical sociology', *Sociology of Health & Illness*, 8 (2): 137–69.

Bury, M.R. (1987) 'Social constructionism and medical sociology: a rejoinder to Nicolson and McLaughlin', *Sociology of Health & Illness*, 9 (4): 439–41.

Freidson, E. (1970) *The Profession of Medicine: The Study of the Applied Sociology of Knowledge*. New York: Dodd Mead.

Nicolson, M. and McLaughlin, C. (1987) 'Social constructionism and medical sociology: a reply to M.R. Bury', *Sociology of Health & Illness*, 9 (2): 107–26.

Nicolson, M. and McLaughlin, C. (1988) 'Social constructionism and medical sociology: a study of the vascular theory of multiple sclerosis', *Sociology of Health & Illness*, 10 (3): 234–61.

Shilling, C. (2005) *The Body in Culture, Technology and Society*. London: Sage.

Williams, S.J. (2001) 'Sociological imperialism and the profession of medicine revisited: where are we now?', *Sociology of Health & Illness*, 23 (2): 135–58.

Orla McDonnell

Lay Knowledge

> *Lay knowledge refers to the ideas and perspectives employed by social actors to interpret their experiences of health and illness in everyday life.*

The concept of lay knowledge within medical sociology is a recent development of the idea of lay beliefs. The study of people's beliefs about illness, health and medical care initially provided a way of understanding different forms of 'illness behaviour' and 'lay referral', particularly where 'non-compliant' behaviour suggested differences between the patient's perspectives and those of his or her physician.

Research on these themes provided an empirical foundation for the argument that a patient's behaviour was influenced by his or her beliefs, and that these beliefs were a reasoned attempt to deal with the sometimes intensely contradictory demands of illness and its treatment in everyday life (Robinson, 1973). However, beliefs are more than antecedents to individual behaviour, and a second line of thought was beginning to conceptualize lay beliefs about health and illness as social representations. Drawing on the Durkheimian tradition of sociological theorizing about the conscience collective, Herzlich (1973) provided an important bridge between the interesting but highly focused empirical studies of individual patients within medical sociology, and the panorama of social theorizing about the relationships between self and society.

With a respectful but sociologically critical eye on her respondents' accounts, Herzlich was able to move away from the methodological individualism characteristic of much of the work on lay beliefs at the time. She argued that individual beliefs about health and illness are representations of the culture and society in which people live. While these representations may include medical ideas about pathology and aetiology, lay perspectives express a certain cultural autonomy and embody a wider theorization of health and illness in relation to society. In analysing her material in this way, Herzlich marked out a set of themes that would remind future social scientists that lay beliefs represented far too fecund a field to be left to the withering attention of health services researchers or government civil servants. The development in the UK of the Expert Patient Programme suggests that policy responses to the acknowledgement of lay knowledge and expertise remain top-down, normative and individualistic, drawing on psychological rather than sociological concepts (Taylor and Bury, 2007).

The work of Herzlich provided the intellectual foundation for two key arguments about lay knowledge. First, that lay ideas are not 'primitive' residuals stuck in the otherwise smoothly functioning bowels of modern 'scientific' societies, but complex bodies of knowledge and forms of rationality that are central to our understanding of culture and society (Good, 1994). Second, 'lay knowledge' has two key dimensions. On the one hand, it contains a robust empirical approach to the contingencies of everyday life; an approach required by people trying to make sense of the occurrences of health and illness in themselves, their families and the wider communities in which they live. On the other, especially in situations in which the illness is particularly serious or frightening, it displays a search for meaning that goes beyond the straightforwardly empirical, situating personal experiences of health crisis in relation to broader frameworks of morality, politics and cosmology.

An illustration of the complexity of this can be found in Comaroff and Maguire's classic (1981) study of 'the search for meaning' in childhood leukaemia. Modern medicine, they argue, supplies an empirical basis for explaining to parents what is happening to their children, but it provides no overarching framework through which parents can 'make sense' of what is happening. The parents in their study were asking not only what causes childhood leukaemia, but also why has my child developed this disease, and why now? Perhaps it is not the business of good doctoring to answer these questions, but it does point to the tension between 'evidence-based' and 'narrative-based' approaches to health knowledge. Lay people need the evidence, but the evidence itself will not be enough to support the wider framework of interpretation needed to make sense of their child's illness.

With the increasing emphasis during the 1990s on public health and health promotion, there has been a growing interest in how lay knowledge relates to ideas about health risks. For Herzlich's middle-class Parisians the 'way of life' in modern societies produces ill health, with way of life being defined more in terms of social and environmental circumstances than individual behaviour. Later work on this theme showed a tendency for personal responsibility explanations for ill health to be prevalent in both 'rich' and 'poor' populations, possibly reflecting the enduring values of a Protestant ethic in some of the communities studied, and the effects of the ideology of 'possessive individualism' that were ripping through Western societies at the time (Blaxter, 1983).

However, the key characteristic of lay knowledge is that it is integrative and holistic, drawing on multiple factors in a syncretic but not indiscriminate fashion and bringing together 'scientific' or other professional sources of knowledge. While this knowledge reflects the cultural values and ideological interests of the times, it can also provide an incisive moral and political critique of them. A good example of this is to be found in Davison et al.'s (1991) study, based on extensive interviews and observational data from naturalistic settings. This study examined the relationships between lay perspectives on coronary heart disease and the orthodox doctrine promulgated in a nationwide health promotion campaign – Heartbeat Wales.

Davison et al. (1991) uncovered a strong strand of lay thinking that emphasized a personal responsibility for health. They also identified a close correspondence between lay views and the simple, linear causal models of health educators, emphasizing the links between diet, exercise, blood pressure, serum cholesterol and heart disease. There was no clear-cut clash of perspectives between lay people and professionals. However, Davison and his colleagues also argued that in situations in which a person becomes ill or a relative dies, when an explanation is *needed*, these lay views become more complex. They coined the term 'lay epidemiology' to describe the way in which people may use a combination of personal, familial and social sources of knowledge, alongside professionally delivered information, to try and make sense of an event or problem. People develop a notion of who is a 'candidate' for a coronary that corresponds quite closely with risk factor epidemiology. However, the reality of lay experience is that we come across many individuals who smoke, eat fatty foods, drink too much alcohol, have a stressful life, take no exercise and live to a ripe old age (the 'Uncle Norman' character); and conversely there are those who live an Aristotelian 'good life' of balance, frugality, virtue and restraint but collapse and die in their forties. Like the parents in Comaroff and Maguire's (1981) study who were faced with their children's leukaemia, abstract descriptions of 'risk factors' are not enough to explain why a much-loved mother or brother has died so young. These problems have taken on a new dimension with the expansion of molecular and genetic models for health in general and specific diseases. These can be seen to have become part of the cultural representations through which sense-making takes place (Emslie et al., 2003).

Much risk factor epidemiology also assumes a freedom to make healthy choices that is out of line with what many lay people experience as real possibilities in their everyday lives. For example, in a study of Salford – a deprived inner-city area in the north-west of England (Williams et al., 1995) – we see how lay people are only too well aware of the 'political' context of explanations for ill health in the community. In this instance, and in stark contrast to much risk factor epidemiology, the lay accounts reported illustrate the need to contextualize risks – smoking, diet, alcohol, a lack of exercise – by reference to the wider material and environmental conditions in which the risks are embedded. The respondents understood the behavioural risk factors that made ill health more likely and for which they were, in a severely limited sense, responsible, but they were also aware that the risks they faced were part of social conditions that they could do little to change. For these working-class Salfordians, as for Herzlich's middle-class Parisians, the 'way of life' – in this case unemployment, poor housing, a low income, stressful and sometimes violent lives – provided a context for 'making sense' of smoking, drinking and drug-taking and all the other 'behaviours' that risk factor epidemiologists calculate and correlate.

This more political expression of lay knowledge finds its most challenging form in the 'popular epidemiology' examined by Brown (1995), and others, where lay knowledge becomes a form of 'civic intelligence' that is deployed in the contestation of scientific expertise (Elliott et al., 2010). Studies of popular epidemiology take situations in which members of local communities have become concerned about a public health problem in their locality – the numbers of children with cancer, the high prevalence of asthma, or an increase in road traffic accidents – and seek some explanation for it. In these circumstances popular epidemiology begins with lay people linking the observed increase in the health problem to some kind of social or environmental hazard: road safety, factory emissions, toxic waste, nuclear power and so on. Having made the connection, the community then tries to take action to do something about it, and finds itself in conflict with local politicians, business corporations or professional experts who disagree, for one reason or another, with the view being expressed by the community, or some sections of it. In these situations, local people are forced to move beyond the statement of a point of view to a process in which a social movement develops, evidence is systematically collected and analysed, and scientific arguments are developed and sometimes tested in the courts. In popular epidemiology we see the blurring of the boundaries between 'lay people' and 'experts' and the nature of the complex relationships between scientific rationality, personal beliefs and political interests.

While the concept of lay knowledge was initially developed as a critical response to the literature on lay beliefs (Williams and Popay, 2006 [1994]), its proponents have been accused both of oversimplifying the sociology of the 'lay expert' and of understating the importance of genuine bodies of expert knowledge (Prior, 2003). However, the exploration of lay knowledge throws into sharp relief some of our major social concerns – the relationship between authority and expertise, the problem of meaning in a pluralistic society, the incommensurability of different frameworks of interpretation, and the difficulties involved in developing a society that is both democratic and knowledge-based.

It is impossible to study lay beliefs as forms of knowledge without first acknowledging – as did the late Roy Porter (2000) in his discussion of the pivotal place of the eighteenth-century coffee-house in the dissemination of 'news, novelty and gossip' – that universities and laboratories are not the only places in which evidence is debated and knowledge generated. Knowledge is a dynamic phenomenon that moves through the home, the street, pubs and bars, the internet and the workplace, often revealing itself only at times of personal or community crisis when the taken-for-grantedness of everyday life is disturbed. What started – to paraphrase the historian E.P. Thompson – as an attempt to rescue lay knowledge from the enormous condescension of professional experts, has become a field of study in which the interaction of different forms of knowledge and expertise, through conflict and consensus, can be seen and understood.

See also: *Illness Narratives; Social Movements and Health*

REFERENCES

Blaxter, M. (1983) 'The causes of disease: women talking', *Social Science & Medicine*, 17: 59–69.

Brown, P. (1995) 'Popular epidemiology, toxic waste, and social movements', in J. Gabe (ed.), *Medicine, Health and Risk*. Oxford: Blackwell.

Comaroff, J. and Maguire, P. (1981) 'Ambiguity and the search for meaning: childhood leukaemia in the modern clinical context', *Social Science & Medicine*, 15B: 115–23.

Davison, C., Davey Smith, G. and Frankel, S. (1991) 'Lay epidemiology and the prevention paradox: the implications of coronary candidacy for health promotion', *Sociology of Health & Illness*, 13: 1–19.

Elliott, E., Harrop, E. and Williams, G.H. (2010) 'Contesting the science: public health knowledge and action in controversial land-use developments', in P. Bennett, K. Calman, S. Curtis and D. Fischbacher-Smith (eds), *Risk Communication and Public Health*, 2nd edn. Oxford: Oxford University Press.

Emslie, C., Hunt, K. and Watt, G. (2003) 'A chip off the old block? Lay understandings of inheritance among men and women in mid-life', *Public Understanding of Science*, 12: 47–65.

Good, B.J. (1994) *Medicine, Rationality and Experience: An Anthropological Perspective*. Cambridge: Cambridge University Press.

Herzlich, C. (1973) *Health and Illness: A Socio-Psychological Approach*. London: Academic Press.

Porter, R. (2000) *Enlightenment: Britain and the Creation of the Modern World*. London: Penguin.

Prior, L. (2003) 'Belief, knowledge and expertise: the emergence of the lay expert in medical sociology', *Sociology of Health & Illness*, 25: 41–57.

Robinson, D. (1973) *Patients, Practitioners and Medical Care*. London: Heinemann.

Taylor, D. and Bury, M. (2007) 'Chronic illness, expert patients and care transition', *Sociology of Health & Illness*, 29: 27–45.

Williams, G. and Popay, J. (2006 [1994]) 'Lay knowledge and the privilege of experience', in D. Kelleher, J. Gabe and G. Williams (eds), *Challenging Medicine*, 2nd edn. London: Routledge.

Williams, G., Popay, J. and Bissell, P. (1995) 'Public health risks in the material world: barriers to social movements in health', in J. Gabe (ed.), *Medicine, Health and Risk*. Oxford: Blackwell.

Gareth H. Williams

> *Within sociological theory and research, reproduction, referring to pregnancy, birth and the use of reproductive technologies, is regarded as a social and cultural process as well as a biological process.*

The shared beliefs, values and practices of any society are central to how women, men and children orient themselves towards the major events of birth, illness and death. By extension, reproduction is an area that reveals the relations between health care as a social practice, dominant social values and gendered beliefs. There is considerable cultural variation in how pregnancy and childbearing are defined and managed in everyday life. In some societies pregnancy is a normal life event and a status passage; in others it is regarded as an illness. Crucial to the sociological view of reproduction is that it happens to, and within, society, as well as to individuals, who may, or may not, be subject to medical control. Thus, the way reproduction is 'managed' has important implications for society as a whole: for how people as social agents view reproduction, and for the position of women, men and family relationships. Furthermore, from the point of view of the individual woman, her 'career' as a pregnant woman is not isolated from her other social roles, such as wife, worker or patient.

An examination of literature in this field shows that an early, narrow definition of the sociology of human reproduction – relating to conception, pregnancy, birth and motherhood – has been broadened. The literature now encompasses the study of sexuality, reproductive technologies, and the social relations involved in the provision of reproductive health services. This has resulted in writings examining the sexual politics of reproduction and the construction of biomedical knowledge (Clarke, 1998). Such writings have aimed to move away from definitions of reproductive processes as biological events, isolated from social reality. At the same time, writings stressing social aspects, including embodiment, have been cautious not to mask the effect the biology has on women's lives, and more recent work has also focused on the relationship between men and reproduction (Lee, 2010).

Macintyre's (1977) review still endures in its identification of four types of sociological approach to the management of childbirth and sets out a sociological research agenda more generally. These approaches are: (1) historical, drawing on the sociology of professions and science perspectives; (2) anthropological, focusing on the management of birth in different cultures; (3) 'patient'-oriented, focusing on user views and experiences; and (4) 'patient'-services interaction. Macintyre's review highlights two key themes that are directly related to areas of debate within the sociology of reproduction. The first has been the concept of *medicalization*, and the second has been a dualistic notion of *competing ideologies of reproduction*.

Medicalization, a key concept in the sociology of health and illness, draws attention to medicine as a powerful instrument of social control. Women have been seen as particularly vulnerable to medicalization, and it is in relation to reproduction that the concept has been much debated. Sociologists have drawn attention to the medicalization of various aspects of the reproductive process. An early development of the medicalization concept was the work of feminists who identified patriarchal society and its extension – patriarchal medicine – as a key force behind the medicalization of women's health issues. These scholars analysed how previous religious justifications for patriarchy were transformed into scientific ones, and described how women's traditional skills for managing birth were expropriated by medical experts at the end of the nineteenth century. Such work examined the way services were organized, reproductive technologies controlled and sexuality constrained as particular manifestations of the patriarchal domination that shaped women's reproductive experiences. This early feminist literature identified the sexual politics of women's health and provided a theoretical basis for reclaiming knowledge about, and control over, women's bodies. It was polemical, intentionally political, and critical of the medical model imposed on pregnancy and birth.

Oakley's (1980) seminal studies of pregnancy and childbirth in Britain have, unusually for sociological texts, provoked a wider public and professional debate. In her early work, she demonstrated the ways in which the discourse of the medical world differs from the everyday language of women and their relatives, and how various understandings are associated with unequal authority and power. In a critical analysis of the profession of obstetrics, she theorized a dualistic notion of *competing ideologies of reproduction*. Here, women see pregnancy as a social process over which they should exert active control, while medicine posits it as a potentially pathological event that must be controlled and managed.

This theory assumed that women of all classes and ethnicities share the same view. This assumption was later challenged by writers who argued that discourses pertaining to reproduction cannot be reduced to dichotomies; rather, reproductive discourses are multiple and complex. For example, Riessman (1983) examined childbirth and reproduction, premenstrual syndrome and mental health. She claimed that what women have gained and lost with the medicalization of 'life problems' has not been documented. Nor has it been noted how women have actively participated in the construction of new medical definitions, or the reasons that led to such participation. Riessman argued that both physicians and women have contributed to the redefining of women's experiences in terms of medical categories. Furthermore, physicians have sought to medicalize experience because of beliefs and economic interests, depending on specific professional developments and market conditions.

The work on childbearing in the 1970s and the 1980s provided the background for work on *New Reproductive Technologies* (NRTs). By the mid-1980s, the focus was moving away from the experiences of the majority of women during pregnancy and birth towards a critique of NRTs. This was spurred on by the birth of Louise Brown, the first test tube baby, in the UK in 1978. NRTs include surrogacy, assisted fertility techniques, prenatal screening and diagnosis, pre-implantation diagnosis and foetal surgery. These were derived from a scientific approach to reproduction, just like

reproduction

older techniques such as contraception which were developed to 'manage' pregnancy and childbirth. Questions asked about NRTs have comprised three dimensions. The first describes their nature and function; the second is the triad of women, gender and science; the third expands the above debates to encompass health system access issues and cross-cultural perspectives.

Drawing on feminist criticisms of scientific knowledge and the medicalization of women's lives, studies of reproduction have highlighted the power relations such practices mediate. Criticisms include: women being used as experimental material; women's bodies being commodified; and the construction of the conflicting status of women and foetuses. Such writings have critiqued state control over access to services, and have also asked in whose interests have technological developments – such as prenatal screening and testing, infertility treatments, test tube babies, foetal imaging and surrogacy – been developed? The debate has focused on the extent to which these new technologies have been beneficial, or a form of oppression to women, setting up a binary divide of 'salvation or damnation'. Yet in reality the picture is more complex. In the USA, in a seminal piece, Rothman (1986) reported that prenatal testing changed the way people thought about childbirth and parenthood. An open mind about the outcome of pregnancy had been replaced with a new norm of *'tentative pregnancy'*, even though perfection could not be offered. She concluded that although prenatal testing had increased women's choices, it had also constructed women as genetic gatekeepers, with a new moral responsibility for the consequences of their decisions which had societal implications.

In the 1990s, contributors considered how bio-medicine constructs the procreative body, the role of associated regulatory practices and how technology allows medical professionals greater jurisdiction over larger areas of reproduction. Stacey (1992) has argued that the new reproductive technologies, such as IVF, GIFT and the 'new genetics' that are based on the discovery of DNA, have opened up new possibilities and created a 'scientific revolution in human reproduction', i.e. the teaming of real science with obstetrics, with implications for the way such technologies are managed and controlled. There has been a concern that women are not just seen as the passive recipients of reproductive technology, and that efforts should be made to explore how they contest and contribute to the construction of new medical definitions and the use of NRTs. Such work has disavowed technological and biological determinism and emphasized human agency. This has involved the delineation of the role of experts and the identification of female resistance. Lock and Kaufert (1998) have pointed out how women make pragmatic use of reproductive technologies and have challenged the representation of women as the passive victims of surveillance. A recent review of the experience of infertility informed by social scientific studies of illness experience, gender, the body and stigma highlighted an increasing focus on the socio-cultural and health systems context (Greil et al., 2010). The infertility literature can also serve to remind us that it is not only women who reproduce, who undergo medicalization and who experience stigma; men should also be included in such research.

The sociology of reproduction raises many other issues. Notably, there are questions about the underlying perspectives of writers in this field, ranging from those who seek to contribute and develop sociological theory, to writers with the explicit aim that their work should improve the experiences of women. This range of perspectives parallels debates within the study of illness narratives as well as public sociology, which is reflective of a broader division of labour where different types of knowledge are formulated for academic and/or extra-academic audiences. In the debate about *competing ideologies of reproduction*, Annandale and Clark (1996) have critically reviewed many of the underlying assumptions of writings in the domain of the sociology of childbirth. In so doing these authors have sought to further conceptual knowledge, though such thinking has also been drawn upon by others to inform public and policy debates. On the basis of a range of broad critiques of writings on the sociology of health and gender, Annandale and Clark have suggested that much of the literature has been sociologically naïve around the use of reproductive technology and the rhetoric of midwifery. Specifically, they have argued that much writing has been preoccupied with abnormalities in women's health; has universalized women's experiences regardless of ethnicity and class; has equated reproductive technology with the medicalization of reproduction; has assumed that an increased use of technology in childbirth is a 'bad' thing for women; and has implied that women are powerless victims or dupes in this process. Furthermore, in juxtaposing midwifery and obstetrics, much writing has given uncritical support to the notion that midwifery is 'better' for women than male-dominated obstetrics; it assumes that midwifery has an underlying feminist viewpoint and implies that midwives are 'with women', ignoring issues of power between women and their female caregivers.

Although feminist perspectives and political action in relation to women's health have been defended from a different epistemological basis – specifically in relation to critiques of reproductive interventions and midwifery – such critiques hold and form the basis for some new directions for research in the sociology of reproduction (Brubaker and Dillaway, 2009). In particular, such writing emphasizes the need to deconstruct notions about what is 'natural' and explore the transformative possibilities of technology.

In summary, some sociological work in the area of human reproduction has played a key role in shaping policy and practice and has been grounded in women's concerns in a reflexive way. Early work that focused on pregnancy and birth has broadened out into an examination of reproductive technologies and the 'new' genetics. Future work in the field of human reproduction that draws on sociological theories of risk and the body would be fruitful, alongside a sociology of science that critically examines the role of pharmaceutical and biomedical industries. In so doing, the sociology of reproduction should develop a global perspective, exploring how such processes unfold in various countries and cultures.

See also: *Medicalization; Medical Technologies; Nursing and Midwifery as Occupations*

reproduction

REFERENCES

Annandale, E.C. and Clark, J. (1996) 'What is gender? Feminist theory and the sociology of human reproduction', *Sociology of Health & Illness*, 18 (1): 17–44.

Brubaker, S.J. and Dillaway, H.E. (2009) 'Medicalization, natural childbirth and birthing experiences', *Sociology Compass*, 3 (1): 31–48.

Clarke, A.E. (1998) *Disciplining Reproduction, Modernity, American Life Sciences, and the 'Problems of Sex'*. Berkeley: University of California Press.

Greil, A.L., Slauson-Blevins, K. and McQuillan, J. (2010) 'The experience of infertility: a review of recent literature', *Sociology of Health & Illness*, 32: 140–62.

Lee, E. (2010) 'Pathologising fatherhood: the case of male post-natal depression in Britain', in B. Gough and S. Robertson (eds), *Men, Masculinities and Health: Critical Perspectives*. Basingstoke: Palgrave Macmillan.

Lock, M. and Kaufert, P.A. (1998) *Pragmatic Women and Body Politics*. Cambridge: Cambridge University Press.

Macintyre, S. (1977) 'The management of childbirth: a review of sociological research issues', *Social Science & Medicine*, 11: 447–84.

Oakley, A. (1980) *Women Confined: Towards a Sociology of Childbirth*. Oxford: Martin Robertson.

Riessman, C.K. (1983) 'Women and medicalization: a new perspective', *Social Policy*, Summer: 3–17.

Rothman, B.K. (1986) *The Tentative Pregnancy: Amniocentesis and the Sexual Politics of Motherhood*. New York: Viking Penguin.

Stacey, M. (ed.) (1992) *Changing Human Reproduction: Social Science Perspectives*. London: Sage.

Jane Sandall

Medical Technologies

> *Medical technologies are social artefacts that may be diagnostic, monitoring, screening, preventive, predictive, therapeutic, prosthetic, palliative, regenerative, rehabilitative or assistive, with contemporary attention being greatly focused on innovations in genetics, information and communication media, and nanotechnology.*

It is impossible to think of contemporary medicine without considering the multitude of technologies that are now integral both to medical practice and to health care worldwide. Such technologies are to be found inside health care systems, in domestic and personal spaces, and in workplaces and public places. Increasingly, medical technology is provided, accessed and consumed outside of traditional medical and health care settings in various forms of self-administered care regimes. Medical technology can lead to the re-shaping and re-defining of the boundaries of health care and 'medicine' itself, and users' subjective identities, be it as patients, consumers, citizens or health activists.

The definition of medical technologies provided above is a composite one, based on the type of action on the human body. It is important to note that the classification of medical technologies is itself a matter deserving of sociological understanding, because different classifications are used by different social actors with different 'stakeholder' agendas. Processes of classification, as shown by social anthropologists, are at the heart of how societies make the world intelligible and meaningful. In the case of medical technologies, the interested actors include, most obviously, national and global medical products industries, medical technology regulators and advisors, and healthcare professionals and citizens or patients. Thus, for example, European Union law currently groups technologies in classes including medical devices, in-vitro medical devices, active implantable devices, and advanced therapies (tissue engineering, cell therapy and gene therapy), and applies regulatory rules of varying stringency dependent on the degree of safety risk associated with particular products. Basic classifications from an industry perspective, on the other hand, involve distinctions between pharmaceuticals and medical devices, and sub-categories such as medical biotechnology which give definition to particular sectors of the contemporary medical products industries which figure in governments' policy making.

Medical technologies have been climbing up governments' policy agendas over the last thirty years. Since the 1980s, partly under the impetus of concerns about cost containment, health care policy internationally has seen a massive increase in movements to assess the suitability of medical technologies. For example, in 1992 in the UK, a report from concerned parties framed these issues in terms of a 'Tidal Wave' of new medical technologies (Hoare, 1992), paving the way for the birth of what is now known as Health Technology Assessment and evidence-based medicine, which attempt to rationalize health care by tying technology to 'robustly' evaluated standards of research evidence. These movements have evolved large infrastructures across industrial countries, deploying complex methodologies for assessing technologies in terms of efficacy, effectiveness, safety and cost-effectiveness. In the UK, the movement is epitomized by the internationally-recognized National Institute for Health and Clinical Excellence (NICE), which commissions technology assessments and makes recommendations about the adoption and clinical use of medical devices and pharmaceuticals, thus acting as a regulator. By having its decisions debated in the public realm, NICE enables 'the politics' of conflicting stakeholders' views about technologies to be ventilated, providing some social legitimacy to the health care technology policy process.

The social science literature relevant to health technologies is massive, comprising many approaches. Given this potentially confusing hinterland, a useful sociological starting-point is to take a more general question that has concerned scholars of the relationship between technology and society, and to apply it to medical technology. The question is: *'Is technology neutral?'* Asking such a question forces us to examine where technologies come from, how they are produced, by whom and with what images of users in mind, and how they are actually adopted, used and given meaning in the context of health and everyday life. Otherwise health technology may be seen as just an unchangeable 'black box' with its own logic which creates its own inevitable consequences (Lehoux, 2006: 42ff). Such simplified images are frequently to be found in the mass media ('new device set to revolutionize heart surgery'), and imply that the 'impacts' of medical technology are straightforward. This image is often associated with uncritical assumptions about the benefits or risks of technological progress. Such a view has been called technological determinism. It is important to note that in spite of its name it is in a sense a 'theory of society'. For a variety of reasons it has been strongly rejected by many sociologists and students of science and technology as, at best, a partial theory, notably because it implies a vision in which social actors – citizens, health care professionals, patients, planners and policymakers – can do little except react and adapt to technological developments (MacKenzie and Wajcman, 1999; Timmermans and Berg, 2003). So technological determinism, associated with the idea of a 'technological imperative', ignores the socially based variability of the design of technologies and what can be called their usership (Faulkner, 2009). To give an example of a controversial issue, a sociological approach is particularly revealing in the field of disease-testing technologies (biomarkers, genetic tests) that can provide clues about asymptomatic disease or the risk of developing a medical condition. Rather than assume that such tests will always be and indeed should be made use of, sociological analysis has shown how complex the decision to undergo them can be, how people think about them in terms of non-medical concerns such as family, social networks and working lives, and how people subjectively consider uncertain issues about 'becoming a patient' or not. The widely used but poor-performing blood test that can indicate latent prostate cancer in men is a good example of this (Faulkner, 2009). Equally, a determinist view is likely to over-simplify the way in which a new device might be adopted in a hospital or in primary care. It is apparent that some technologies are quite closely aligned with an existing profession (for example, stents in cardiovascular surgery), while others are much more 'configurational' in the sense that there are various ways of organizing their use and adapting the technology itself. Note, for example, telemedicine systems, which often are not implemented according to their original vision, and which require the active participation of multiple medical and nursing specialties as well as a connection with clinical data systems.

Sociologists' critique of technological determinism has been productive, in the sense that we can now point to more flexible ways of thinking theoretically about the relationship between medical technology and society. It is useful to consider these approaches in the context of simple distinctions between, first, the production and development of medical technologies; second, their introduction, adoption and regulation; and third, their usership and patients' experiences. In considering production and development, 'social shaping' is the counterpoint to technological determinism (MacKenzie and Wajcman, 1999; Timmermans and Berg, 2003). This term represents the opposite extreme, but as MacKenzie and Wajcman note: 'the social shaping of technology is … (usually) … a process in which there is no dominant shaping force' (1999: 16). These authors approach technology-society in a flexible way, pointing to economic shaping and the role of the state, and to the 'mutual constitution' of technology and society. The latter approach has steadily gained ground, conceptually indicating the inseparability of artefacts and society, or technologies and social relations. Timmermans and Berg (2003) refer to this as the 'technology-in-practice' approach, and it is now widely used in medical sociology, although it is, arguably, more applicable to usership and experience than it is to design, production and development. The mutual constitution approach is associated especially with 'actor-network theory' – the key feature of this is that it enables us to see the characteristics of medical technologies as playing one part amongst the other individual, social, and institutional 'actors' that produce the socio-medical realities with which we live. An implication of this theory is that any medical technology must be studied 'in action', that is, in the process of its design or adoption, and in the variably organized and specialized practices of its use. A good example comes from research into the management of childhood asthma, where the commonly used metered-dose inhaler was shown to be a significant actor in a complex network that also included parents, clinicians, scientists, children's lungs, aerosol gases and mechanical valves (Prout, 1996). Out of this ensemble, to simplify greatly, emerged novel skills, novel biomedical organization and novel social identities, as well as care regimes.

One of the criticisms made of 'social shaping', and 'mutual constitution' or 'network' approaches is that they fail to allow issues of political economy to be given due weight. Considering the innovation of medical technologies, the role of the state and industry is often important in shaping the direction of technologies. Contemporary medicine internationally shows significant trends that have been summarized as the medico-industrial complex and 'corporate health' (Webster, 2007). In this respect, the USA is both the largest producer and consumer of medical devices, followed by Japan and the western European countries; developing economic powers such as China and India are also becoming increasingly influential. State governments internationally are developing economic and health policies in order to promote technologies such as tissue engineering, cell therapy and medical nanotechnology, though some evoke ethical concerns which challenge existing regulations, sociomedical practices and social values. Sociologists can study in detail how medical technology innovation occurs, and it is recognized that central to this process is the forging of affiliations between a variety of social institutional actors, especially industry and academic scientists or clinicians. This has been shown, for example, through detailed historical and interview methods, in the case of the diagnostic imaging devices such as MRI and CT scanning that have become routine in advanced health care over the last thirty years (Blume, 1992).

Medical technologies also enter into everyday 'lifeworld' experiences (Lauritzen and Hydén, 2006) of usership and citizenship. Users of technologies may be construed as patients or citizens with subjective and social capacities and identities. Patients may also organize themselves around technologies, for example cardiac pacemaker groups, and in some cases will actively resist the 'inscriptions' built into them, as have parents in many countries who resisted projects to introduce cochlear implants (the 'bionic ear') for children. This resistance has been exercised on the grounds that cochlear implants disrupt the everyday family practices and social identity associated with the Deaf community and sign language. The lifeworld of health care practitioners also changes in negotiating technological innovations. Devices such as ultrasound scanning become part of clinical encounters, but may give rise to moral issues regarding troublesome pre-diagnostic information. Also, as the data and tissues of the human body are exposed to complex and fragmented screening, testing, diagnostic and monitoring technologies, then clinical professional boundaries, skills and multidisciplinary interactions are renegotiated.

Medical technologies are moving centre-stage in medical sociology and in contemporary societies. Sociological analysis can show the many ways in which they are not 'neutral' tools. Innovative devices and products disrupt existing social subjectivities, care organization and skills, and may be associated with classical sociological concerns of inequalities, medicalization, privatization and identity. Scientific trends such as molecularization, proteomics and medical nanotechnology, produced through international innovation networks, are of undoubted importance for medicine's future. Nevertheless, an even-minded sociological approach should not be too distracted by high-tech visions. For a sociological understanding, it is important to consider also 'mundane', under-the-radar, taken-for-granted technologies. In such a view, the bandage or the wheelchair may be as sociologically interesting, and have just as much social significance, as the bioreactor or the latest cardiac surgery device.

See also: *Geneticization; Bioethics; Medicines Regulation*

REFERENCES

Blume, S. (1992) *Insight and Industry: On the Dynamics of Technological Change in Medicine*. Cambridge, MA: MIT Press.

Faulkner, A. (2009) *Medical Technology into Healthcare and Society: A Sociology of Devices, Innovation and Governance*. Basingstoke: Palgrave Macmillan.

Hoare, J. (1992) *Tidal Wave: New Technology, Medicine and the NHS*. London: King's Fund Centre.

Lauritzen, S.O. and Hydén, L-C. (eds) (2006) *Medical Technologies and the Life World: The Social Construction of Normality*. Abingdon: Routledge.

Lehoux, P. (2006) *The Problem of Health Technology: Policy Implications for Modern Health Care Systems*. Abingdon: Taylor & Francis.

MacKenzie, D.A. and Wajcman, J. (1999) *The Social Shaping of Technology*, 2nd edn. Buckingham: Open University Press.

Prout, A. (1996) 'Actor-network theory, technology and medical sociology: an illustrative analysis of the metered dose inhaler', *Sociology of Health & Illness*, 18 (2): 198–221.

Timmermans, S. and Berg, M. (2003) 'The practice of medical technology', *Sociology of Health & Illness*, 25, Silver Anniversary Issue: 97–114.

Webster, A. (2007) *Health, Technology and Society: A Sociological Critique*. Basingstoke: Palgrave Macmillan.

Alex Faulkner

eHealth refers to the use of information and communications technology (ICT) to provide and create health information and services.

eHealth (or e-health) is a relatively recent concept in medical sociology. The inclusion of it here reflects the now ubiquitous role of computers and digital communications technologies in medical practice, the organization of health care, and everyday life. However, the concept is not clearly defined (Pagliari et al., 2005). In the sociological literature, the label 'eHealth' is mainly used broadly to indicate the intervention of some form of digital mediation. This umbrella usage covers all aspects of digital health technologies, from patients researching symptoms on the internet to the use of remote body sensors. In a similar fashion, the label 'health informatics' is used to indicate information management and, in particular, patient records and medical library systems. However, different labels are used within other disciplines to denote particular areas of health technology. For example, telemedicine has a history that can be traced back to the 1900s and the early use of the telephone to transmit clinical information across geographical boundaries. Today the term is used to denote clinical applications of information and communication technologies (ICT) that may include patient monitoring devices (especially remote monitoring) and medical education applications. Congruent with Giddens' (1991: 124) observation that high levels of specialization (differentiation) are characteristic of medical science (and expert systems in general) in high modernity, the suffix 'tele' is now attached to a range of clinical areas including telepsychiatry, teleradiology, and telepathology.

Reflecting traditional concerns within medical sociology, a persistent theme in eHealth is the impact ICT might have upon patients' engagement with health information. In a sense medical knowledge has 'e-scaped' onto the internet, thus giving the public unprecedented access to information about health (Nettleton and Burrows, 2003). Under these conditions it is tempting to regard the internet as a resource that empowers patients and changes the doctor–patient relationship. The provision of reliable health information is central to the creation of the 'informed patient' and most centrally organized health care systems have developed a presence on the internet where people can access health information. For example, in the UK, NHS Direct provides users with the means to identify information that relates to their symptoms as well as the opportunity to telephone a nurse advisor. However, sociologists have been critical of the assumption that access to digitized medical knowledge necessarily empowers patients and changes the nature of the medical profession.

Lay ideas and advice about health and illness have always been exchanged quickly through word-of-mouth and such conversations are now conducted online. Often organized around a particular condition, for example diabetes or HIV, the conversations and information within such 'virtual self-help groups' enable people to discuss and share information anonymously with a global audience. This is important because it allows individuals who might otherwise be subject to stigma or discrimination to share experiences. Information shared within these groups may also encourage socially censured practices. Perhaps the starkest example can be found in the online suicide groups that are used by strangers to coordinate suicide attempts. Other examples include 'proana' groups that provide information and support to those wanting to lose weight to a degree that may result in a clinically dangerous outcome.

Much research related to eHealth reflects the diversity and proliferation of information, authors and formats (Hardey, 1999). Since the late 1980s doctors, policy makers and others have been concerned with the quality of health information available on the internet. In particular, it is argued that people may change their health behaviour on the basis of wrong or misleading information (European Commission, 2002). Note that what constitutes 'wrong' information is contentious in that, for example, alternative health practices may only be incorrect from a biomedical perspective. Consequently, various standards, shaped by evidence-based medical methodologies, have been developed and used as kite marks for approved websites (for example, the Health On the Net (HON) code of conduct). In effect such mechanisms seek to reinforce the division between lay and medical knowledge. This suggests that the apparent equality of information on the internet is an illusion and that the way search engines work to identify information should be considered. For instance, Google operates through a PageRank algorithm based on the number and quality of links a website receives as an indicator of its value. This algorithm produces a bias towards large and better-connected sites (Seale, 2005). Consequently, information from well-funded websites is privileged over others, and especially those maintained by small groups or an individual. However, research that has focused on patients' actions and how they identify useful health information suggests that they are not 'search engine dupes' but have their own strategies for finding information that are shaped by their embodied knowledge and experiences (Henwood et al., 2003).

The global nature of eHealth may bring people together who share the same health needs but it also undermines national regulations and practices. For example, people can obtain drugs and other items that may not be available without a prescription in one country from another. This globalization of health information and products has also opened up a new market for health services whereby medical tourists can obtain surgical and other procedures in, for example, India and for considerable less cost than in Europe or the USA. Further evidence of the commodification potential of eHealth can be found in the increasing number of user review websites. Highly popular amongst tourists seeking recommendations about hotels, there are similar sites that enable patients to rate and comment on their doctor. Doctors are identified on some sites while the patients remain anonymous and on others only a unit (for example, a hospital ward) is indefinable.

Medical tourism and user review sites may provide choices for some but it is the potential such choices may have to further disadvantage those from poor households that has been the focus of much sociological attention. Arising out of the considerable volume of work on health inequalities, lack of access to the internet has been recognized as an important social and policy problem. What is described as a 'digital divide' reflects the cost, availability (especially in rural areas or less developed parts of the globe), and sometimes the lack of skills that act as a barrier to the internet. With the spread of broadband and an increasing range of services using the system (for example, broadcast media), many countries have policies in place to support the connection of hard-to-reach communities. However, in some parts of the globe poorly wired infrastructure has led to people using mobile phones as their main way of connecting to the internet. What is referred to as 'community informatics' has evolved around various initiatives to provide people with the skills, if not the equipment, to access the internet (Office of the e-Envoy, 2001). This is important as a disproportionate number of people with chronic and other persistent health problems are situated in the poorer sections of the population. If an increasing number of government health and social services are to provide information, choices and other resources through the internet, it is essential that potential users of these services have adequate access to them. The risk here is the creation of a digitally excluded group of people with high health and other needs who will be further marginalized in a network society.

During the first decade of the web (from the early 1990s) the majority of content resembled traditional published material: most web users were consumers of content that was created by a relatively small number of providers or authors. In the early 2000s a significant transition to what is called Web 2.0 took place. Briefly, this highlighted the importance of user-generated content and user-centred services that could be accessed through any device that was connected to the internet. Social media domains – including blogs, microblogging (for example, Twitter), social bookmarking sites, Social Network Sites (for example, Facebook), and photo and video sharing communities (for example, Flickr and YouTube) – now contain an ever-evolving mass of health information. Correspondingly, 'groups' organized around a shared health interest within a social network site may replicate some of the features of virtual self-help groups. However, the members of these groups are never anonymous as participation and information are shared across known networks. The popularity of social media has created a new intensity of communication whereby people may instantly receive and respond to information from friends and organizations. Under these conditions the division between providers and users of eHealth information is blurring. In particular, information is routinely tagged, reproduced, and otherwise fragmented and disembedded from its origins. Critics have argued that a process of 'informationalization' (Lash, 2002: 154) is taking place whereby 'informational knowledge' becomes de-contextualized, ephemeral, and partly meaningless. To put it simply, people are presented with a landscape of ever-changing information, often with unclear origins, content, and value. Such critical perspectives are a useful reminder that eHealth may create new risks as well as opportunities for the public, health professionals, and providers. In that respect, eHealth is an area of increasing relevance for medical sociologists who are interested in health, knowledge, and practice.

See also: *The Sick Role; Lay Knowledge; Medical Technologies*

REFERENCES

European Commission (2002) *eEurope 2002: Quality Criteria for Health Related Websites*. Brussels, 2002-11-29, COM 667 final.

Giddens, A. (1991) *Modernity and Self-Identity*. Cambridge: Polity Press.

Hardey, M. (1999) 'Doctor in the house: the Internet as a source of lay health knowledge and the challenge of expertise', *Sociology of Health & Illness*, 25 (6): 589–607.

Henwood, F., Wyatt, S., Hart, A. and Smith, J. (2003) '"Ignorance is bliss sometimes": constraints on the emergence of the "informed patient" in the changing landscapes of health information', *Sociology of Health & Illness*, 25(6): 589–607.

Lash, S. (2002) *Critique of Information*. London: Sage.

Nettleton, S. and Burrows, R. (2003) 'E-scaped medicine? Information, reflexivity and health', *Critical Social Policy*, 23 (2): 165–85.

Office of the e-Envoy (2001) *UK Online Annual Report*. London: Office of the e-Envoy. Online: www.e-envoy.gov.uk

Pagliari, C., Sloan, D., Gregor, P., Gregor, G., Sullivan, P., Detmer, D., Kahan, J., Oortwijn, W. and MacGillivray, S. (2005) 'What is e-health (4): a scoping exercise to map the field', *Journal of Medical Internet Research*, 7 (1): e9.

Seale, C.F. (2005) 'New directions for critical internet health studies: representing cancer experience on the web', *Sociology of Health & Illness* 27 (4): 515–40.

Michael Hardey

········· Geneticization ·········

> Geneticization refers to the way in which diseases, conditions and behaviours may come to be regarded as being determined, wholly or in part, by genetic factors.

Geneticization describes the extension and significance of genetic explanations within medical and social discourse (Lippman, 1991). The concept is associated with the rise of the 'new genetics': 'the body of knowledge and techniques arising since the invention of recombinant DNA technology in 1973' (Cunningham-Burley and Boulton, 2000: 174). Geneticization refers to the process by which disorders and behaviours deemed 'problematic' are increasingly described as genetically determined. The consequence of this genetic essentialism is that research agendas, public policies and resources become oriented towards biological rather than social tenets. From a critical sociological perspective, such discourses are themselves problematic insofar as alternative contexts, models of health and sources of treatment become discarded, reproducing existing debates about medicalization in a genetic context. Casting this dualistic approach as unproductive, Hedgecoe (1999) argues for a more neutral case-by-case analysis that frames genetic technology as neither inherently critical nor fundamentally essentialist.

In 2003 the Human Genome Project (HGP) produced a 'map' of the human genome (less than 30,000 genes) which was expected to contribute to the identification of a genetic basis for many diseases and give rise to increased treatments and cures. However, these 'promissory futures' of genetic research remain, for the most part, unfulfilled. Although the Cystic Fibrosis gene was identified in 1989, scientists are still unable to predict with any certainty the severity of the disease or the survival age for any individual. Despite extensive research the promise, rather than the reality, of gene therapy continues more than twenty years later. Pharmacogenetics and personalized medicine, where drugs are targeted to individuals and groups on the basis of genetic markers, remains in its infancy (Hedgecoe, 2004). Knowledge of genetic factors is of uncertain value in the management of many common conditions such as cancer, chronic heart disease, diabetes and the major mood disorders (for example, schizophrenia and bipolar affective disorder). There is an increasing awareness that these are complex multifactorial diseases which depend on the behaviour of several genes in combination with the environment, factors which are not easily identified or manipulated. However, the suggestion of an underlying genetic cause is met with extensive media coverage: alcoholism, homosexuality and obesity have all been described as 'genetic' without subsequent confirmation or a clear clinical application. Clinical treatment is limited for most 'disorders' thought to have a genetic component, and this raises the issues of (i) what impact genetic knowledge has for populations and (ii) the implications for medical policy and practice.

Geneticization reflects how genetic interventions become normalized and this is particularly so within the field of reproductive technology. National prenatal screening programmes are routine, and techniques such as in vitro fertilization (IVF) and pre-implantation genetic diagnosis (PGD) enable embryos to be identified on the basis of disease status, carrier status, and disease susceptibility status. These technologies can also be employed to support cultural norms, such as gender preference. For example, the use of sex selection techniques in China and India has led to the 'gendercide' of female embryos and contributed to a gender imbalance in these populations. Within developed countries, lower fertility rates and the increasing age of motherhood have resulted in a high demand for technical solutions such as IVF and surrogacy. Pressure to conform to societal expectations may mean that individual choice and consent regarding the use of new genetic technologies is constrained and raises questions about the commercialization of these techniques and equality of access. Particular concerns are voiced about the potential for 'designer babies'. The creation of 'saviour siblings', where an embryo is specifically selected as a genetically identical match for a seriously ill child, has been extensively contested. Likewise, the positive selection of deafness, as has been supported by some sections within the deaf community, raises questions about the rights of the unborn child, as well as confronting societal understandings of illness and disability (Scully, 2008). There is no global consensus on the use of genetic technologies. The increase in internet-based 'direct to consumer' personal genome testing and the growth of medical tourism highlight the demand for such technologies and the difficulties of regulation. Techniques such as sex selection, stem cell therapy and disease susceptibility testing are routinely available for those with resources, although these procedures might be expensive, unproven, and illegal within certain jurisdictions.

Techniques allowing for the large-scale collection of DNA samples provide opportunities to increase knowledge of specific diseases and develop diagnostic and predictive tests and treatments. Numerous public and private 'biobanks' have been created, within and beyond national borders, raising questions about ownership and the use of genetic data. The patenting of some genes, for example BRCA1 and BRCA2 (associated with inheritable forms of breast cancer) has also taken place, although the right to do this for commercial purposes has been contested. The ethical and legal implications of genetic databases have been extensively debated in the context of criminal proceedings. Unsolved cases and miscarriages of justice have been successfully concluded with the advent of DNA technology and its facility for storage. However, within the UK the legality of retaining DNA samples from those arrested but not charged was successfully challenged in the European court in 2010.

Historical and cultural understandings of individual health and collective responsibility have been re-framed through genetic technology. Diagnostic tools such as prenatal diagnosis, newborn screening techniques, carrier testing and personal genomic testing kits have extended the patient population by blurring the boundaries between health and illness. These 'patients without symptoms' include carriers of a genetic 'disorder', those 'at risk' of developing a late onset condition, and individuals identified as 'susceptible' to a particular disease in later life (Finkler et al., 2003). The diagnosis of a potentially serious and life threatening condition has implications for self-identity and stigma, disclosure practices, and access to employment and insurance. The 'genetically responsible patient' is expected to make informed decisions in the light of new knowledge. Genetic disease stands in marked contrast to other types of illness because of the association with 'family'. Within these 'webs of genetic connectedness' (Novas and Rose, 2000), sociological enquiry has focused on the negotiation of guilt and blame, understandings of genetic risk, and familial communication strategies. Whether an individual's genetic profile should be disclosed to other family members has been fiercely contested, raising the question of ownership, confidentiality, the right to know, and the right not to know (Featherstone et al., 2006). Genetic citizenship encapsulates a movement from patient to active citizen, where patients express their biosociality by influencing the direction of scientific work and becoming active contributors in the production of biomedical knowledge (Taussig et al., 2003). Expanding on Foucauldian thinking, Heath et al. (2004: 11) describe the expansion of health regimes involving surveillance of the body and mind as a 'genetic panopticon', where 'health activists, scientists, politicians, physicians, tissue banks, bioinformatic databases, websites, confessional talk shows, and bio-engineered medical devices are brought together to forge innovative "technologies of the self"'.

By focusing on the significance of genetic knowledge, there is a danger that the complex reality of diagnostic negotiations, diverse patient experiences, and the possibility of resisting genetic explanations might be forgotten. For example, the impact of genetic technology on medical work has been characterized by a shift away from the 'clinical gaze' towards the 'molecular gaze', suggesting a relocation of the diagnostic process from clinic to genetic laboratory. However, detailed studies of clinical work identify the continued significance of the clinic (Latimer et al., 2006). Likewise, there may appear to be public support for genetic screening programmes but in practice their uptake is low. This was the case when a test to identify the Huntingdon's Disease gene became available in 1993, yet the uptake of predictive testing still remains lower than 20 per cent of the 'at risk' population. Patients may find the genetic nature of disease becomes a significant challenge at certain times, for example when planning to have children, or communicating risk information to other family members (Petersen, 2006). However, genetic knowledge does not always dominate identity, experience, and activity (Bharadwaj et al., 2007).

The 'new genetics' raises fears of a recurrence of eugenic policies. Such policies began in the late nineteenth century and remained popular across Europe and the USA until the 1940s. The disability movement, among others, has highlighted how the prevention of difference through genetic manipulation has the potential to devalue the lives of people living with a disability. There remains concern that the acceptance of genetic interventions could stigmatize sections of society and lead to a genetic 'underclass'. Secular and religious social movements have emerged all over the world, raising 'moral arguments' about what life is, the right to life, and the right to manipulate human and animal cell material. Many of the issues arising from geneticization and the 'new genetics' are not completely new. Further sociological research is needed to recognize the diverse meanings, implications, and use of genetic knowledge, and the impact of regulatory frameworks.

See also: *Stigma; Disability; Reproduction; Medical Technologies*

REFERENCES

Bharadwaj, A., Atkinson, P., Clarke, A. and Worwood, M. (2007) 'Medical classification and the experience of genetic haemochromatosis', in P. Atkinson, P. Glasner and H. Greenslade (eds), *New Genetics, New Identities*. London: Routledge.

Cunningham-Burley, S. and Boulton, M. (2000) 'The social context of the new genetics', in G.L. Albrecht, R. Fitzpatrick and S.C. Scrimshaw (eds), *The Handbook of Social Studies in Health and Medicine*. London: Sage.

Featherstone, K., Atkinson, P., Bharadwaj, A. and Clarke, A.J. (2006) *Risky Relations: Family and Kinship in the Era of New Genetics*. Oxford: Berg.

geneticization

139

Finkler, K., Skrzynia, C. and Evans, J.P. (2003) 'The new genetics and its consequences for family, kinship, medicine and medical genetics', *Social Science & Medicine*, 57 (3): 403–12.

Heath, D., Rapp, R. and Taussig, K.S. (2004) 'Genetic citizenship', in D. Nugent and J. Vincent (eds), *A Companion to the Anthropology of Politics*. Oxford: Wiley-Blackwell.

Hedgecoe, A. (1999) 'Reconstructing geneticization: a research manifesto', *Health Law Journal*, 7: 5–18.

Hedgecoe, A. (2004) *The Politics of Personalised Medicine: Pharmacogenetics in the Clinic*. Cambridge: Cambridge University Press.

Latimer, J., Featherstone, K., Atkinson, P., Clarke, A.J. and Shaw, A. (2006) 'Rebirthing the clinic: the interaction of clinical judgement and molecular technology in the production of genetic science', *Science, Technology and Human Values*, 31: 599–630.

Lippman, A. (1991) 'Prenatal genetic testing and screening: constructing needs and reinforcing inequities', *American Journal of Law and Medicine*, 17: 15–50.

Novas, C. and Rose, N. (2000) 'Genetic risk and the birth of the somatic individual', *Economy and Society*, 29 (4): 485–513.

Petersen, A. (2006) 'The best experts: the narratives of those who have a genetic condition', *Social Science & Medicine*, 63 (1): 32–42.

Scully, L.J. (2008) 'Disability and genetics in the era of genomic medicine', *Nature Reviews Genetics*, 9 (10): 797–802.

Taussig, K.S., Rapp, R. and Heath, D. (2003) 'Flexible eugenics: technologies of the self in the age of genetics', in A.H. Goodman (ed.), *Genetic Nature/Culture: Anthropology and Science Beyond the Two-Culture Divide*. Berkeley: University of California Press.

Rebecca Dimond and Jacqueline Hughes

Bioethics

> *Bioethics is the philosophical study of the ethical controversies brought about by advances in biology and medicine. The modern field of bioethics emerged when medical/scientific/technical advances in morally contested areas, including organ transplantation and end-of-life care, began posing new and novel questions.*

Sociology has had a long and distinguished engagement with normative issues, that is, with what *ought* to be done. Indeed, the notion of not just understanding the world but also changing it is central to the disciplinary ethos of sociology. From this perspective, 'doing sociology' is an ethical project. However, the relationship between sociology and ethics has come to mean something much narrower. Bioethics is now a growing topic of sociological investigation, and this research can be conveniently divided into two main areas: sociology *in* bioethics, and sociology *of* bioethics (Orfali and De Vries, 2010).

Sociology *in* bioethics explores the links between bioethics, medicine, science and society and aims to ground more abstract philosophical ethical debates in empirical case studies which explore and describe the embodied ethics of 'real actors' in particular social worlds. Sociological approaches to bioethics thus examine the social processes that frame the making of ethical problems, analysing the ways in which ethical problems are identified, managed, and resolved in clinical and scientific settings. Classic ethnographic studies illustrating this approach to ethical issues and reasoning in the clinic include Anspach (1993), on difficult choices in neonatal intensive care, and Chambliss (1996), on ethical decision making in adult intensive care units.

In contrast, sociology *of* bioethics charts the social forces that have helped shape particular (dominant) varieties of philosophical bioethics (for example, principlism, utilitarianism, etc.), examining the ways in which certain kinds of ethical questions are privileged, promoted and funded within bioethics whilst other questions and approaches tend to be marginalized. From this perspective, the professional field of bioethics can be seen as constraining the types of questions that can legitimately be asked and researched (Fox and Swazey, 2008). It has been argued that there has been a 'seeping out of the social', particularly in mainstream US bioethics. This has limited ethical debates to questions around means rather than questions about ends, thus ignoring discussion of what some see as the central question of ethics, namely, 'what counts as a good life'.

Turning first to some examples of sociology *in* bioethics, Wainwright et al. (2006) developed the concept of 'ethical boundary-work' to analyse how scientists involved in human embryonic stem cell science practise ethics in the lab. They examined how scientists present themselves as ethical, as well as expert actors, by drawing the boundaries of 'ethical scientific activity' around three key issues: what scientists themselves view as ethical sources of human embryos and stem cells; their definitions of human embryos and stem cells; and how they perceive regulatory frameworks in stem cell research. Practical ethics here takes the form of a number of choices over how to conduct oneself in a complicated political, moral, and scientific context. Ethical boundary work means maintaining the distinction between 'real science' and 'associated ethics', whilst at the same time incorporating ethical acceptability into the heart of the scientific work. Other recent work on social understandings of the complexities of 'ethics in practice' include: studies of clinical trials; the ethics of sex selection; the financial context of ethical decision making; ethics in the health policy process; and ethical standards for medical research in developing countries (see De Vries et al., 2007).

Turning next to some key examples of sociology *of* bioethics, Evans (2002), in his seminal monograph, examined the ways in which debates about human genetic engineering in the USA in the second half of the twentieth century have been deprived of an important social dimension. Evans argues that a narrow focus on the analytical philosophy of the means for achieving assumed ends, rather than a public discussion about the ends themselves, has occurred. Such discussions about means, which are dominated by philosopher/lawyer bioethicists, structure a debate that is reduced to a set of technical decisions over a restricted list of ethical choices: in other words, individual autonomy is being privileged over broader societal ends in a process that is, for sociologists like Evans, more about the rise to power of a new profession of bioethicists than it is about promoting public debate on 'the good life'. In a recent paper, Hedgecoe (2010) has argued that bioethicists tend to unquestioningly accept scientists' expectations about the ethical issues raised by pharmacogenetics, whilst ignoring the few contributions from bioethicists who do question these views. In short, Hedgecoe highlights the ways in which the practice of philosophical bioethics tends to support rather than question the scientific status quo. Debates in the sociology *of* bioethics are, therefore, concerned with *bioethicization* (in similar ways to sociological studies of *medicalization*). What is key to these debates are social processes of jurisdiction (defining what counts as ethical) and also of legitimacy (defining who is the right person to discuss 'ethics'). These processes, in turn, are linked with those of institutionalization and professionalization that are two of the crucial engines driving the making of bioethics as a field (Fox and Swazey, 2008).

We now turn to some of the problems identified by sociologists in the emerging literature on sociology and bioethics. Sociologists have proven adept at unpacking the social complexities and meanings associated with what can, in the hands of some philosophical bioethicists, seem like a set of unproblematic ideas such as informed consent and the right to choose. In contrast, sociologists have shown how philosophical debates on informed consent can be inadequate when they run up against the complexities of the real social worlds of the clinic (Corrigan, 2003). In a similar vein, a whole cluster of studies around antenatal screening and testing has analysed the socially conditioned nature of the problems that practitioners and patients encounter in relation to choice, non-directive counselling, and drawing boundaries around which children should be born (see, for example, Williams, 2006).

These studies are all examples of what philosophers sometimes disparagingly describe as 'empirical ethics', although we think they are better described as 'sociology *in* bioethics'. For some philosopher bioethicists, such social research lacks a normative dimension: it describes the complexities of ethical issues rather than offering guidance on what *ought* to be done. One typical riposte from sociologists to this potential objection is to argue that philosophical analysis is of little value in helping 'real people in real settings' make ethical judgements, as the complexities of the social world undermine the premises and assumptions of many philosophical arguments (Cribb et al., 2008). The danger here is that such extreme versions of sociologists and bioethicists will only talk *at* each other rather than *with* one another. There are, however, signs that bioethicists and sociologists are engaging in efforts to leave the cul-de-sacs of the 'merely empirical' and the 'purely philosophical' (Cribb et al., 2008). For instance, sociologists and philosophers including De Vries et al. (2007) and Draper and Ives (2007) have argued that we should explore how philosophy and the social sciences could be brought together in happy, rather than dysfunctional, 'marriages'.

We would contend that descriptive, empirical sociology *in* bioethics is valuable in its own right. However, it has been suggested that sociology *in* bioethics research could usefully incorporate a more philosophical normative approach. For instance, sociologists could begin to develop ethical *frameworks* with colleagues from philosophical ethics, by drawing on a mix of empirical data and philosophical arguments (Parker, 2007). These ethical frameworks would provide a template for practitioners of, for example, experimental biomedicine, against which they could evaluate morally contentious clinical and scientific issues. It is also possible in principle to go a step further and begin to *test* such ethical frameworks against established 'hard cases' that are typically employed to evaluate purely philosophical ethical reasoning (Draper and Ives, 2007). One way to think about these developments is as a continuum of normative empirical ethics where *exploration*, *frameworks* and *testing* become key features of a sociologically informed interdisciplinary bioethics. That said, we would also urge sociologists to continue to work on the twin sociological traditions outlined earlier: of critical sociologies *of* the field of bioethics, and rich sociological case studies of 'ethics-in-action' *in* the social worlds of the laboratory, the clinic, and beyond.

See also: *Medicalization; Geneticization*

REFERENCES

Anspach, R. (1993) *Deciding Who Lives: Fateful Choices in the Intensive Care Nursery*. Berkeley: University of California Press.

Chambliss, D. (1996) *Beyond Caring: Hospitals, Nurses and the Social Organization of Ethics*. Chicago: University of Chicago Press.

Corrigan, O.P. (2003) 'Empty ethics: the problem with informed consent', *Sociology of Health & Illness*, 25: 768–92.

Cribb, A., Wainwright, S.P., Williams, C., Michael, M. and Farsides, B. (2008) 'Towards the applied: the construction of ethical positions in stem cell translational research', *Medicine, Health Care & Philosophy*, 11: 351–61.

De Vries, R., Turner, L., Orfali, K. and Bosk, C. (2007) *The View from Here: Bioethics and the Social Sciences*. Sociology of Health & Illness Monograph. Oxford: Blackwell.

Draper, H. and Ives, J. (2007) 'An empirical approach to bioethics: social science "of", "for" and "in" bioethics research', *Cognition, Brain, Behaviour*, XI: 319–30.

Evans, J.H. (2002) *Playing God? Human Genetic Engineering and the Rationalization of Public Bioethical Debate*. Chicago: University of Chicago Press.

Fox, R.C. and Swazey, J.P. (2008) *Observing Bioethics*. New York: Oxford University Press.

Hedgecoe, A. (2010) 'Bioethics and the reinforcement of socio-technical expectations', *Social Studies of Science*, 40: 163–86.

Orfali, C. and De Vries, R. (2010) 'A sociological gaze on bioethics', in W.C. Cockerham (ed.), *The New Blackwell Companion to Medical Sociology*. Oxford: Wiley-Blackwell.

Parker, M. (2007) 'Ethnography/ethics', *Social Science & Medicine*, 65: 2248–59.

Wainwright, S.P., Williams, C. Michael, M. Farsides, C. and Cribb, A. (2006) 'Ethical boundary work in the embryonic stem cell laboratory', *Sociology of Health & Illness*, 28: 732–48.

Williams, C. (2006) 'Dilemmas in fetal medicine: premature application of technology or responding to women's choice?', *Sociology of Health & Illness*, 28: 1–20.

bioethics

Clare Williams and Steven P. Wainwright

Within the context of health promotion, medical sociologists use the term 'surveillance' to refer to activities such as surveys, screening and public health campaigns, which are designed to monitor, regulate and induce good health practices in both individuals and the population in general.

Health promotion refers to those planned activities that are designed to prevent illness and improve the health of the population. Such activities comprise: assessing health needs; developing and evaluating interventions which aim to facilitate the improvement of people's health status; and supporting health professionals and the public by providing information on putatively the most effective means to achieve good health. The goal of health promotion is to bring about change at both an individual level (by encouraging people to lead 'healthy' lives) and a societal level (by bringing about institutional changes which will make for a healthier social and, physical environment). It is closely aligned to a branch of medicine called 'public health', which deploys the disciplines of social science, biology, epidemiology, immunology and environmental science to deal with complex health matters such as: controlling infections; improving access to services; handling environmental hazards; and reducing the prevalence of threats to good health. Such threats might include substance misuse, unhealthy eating, accidents and injury, and so on.

This concept of surveillance finds its origins in the work of Foucault (1979), and, in particular, his novel notion of 'disciplinary power' that he most vividly articulated in his book *Discipline and Punish*. Disciplinary power refers to the way in which bodies are regulated, trained, understood and empowered, and is most evident in social institutions such as schools, prisons and hospitals, though it also permeates throughout society. It is within social institutions that knowledge of bodies is produced. For example, the observation of bodies in prisons yielded criminology, the observation of bodies in hospitals contributed to medical science, and the observation of people in social settings forms the basis of sociology. Foucault refers to this process as power/knowledge. Disciplinary power – a form of surveillance – works at two levels. First, individual bodies are trained and observed (Foucault refers to this as the anatomo-politics of the human body). Second, and concurrently, populations are monitored by regulatory controls – the 'bio-politics' of the population. A pivotal idea here is that examining individuals and populations in tandem gives rise to social, medical and statistical norms, and those who deviate from these norms are deemed to be in need of treatment, rehabilitation, or correction.

Health promotion, and indeed public health, therefore form the political and practical manifestations of what has come to be conceptualized as 'surveillance medicine', which emerged as a dominant form of health and medical care in the latter half of the twentieth century (Armstrong, 1995). Armstrong states that a 'cardinal feature of surveillance medicine . . . is its targeting of everyone', and that health care is concerned not just with those who are ill but also with those who are well. It is not only orientated towards treating the symptoms of disease, it also seeks to identify and monitor those risk factors which serve as markers of diseases that may be more or less likely in the future. The French philosopher Castel (1991) makes a similar observation but uses the term 'epidemiological clinic' instead of 'surveillance medicine', suggesting that since the latter half of the twentieth century we have moved away from a health care system that was premised upon 'dangerousness' towards one based upon 'risk'. In the past, the dominant mode of working among health professionals was to err on the side of caution in order to prevent the development of symptoms following the onset of disease. Patients who were ill could be 'dangerous' to those who might come into contact with them and of course to themselves. Today, however, health care focuses on the social and behavioural characteristics of the person (rather than the patient), and this in turn involves a mode of surveillance which – with the aid of technological advances – makes the calculation and possibilities of 'systematic pre-detection' increasingly sophisticated. These surveillance activities create a whole new range of risk factors. The mechanisms of health promotion surveillance therefore identify those individuals and groups who are 'at risk'. The concepts of surveillance and risk, within the context of health promotion, are mutually constitutive, with the former resulting in what Skolbekken (1995) has described as a 'risk epidemic'.

Skolbekken (1995: 296) argues that health promotion provides 'the ideological frame needed to explain the present emphasis on factors regarded as risks to our health. Through the ideological frame of health promotion we get a glimpse of some of the functions served by the risk epidemic'. He cites these functions as follows. First, to predict disease and death – in other words, to gain control over disease which in turn confirms our faith in medical science. Second, it is sometimes assumed that the findings of this type of research may help to save money as people are less likely to require acute, and therefore expensive, services. Third, it contributes to medicalization. Risk factors that are hypothesized to be linked to disease come to be treated as 'diseases to be cured' (p. 299).

A number of sociologists have pointed to the fact that society today is characterized by a 'politics of anxiety', indeed, that it is a risk society (Beck, 1992). A point on which all these authors appear to agree is that the risks associated with modern-day living are person-made – they are a product of social organization and human actions. Armstrong (1995) contrasts the health risks of today with the health risks present in the nineteenth century. While in that earlier century such risks were associated with the 'natural' environment and dangers lurked within water, soil, air, food and climate, today the environmental factors that impinge on health, such as acid rain and global radiation, are the (unintended) consequence of human actions. Of course, not all contemporary health risks are 'purely' human products. AIDS, for example, is the consequence of a virus. Nevertheless, the condition has come to be conceptualized within a social matrix: it exists within a wider context of social activities and is typically envisaged in terms of complex social interactions between gay men, intravenous drug users and those requiring and administering blood transfusions. In this respect, it has increasingly become articulated in the same terms as humanly created risks which need to be monitored and regulated – or subjected to surveillance.

The techniques deployed in the scrutinization of these 'risk factors' within the context of public health and health promotion are primarily: screening for a range of diseases and symptoms; the collection of information on patients by health professionals; epidemiological studies; social surveys; and qualitative studies. Once a 'factor' such as eating 'fatty foods' is found to be statistically associated with another indicator of ill health (or risk factor), such as cholesterol levels, it is deemed to be a 'risk factor'. The social aspects of eating fatty foods may then be explored by sociologists and anthropologists who aim to answer questions such as: Why do people eat fat? What does eating fatty foods mean to them? What is the social and symbolic significance of eating fatty foods? This information is considered to be crucial to the development of effective health promotion. The findings of the epidemiologists and the social scientists are drawn upon by health promoters to encourage people to eat less fatty foods. The government will keep an eye on the population's fat consumption and set nutritional targets. Thus, surveillance techniques and the management (or, even, social construction) of risks go hand in hand. Mechanisms of surveillance orientated towards individual risk factors may contribute to the formation of a new individual 'risk identity' (Armstrong, 1995).

The advent of the new millennium has seen a further development in relation to the calculation of health risks and surveillance. In the late twentieth century, health risk factors tended to be associated with lifestyles and broader social determinants. By the early twenty-first century, the advent of technologies used to identify the genetic bases and/or genetic influences on people's health has meant that the management of health risks has permeated biological as well as social bodies. Referred to as the 'new genetics', these developments add a further twist to the risk identity and give rise to what Rose and Novas (2005) term 'biological citizenship'. Myriad opportunities for genetic testing mean that individuals are encouraged to be aware of, and informed about, their own genome. This gives rise to a series of moral and ethical dilemmas that are too numerous to discuss here. However, what is pertinent in relation to surveillance and health promotion is the way in which biological citizens are able to undertake genetic tests to identity and become informed about any genetic predisposition to disease that they might have. But this is far from straightforward; for example, it is not at all clear what people should do with this information, nor how they could alter their actions in order to compensate for any genetic predisposition.

A particularly troubling example pertains to the way some individuals or groups who are at greater risk of being 'carriers' of genetic conditions are encouraged to opt for testing, when this is invariably *within* the wider context of medical discourses on prevention which seek to reduce the prevalence of these same conditions (Atkin, 2003). The rhetoric is one of informed choice, yet in practice there is the spectre of discrimination and for some even eugenics. For the most part, in relation to genetic testing for the vast majority of diseases diagnostically clear cut genetic information is very rare indeed, and so all that can be determined through the 'genetic anotomo-politics' of the body are calculations of the relative risks of people's predisposition towards the occurrence of diseases and/or conditions. Everyone has a propensity towards at least some diseases and no one has a normal genome. As Rose (2009: 74) puts it, 'there is no normal genome; variation *is* the norm'. Surveillance therefore takes a new twist: technologies of pre-detection and prevention are no longer only limited to rehabilitating those who deviate from the norm. The irregular is the new norm and individuals are encouraged to become informed about and take responsibility for their personal genome and exercise what Rose calls 'genetic prudence'.

The sociological notion of surveillance, informed by Foucault's work, is not without its critics. Arguably, the idea of disciplinary power is itself inappropriate as it under-estimates the impact of other forms of power which may be wielded by those groups who have greater resources and, thereby, the capacity to control and dominate others. Second, and relatedly, it is suggested that to say the mechanisms of surveillance simply generate knowledge of people's health and illness excludes the possibility that certain interest groups might generate particular forms of knowledge about health, disease and illness, which may serve to enhance their commercial or professional status. Finally, it is claimed that the notion of surveillance is overly descriptive and fails to account for the origins and motivations of change, as well as underplaying the influence of human agency. The concept of surveillance, however, provides a valuable analytic tool with which to make sense of contemporary developments within health care more generally and health promotion in particular (Lupton, 1995). Surveillance procedures can contribute to existing forms of repression; for example, they have negative consequences for the health experiences of women (Nettleton, 1996). The concept of surveillance is also useful in contributing to an appreciation of the ways in which collective, societal levels of intervention (for example, screening or education campaigns) can have an impact upon individuals in terms of the development of their 'risk identities' and the nature of their interactions with health professionals (see, for example, a study of two types of health surveillance in Sweden by Lauritzen and Sachs, 2001). Finally, the concept can enable health practitioners and health researchers to gain an analytic appreciation of some of the societal implications of the routine day-to-day practices of health promotion.

See also: *Medicalization; Risk; Geneticization*

REFERENCES

Armstrong, D. (1995) 'The rise of surveillance medicine', *Sociology of Health & Illness*, 17 (3): 343–404.

Atkin, K. (2003) 'Ethnicity and the politics of the new genetics: principles and engagement', *Ethnicity and Health*, 8 (2): 91–109.

Beck, U. (1992) *Risk Society: Towards a New Modernity*. London: Sage.

Castel, R. (1991) 'From dangerousness to risk', in G. Burchell, C. Gordon and P. Miller (eds), *The Foucault Effect: Studies in Governmentality*. Brighton: Harvester Wheatsheaf.

Foucault, M. (1979) *Discipline and Punish: The Birth of the Prison*. Harmondsworth: Penguin Books.

Lauritzen, S.O. and Sachs, L. (2001) 'Normality, risk and the future: implicit communication of threat in health surveillance', *Sociology of Health & Illness*, 23 (4): 497–516.

Lupton, D. (1995) *The Imperative of Health: Public Health and the Regulated Body*. London: Sage.

Nettleton, S. (1996) 'Women and the new paradigm of health and medicine', *Critical Social Policy*, 16 (3): 33–53.

Rose, N. (2009) 'Normality and pathology in a biomedical age', *Sociological Review*, 57 (s2): 66–83.

Rose, N. and Novas, C. (2005) 'Biological citizenship', in A. Ong and S.J. Collier (eds), *Global Assemblages: Technology, Politics and Ethics as Anthropological Problems*. Oxford: Blackwell.

Skolbekken, J. (1995) 'The risk epidemic in medical journals', *Social Science & Medicine*, 40 (3): 291–305.

Sarah Nettleton

Part 4

Health Work and the Division of Labour

Medical Autonomy, Dominance and Decline

Medical autonomy is the publicly accepted control that the medical profession exercises over the terms and conditions of its work. Medical dominance is a relative concept, indicating the authority that the medical profession can exercise over other occupations within the health care division of labour, patients or society. Since the 1980s, many medical sociologists have suggested that these characteristic expressions of professional power have been reduced by external challenges.

The concepts of autonomy and dominance inform discussions of professional power, especially in relation to the medical profession. Indeed, they have often been used as if they were interchangeable. Clearly, they are very closely related – logically and empirically. In a complex division of labour, only an occupation able to exercise dominance over others can have very high levels of publicly accepted or legitimated autonomy and vice versa. But keeping an analytic distinction between the two is useful when analysing professional power – a recurrent theme within medical sociology over the past fifty years. Although the theme has recurred, the emphasis has changed. From the 1960s to the 1980s, medical sociologists' primary interest was in the origins and persistence of medical autonomy and its social consequences. By the 1990s, the questions medical sociologists asked were more concerned with the possible decline of medical autonomy and dominance and, to some extent, with the possible negative consequences of this.

The American sociologist Eliot Freidson has made a major contribution to this debate. In a landmark book on the American medical profession published in 1970, he argued that only certain professions, like medicine, have been '*deliberately* granted autonomy, including the exclusive right to determine who can legitimately do its work and how the work should be done' (1970: 72, original emphasis). For Freidson, possession of a high level of state-sanctioned autonomy, and, by implication, institutionalized expectations of societal trust in the occupation's claims, were the defining characteristics of a true profession. This autonomy had been achieved, he argued, through an essentially political process of professionalization. This entailed convincing, over time, the public – or at least socially powerful groups – that the profession's services were of value and then obtaining the legal sanction for its autonomy. The latter was expressed in the establishment of statutorily-defined, self-regulating professional licensing and disciplinary systems, such as the UK's General Medical Council, first established in 1858 as an entirely medical institution.

Various typologies of autonomy have been put forward in the sociological literature but three main categories are usually identified: (1) clinical or technical autonomy – the right of the medical profession to set standards and evaluate clinical performance; (2) political autonomy – the right to make policy decisions as the legitimate experts on health and medicine; and (3) economic autonomy – the right to determine levels of personal remuneration or the level of resources available for their work (Elston, 1991: 61). Historical and comparative analysis suggests that these different aspects of autonomy can, to some extent, vary independent of each other. For example, hospital doctors in the USA enjoyed a much higher level of economic autonomy compared to their UK counterparts during the later part of the twentieth century. While doctors in the USA could charge a fee for services, doctors working in the UK's National Health Service (NHS) hospitals were salaried. However, the experience of doctors working for the UK state did not reflect a marked diminution in other aspects of their autonomy. For example, they had more clinical autonomy to decide how resources were spent and allocated than their counterparts in the USA because they were not constrained by patients' varying ability to pay directly. It is also important to recognize that not all segments of the medical profession within the same society are likely to enjoy equal levels of autonomy. There may be differences between specialisms and positions in occupational structures and these can be related to social group membership. When discussing whether medical autonomy is increasing or diminishing, these complexities need to be recognized.

Medical dominance is also a concept that has been applied in a variety of contexts and to refer to different aspects of medical power. Three aspects have been particularly significant within medical sociology: (1) medical dominance within society generally, i.e. the profession's cultural authority to determine, for example, what is to be counted as sickness; (2) medical dominance over patients; and (3) medical dominance over other occupations in the increasingly complex division of health care labour and in the policy-making process. The first of these aspects can be subsumed, for our present purposes, under the concept of medicalization and the second under 'the doctor–patient relationship'. It is the third aspect, medicine's state-sanctioned dominance over other health occupations, that is closely associated with claims about medical autonomy – particularly in Freidson's work. For Freidson (1970), a crucial part of the professionalization process for medicine (that is, its achievement of autonomy) was the gradual subordination of other occupations, such as nursing, to medical control. As a result, although nursing in the mid-twentieth century had considerable control over some aspects of its work, it was suggested that it still lacked full professional status because its work was subject to 'doctors' orders' – a state of affairs that was likely to continue as medicine would seek to defend its autonomy from nursing's encroachment.

Since the late 1980s a substantial literature has been published questioning the future of medical autonomy and, more generally, professional power and authority (Harrison and Ahmad, 2000; Kelleher et al., 2006). As outlined below, contributors to this literature have employed a variety of concepts, drawn from different theoretical perspectives. Before these are discussed, some preliminary points need to be made to set the context in which these concepts have been put forward.

The first, self-evident point is that to speak of the decline of medical or professional autonomy implies that there is or was this autonomy to lose. Some have argued that the extent of medical power and its imperialistic tendencies over society or other occupations may have been overstated in the 1970s. However, few would dispute that, compared with most other occupations, the social and cultural authority exercised by the medical profession has been considerable and remains so. Even those who would argue that major change is taking place see this as a process that is under way, not a completed transformation. Moreover, in most cases, those who would claim a decline in medical autonomy are linking this to transformations that affect society generally and hence most, or even all, occupations. In this way, medical autonomy could decline while the relative dominance and advantage of medicine over other occupations would remain unchanged. Furthermore, there is relatively little agreement among contributors to these debates about what would count as firm evidence for or against such a decline, or how much of this would mark a significant change.

So, this is currently a very lively but somewhat speculative area of debate. Sociologists agree that medicine in the early part of the twenty-first century has been challenged on a number of fronts. The debate is over which, if any, of these are significant and how they can be explained theoretically. The challenges discussed in the literature can be categorized as arising from three main sources. The first is the growing and changing form of involvement of third parties in the funding or organizing of health care. Thus, in the UK, the major reforms to the NHS that have been introduced since the 1980s – including the introduction of a more market-driven ethos and structure – have been seen by many as constituting an attack on producer dominance and professional exemption from external scrutiny. In the USA, the expansion of for-profit health care corporations, the move to managed care and associated new financial management of medical practice, have been widely hailed as representing an encroachment on the professional prerogative, by those organized interests who increasingly buy medical services on behalf of patients.

A second type of challenge comes directly from the users of health care, the public. On the one hand, there is the apparent rise of consumerism with individual users rejecting, or being encouraged to reject, a passive trust in medical expertise and medical reputations: a rejection expressed in increased complaints and malpractice allegations and in a more active involvement in clinical decision making, or in an increased resort to alternative medicines. There is also a more collective consumerist challenge in the form of critical self-help groups and social movements, such as the women's health movement or gay rights activism in relation to HIV/AIDS.

The third form of challenge identified is that from other health care occupations. For example, there have been many recent developments in nursing practice, such as the move to develop nurses' clinical skills and expand their role into areas previously regarded as medical responsibilities. Similar developments have occurred in some of the other occupations characterized as 'professions allied to medicine', such as physiotherapy or pharmacy. These have been seen by some commentators as moves in a professionalizing strategy on the part of these occupations. That there are new areas of inter-professional boundary blurring in delivering care involving medicine and nursing, and other fields, is clear. However, it is probably most helpful to follow Witz and Annandale (2006) and see many of these changes as being themselves related to the first kind of challenge – that from third parties, such as the state in the UK.

Different concepts, drawing on different broad theoretical approaches, have been used to elaborate and explain these different types of challenge. Here, there is space to outline only the concepts particularly associated with third party and user/public consumer challenges, and two critical alternative positions.

According to some early American contributors to the debate (notably McKinlay and Arches, 1985), the effect of third party commercial purchasers of medical services on doctors' ability to determine their terms and conditions of work was tantamount to the incipient proletarianization of the medical profession. Drawing explicitly on Marxist theories of the logic of capitalist development, it was argued that the reduction in professional prerogatives such as the right to set remuneration was evidence that medicine was being incorporated into the class of those who produced surplus value for capital. Initial formulations of this position were controversial, not least because American doctors did not greatly resemble typical 'wage-slaves' and because the underlying Marxist theory is itself highly contested. Subsequent formulations from a similar perspective have tended to use the concept of corporatization as less contentious and more indicative of the putative cause of the changes than proletarianization (McKinlay and Marceau, 2002). Neither of these concepts can be unproblematically applied in societies where health care is mainly state-funded or provided but, arguably, some of the same rationalizing principles that underpin corporate managed care are in evidence here. Thus, in the UK, the concepts through which the changing fortune of medical autonomy in relation to the state has been considered include managerialism and privatization.

For those sociologists who see the challenge to medical autonomy as mainly arising from the public, either as individual users of services or collective groups, what is identified is a process of cultural change for which the term 'deprofessionalization' has been coined. On the one hand, exponents of this position argue that there is a more informed, critical public, less inclined to be deferent to experts and to express unconditional trust, a process fostered by the extensive media coverage given to specific incidents of gross medical malpractice. On the other hand, through increasing computerization and bureaucratic regulation (for example, in the form of performance indicators), expert knowledge is itself regarded as becoming more accessible to outsiders, enabling their trust in doctors to be better informed. It is claimed, therefore, that there is a reduction in the knowledge gap between profession and public and in the areas of indeterminacy that support the exercise of professional discretion.

Both the corporatization and deprofessionalization theses have attracted considerable criticism. For example, they have been seen as insufficiently historically grounded and as generalizing too much from specific, short-term American developments. Freidson (1994) has argued that both sets of claims tend to underplay the significance of the organized character of the medical profession. He has suggested that, rather than the external control of medicine being of growing significance, it was the increasing internal re-stratification of the profession that sociologists should attend to. Through enhanced disciplinary procedures, the promulgation of clinical guidelines and protocols and the emergence of new cadres of medical managers, a professional elite is, according to Freidson (1994, 2001), becoming increasingly dominant over rank-and-file medical practitioners. This in itself may weaken the coherence and hence the autonomy of the profession over time.

Light (2010) has suggested an approach based on a more pluralist view of modern societies (or at least of the USA) than the neo-Marxism of the corporatization thesis. He proposes that rather than presume medical dominance as the starting point for analysis, the medical profession should be seen as only one of several major countervailing powers in society with interests in health care, with the other powers including the state, the health care industry, patient advocacy groups and consumers. Light depicts a system in which these different interests compete for power, influence and resources and, if one becomes predominant, a counter-movement will develop over time. The model has the merit of including more than the buyers and sellers of medical services – and the rise and putative fall of medical autonomy can be set in the same explanatory framework. What is less clear is how adequately the theory explains which interests predominate at particular times.

There is general recognition among medical sociologists that the accounts of medical power and autonomy that seemed appropriate to the 1970s are no longer so clearly applicable forty years later. There are undoubtedly new challenges to medicine's authority, some of which have been discussed here. There is less consensus however on what their significance is for the future of medical autonomy and dominance. Time will tell whether medicine will retain its power and authority, by developing a new form of professionalism, based on active trust and a partnership with patients, or whether its power has been irretrievably weakened by the challenges it is now facing.

See also: *Medicalization; Practitioner–Client Relationships; Trust in Medicine; Consumerism*

REFERENCES

Elston, M.A. (1991) 'The politics of professional power', in J. Gabe, M. Calnan and M. Bury (eds), *The Sociology of the Health Service*. London: Routledge.

Freidson, E. (1970) *Profession of Medicine*. New York: Dodds Mead.

Freidson, E. (1994) *Professionalism Reborn: Theory, Prophecy and Policy*. Cambridge: Polity Press.

Freidson, E. (2001) *Professionalism: The Third Logic*. Cambridge: Polity Press.

Harrison, S. and Ahmad, W. (2000) 'Medical autonomy and the UK state', *Sociology*, 34: 129–46.

Kelleher, D., Gabe, J. and Williams, G. (eds) (2006) *Challenging Medicine*, 2nd edn. London: Routledge.

Light, D.W. (2010) 'Healthcare professions, markets and countervailing powers', in C.E. Bird, P. Conrad, A.M. Fremont and S. Timmermans (eds), *Handbook of Medical Sociology*, 6th edn. Nashville, TN: Vanderbilt University Press.

McKinlay, J.B. and Arches, J. (1985) 'Toward the proletarianization of physicians', *International Journal of Health Services*, 15 (2): 161–95.

McKinlay, J.B. and Marceau, L. (2002) 'The end of the golden age of doctoring', *International Journal of Health Services*, 32 (2): 379–416.

Witz, A. and Annandale, E. (2006) 'The challenge of nursing', in D. Kelleher, J. Gabe and G. Williams (eds), *Challenging Medicine*, 2nd edn. London: Routledge.

Mary Ann Elston and Jonathan Gabe

.... Trust in Medicine ....

> *Trust refers to a state of favourable expectations around people's actions and motives as embedded and constituted within social institutions and relationships.*

The concept of trust has been a prominent and recurrent theme in both social theory and medical sociology. From a sociological standpoint it is best seen as a form of social action, involving individuals or institutions in a social relationship, rather than a mental state. According to Sztompka (1999), trust involves an 'optimistic bet' about the unknown, contingent actions of others and, as such, involves a degree of uncertainty. As with all bets, there is a chance of losing which may create distrust.

Much of the work of social theorists (for example, Luhmann, 1979; Giddens, 1990; Beck, 1992) has revolved around three themes (Elston, 2009). First, it has been argued that trust is becoming increasingly important for managing life in a world which is rapidly changing and becoming more risky. Second, while the increase in bureaucratic rationalization and an enhanced sense of risk in late modern society are generating a need for more trust, the basis for trusting has become more precarious. People are becoming less deferential and more critical of experts, resulting in trust having to be actively earned in particular situations. It is not only now dependent on day-to-day experience providing the reasons for trusting someone, but it is also dependent on a capacity to momentarily bracket-off uncertainty and the unknowable, in what Möllering (2001) describes as a 'leap of faith'. Such leaps of faith are common in decisions involving doctors and patients where there is uncertainty and a degree of risk regarding a doctor's competence and intentions. Third, in contemporary society there is a growing need to trust abstract systems – what is termed 'distanciated trust' (Giddens, 1990) – alongside interpersonal trust. For such abstract systems, people occupying 'key access points' play a crucial role in developing trust. Doctors can be seen to occupy such a position, representing the 'faceless' abstract system of biomedicine, though trust in doctors is no longer automatic or taken-for-granted.

In the above account, a distinction has been made between interpersonal trust and distanciated trust in a system. The former is achieved through effective communicative 'face-work' between a clinician (for example, a doctor or nurse) and their patient, and also between one clinician and another and between a clinician and a manager. This needs to be distinguished from trust in a particular health care organization or health care system (Calnan and Rowe, 2008a). These levels of trust are interconnected and may be mutually reinforcing (Stevenson and Scambler, 2005), although it is possible to trust one's clinician while also distrusting the hospital they work in and vice versa.

Empirical research to date has focused primarily on assessing trust from the patient's point of view. Some have studied the nature of trust and distinguished between new patients, who may rely on 'network trust' – the views of trusted family members or friends about a physician – and continuing patients who call on 'experiential trust'. Others have talked about the 'naïve' or unconditional trust of those seeing a physician for the first time and 'reconstructed trust', established when a patient embarks on a relationship with a new clinician after experiencing dissatisfaction with their previous doctor. More often researchers have focused on levels of trust and whether trust in health care professionals or the health care system has declined in recent years. According to Calnan and Rowe (2008a), there is little empirical evidence that trust in such professionals has eroded. They report that studies in the USA and UK have found that trust in doctors is still high, with interpersonal skills and technical competence both being valued by their patients. At the same time, there is evidence that the level of trust may vary to some extent depending on the type of illness, degree of risk and experience of medical care. Those with a life-threatening illness like breast cancer seem to have higher levels of trust compared with those with a condition where a diagnosis is difficult to establish (such as Lyme disease). Also, lower levels of trust are reported when members of the public are questioned compared with patients using the health care system, suggesting that while patient trust in doctors remains high, public trust has fallen. Trust in the medical system, on the other hand, is regularly found to be lower than for individual doctors. And in the UK this lower level of trust in the health care system seems to be mirrored by a low level of trust in health service managers. The latter pattern has been explained by low levels of trust in the performance of the system (National Health Service (NHS)), especially around waiting times and the effects of cost cutting.

According to Calnan and Rowe (2008a), patient characteristics have much less bearing on trust than relationship factors such as the doctor's interpersonal skills. However, some studies have noted that older and less educated people have higher levels of trust and that those from minority ethnic groups have less trust. Research on masculinities also suggests that one of the reasons why men avoid health care is because of their distrust of clinicians (Davidson and Meadows, 2010).

The different levels of trust in doctors and the system may reflect the different significance patients attach to embodied trust and informed trust. The former involves a reliance on reputation, competence and empathy, while the latter refers to new tools of bureaucratic regulation, such as performance indicators, which act as signifiers of quality (Kuhlmann, 2006). A further distinction can be drawn between affective and cognitive factors, with embodied trust relying on individual perceptions, desires and emotions, and informed trust emphasizing 'rationalized', instrumental factors (Kuhlmann, 2006). It has been suggested that structural changes in the provision of care, such as an increase in points of access to primary care (for example, through walk-in centres, NHS Direct/NHS111 call centres and nurse triage clinics), may make embodied trust, based on an enduring relationship with a 'family doctor', less relevant in future. Faced with care being provided by an increasing variety of health care professionals, status, qualifications and reputation may become an insufficient basis for trusting the quality of care on offer. Rather, trust may be contingent and based on the information provided, with patients rationally weighing up the costs and benefits before accepting a proposed course of action.

Taylor-Gooby (2006) suggests that the decline in institutional or system trust has policy implications insofar as it may undermine welfare reform. He bases this assessment on the view that attempts to reinvigorate trust in institutions like the UK NHS, based on policies grounded in rational choice and instrumental judgements, may, like the structural changes mentioned above, have the unintended effect of undermining so-called 'non-rational trust' (grounded in interpersonal relationships). The focus is on incentivizing managers and professionals to meet targets at the expense of any consideration of the feelings of service users. Others have suggested a more complex picture. For instance, the decision to disclose performance data about individual surgeons on the internet may have unexpected consequences. In a case study of the provision of care for elective hip surgery among patients in English hospitals, patients considered the performance data to be unreliable and as likely to be massaged by managers to create as favourable an impression as possible (Calnan and Rowe, 2008a, 2008b). This lack of trust in the data may therefore have the effect of reinforcing interpersonal trust in doctors rather than increasing confidence in abstract systems, as claimed by Harrison and Smith (2004) in the context of discussing developments in clinical governance. As Calnan and Rowe (2008b: 202) put it, 'patients do not demand "proof" of trustworthiness; rather they assess for themselves the quality of service provision based on their personal experience of care'.

Rather less research has been undertaken on interprofessional trust. It has been suggested by Calnan and Rowe (2008a) that trust relations between hospital doctors and other practitioners may be changing as clinical and professional boundaries shift and professionals allied to medicine are given increasing discretion for the delivery of services. Within clinical teams the extent of trust may depend on the quality of communication and the sharing of knowledge. With the increased regulation of working hours for both junior and senior hospital doctors in the UK, there may be a greater reliance on formal as opposed to experiential knowledge. In the aforementioned study of elective hip replacement in secondary care, it was reported that trust was indicated by the degree of delegation and supervision that senior doctors felt was necessary and possible (Calnan and Rowe, 2008a). Initially, junior doctors in the surgical team were given a narrow range of tasks but this widened as senior doctors came to trust their competence and reliability. When it came to relations between clinicians and managers, distrust was more common than trust, as managers sought greater influence over clinical activity. However, managers could earn trust by acknowledging shared interests, by demonstrating competence, and by making themselves visible on the wards.

While much of the attention in medical sociology has been focused on the extent to which patients trust their doctor or the health care system, there has been rather less attention given to trust relations between medicine and the state. Elston (2009) has provided such an analysis. She argues that a series of medical malpractice scandals which came to light in the UK in the mid-to-late 1990s (for example, regarding the general practitioner Harold Shipman in Manchester and paediatric surgeons at the Bristol Royal Infirmary) resulted in medicine's regulatory institutions ceasing to be seen as trustworthy by the state. The response of the profession, or at least its leadership, has been to seek to craft a 'new professionalism', as reflected in the report of the Royal College of Physicians in 2005. This new position involves stressing patient partnership, accountability and transparency as the basis for renewed trust. Such a response can be seen as primarily a defensive move by the medical profession to head off challenges to their autonomy from the state, against a background of growing distrust. But it can also be seen in part as an attempt by the profession to develop new disciplinary mechanisms through self-regulation at the individual level and through institutionalized procedures at the meso (organizational) level (Elston, 2009).

Interestingly, medical sociologists have also come to the defence of the medical profession in the past decade. Freidson (2001), for example, has shifted his position from antagonist to ally. Instead of seeing professionalism as an ideology and professionalization as a competitive power struggle, he now emphasizes the virtues of professionalism as a way of controlling expert services, in contrast to markets and bureaucratic mechanisms. Likewise, Harrison and Smith (2004) have discussed the dangers of distrusting doctors and imposing excessive regulations on them. These authors reflect a shift among some sociologists from challenging medical power to acknowledging the importance of trusting the medical profession and the problems posed by its reported decline.

While such sociologists can be said to be basing their arguments on normative judgements about the benefits of trust for both patients and doctors, it is important to ask whether there is a dark side to trust. Some have suggested that it can lead to an abuse of power, as trust usually involves an asymmetrical relationship between the truster (the subject) and the trustee (the object). In such circumstances trust may be used to legitimate the exercise of power and even to facilitate corrupt practices or cover up malpractice. These abuses of power may be less common, however, if trust now has to be constantly earned, whether at the micro level of the clinician–patient relationship or the macro level of the relationship between the medical profession and the state.

While considerable progress has been made in studying trust, more studies are needed regarding the nature of the relationship between patients' interpersonal trust in clinicians and institutional trust in health care organizations and health care systems. And further research is also required into the changing nature of interprofessional trust. The consequences of changes in service delivery such as walk-in clinics for patient–clinician trust need further exploration as well.

See also: *Risk; Medical Autonomy, Dominance and Decline; Hospitals and Health Care Organizations; Managerialism*

REFERENCES

Beck, U. (1992) *The Risk Society: Towards a New Modernity*. London: Sage.

Calnan, M. and Rowe, R. (2008a) *Trust Matters in Health Care*. Maidenhead: Open University Press.

Calnan, M. and Rowe, R. (2008b) 'Trust, accountability and choice', *Health, Risk & Society*, 10 (3): 201–6.

Davidson, K. and Meadows, R. (2010) 'Older men's health: the role of marital status and masculinities', in B. Gough and S. Robertson (eds), *Men, Masculinities and Health: Critical Perspectives*. Basingstoke: Palgrave Macmillan.

Elston, M. (2009) 'Remaking a trustworthy medical profession in twenty-first century Britain?', in J. Gabe and M. Calnan (eds), *The New Sociology of the Health Service*. London: Routledge.

Freidson, E. (2001) *Professionalism: The Third Logic*. Cambridge: Polity Press.

Giddens, A. (1990) *The Consequences of Modernity*. Cambridge: Polity Press.

Harrison, S. and Smith, C. (2004) 'Trust and moral motivation: redundant resources in health and social care?', *Policy & Politics*, 32 (3): 371–86.

Kuhlmann, E. (2006) *Modernising Health Care: Reinventing Professions, the State and the Public*. Bristol: Policy Press.

Luhmann, N. (1979) *Trust and Power*. Chichester: Wiley.

Luhmann, N. (1984) *Trust and Power: Two Works by Niklas Luhmann*. Chichester: Wiley.

Möllering, G. (2001) 'The nature of trust: from Georg Simmel to a theory of expectations, interpretations and suspension', *Sociology*, 35 (2): 403–20.

Stevenson, F. and Scambler, G. (2005) 'The relationship between medicine and the public: the challenge of concordance', *Health*, 9 (1): 5–21.

Sztompka, P. (1999) *Trust: A Sociological Theory*. Cambridge: Cambridge University Press.

Taylor-Gooby, P. (2006) 'Trust, risk and health care reform', *Health, Risk & Society*, 8 (2): 97–103.

Jonathan Gabe

Nursing and Midwifery as Occupations

Nursing is an occupation involving the provision of care to facilitate the maintenance of, or improvement in, health and/or recovery from illness and the maximum quality of life until death. Midwifery as an occupation aspires to provide independent woman-centred care to healthy parturient women.

Sociological interest in nursing and midwifery as occupations has centred on issues of gender and professional power, and, in particular, on the complex historical relationship each occupation has with biomedicine which affects its relative autonomy and authority in clinical settings. Let us first consider nursing in this regard before turning to midwifery.

The origins of the nursing system we see today in developed countries date from the mid-1800s, when several societal changes prompted a new way of caring for the sick. These changes included the institutionalization of care owing to rapid urbanization, the transformation of biomedicine into a unified and collegiate profession that required a new type of support worker, and the need to create 'suitable' work for middle-class women. Nursing work was associated with the female realm of nurturing and caring, and medicine with culturally masculine labour, namely, the 'objective' scientific work of diagnosis and treatment (Gamarnikow, 1978). Moreover, physicians exercised power over nurses, with the latter formally taking orders from the former (Wicks, 1998).

Early attempts to professionalize nursing in Britain and the USA included the regulation of training, culminating in nurse registration in the first quarter of the twentieth century. This enabled occupational closure (Witz, 1992), that is, control over entry to the occupation. However, the two key challenges that continue to face elites intent on professionalizing nursing are the creation of a unique body of nursing knowledge, and gaining autonomy from biomedicine in the use of this knowledge. Nursing diagnosis, the idea that nursing-specific problems can be identified and mapped onto particular nursing interventions for which a registered nurse is accountable, potentially offers nurses the formal autonomy to control a realm of patient care.

Some studies have found that nursing has made strides in terms of control over the social aspect of care, especially through the notion of teamwork (Svensson, 1996). However, the 'team' concept has been rendered problematic because doctors, as team members, have been found to define work in a manner that undermines the relevance of the social, thereby reproducing traditional hierarchies. In real-life clinical contexts, Davies (1995: 103) argues, the gendered logic of the institution equates nursing work with 'women's work', and has led to the failure to take nursing seriously, instead relegating to it a secondary status relative to medicine. As Davies (1995: 61) puts it: '[nursing] has clearly not had first bite at the cherry in defining its work', forcing it to sweep up whatever areas are left after medicine has carved out its territory. Davies critiques the notion of the old professionalism with its masculine logic and favours for nursing a model that transcends gendered thinking and promotes nurses who are engaged and interdependent and can reflectively use their experience and expertise.

The complexity of clinical contexts has also been considered in relation to the 'gray' area where it is difficult to distinguish between nursing observations and medical diagnosis (Allen, 1997) and where a *de facto* blurring of boundaries has been found to occur (Carmel, 2006). As Gamarnikow (1991) has proposed, it is through nursing practice that the medical 'gaze' is articulated. What we know from a range of empirical studies in clinical settings in the UK (see, for example,

Allen, 1997) and Australia (see, for example, Wicks, 1998) is that senior nurses tend to be assertive in decision making about patient treatment and care but that this power is largely *informal* as doctors may overrule nurses' decisions when it comes to medical diagnosis. It is the case that a growing number of nurses have expanded their role to take on doctor-devolved duties such as independent medication prescribing, and as a group appear to wield a great deal of informal influence over decision making, including in some contexts the formation of local organizational alliances with medicine (Carmel, 2006). Nonetheless, nursing as an occupation appears to have made limited real gains in the ability of its members to exercise power in *formal* decision making about patient care.

In turning attention to the occupational status of midwifery, we can see some rather different issues emerging compared with nursing, as well as some shared concerns. The greatest difference is that midwifery stakes its claim over 'natural' childbirth. It is the aspiration of those in what has come to be called the 'new midwifery' movement, particularly active in Canada, New Zealand and Britain, that appropriately educated midwives should exercise exclusive control over the care of healthy pregnant woman and the process of childbirth. The current situation in many industrially-developed countries is that obstetricians control and manage almost 100 per cent of pregnancies and deliveries (even where midwives actually undertake the deliveries). However, according to new midwifery discourse, obstetricians would only be needed to manage the relatively small number of pregnancies and births that midwives have assessed as abnormal or potentially problematic. Central to the discourse of new midwifery is woman-centeredness, framed in terms of choice, autonomy and partnership between the midwife and woman. Moreover, new midwifery proponents draw on conventional scientific evidence to support their claims that their proposed system of care, which views the routine use of technology in pregnancy and childbirth as unnecessary, is no more risky in terms of birth outcomes than obstetric care. So why is it that this new midwifery has only had limited success in selling itself? To understand the reasons why change has been slow, we need to turn to history and consider issues of power and knowledge as exercised through the discourses that obstetric medicine employed in order to sustain its dominance over pregnancy and childbirth.

Up until the 1800s in many Western nations childbirth was a woman-centred event, with female midwives overseeing childbirth without the use of technology. During the nineteenth century, a new male-dominated science of obstetrics as a branch of Western biomedicine developed that came into competition and conflict with traditional midwifery. Armed with 'new-fangled' instruments that we now know caused more harm than good, and with political allies that funded and supported it, obstetric medicine gained dominance over midwifery to the extent that midwives were relegated to the status of an ancillary occupation working under biomedical control. It was not until the 1970s that feminist sociologists and new midwives problematized what they argued was a spurious relationship between the impressive improvements in mortality figures during the 1900s and the rise of obstetric medicine (Tew, 1998). They pointed to wider

societal factors such as better nutrition, a better standard of living and ameliora-
tion in the overall health of women to account for such improvements. Moreover, the biomedical model of childbirth was criticized for processing parturient
women through a mechanical and impersonal system that socialized them to
believe that they could not give birth without technical assistance (Oakley,
1980). New midwifery discourse has emphasized the benefits of the normalizing
and humanizing potential of midwife-led models, as indicated in a recent
Cochrane review of the quality and safety of midwife-led care in Australia,
Canada and the UK (Hatem et al., 2010).

As expected, the obstetric camp has retaliated with counterclaims to defend its
position. It argues that, based also on scientific evidence, obstetric care is necessary
for all women for the following reason: since one can only define a birth as being
'safe' in retrospect, all pregnancies are potentially risky. Thus, we have two sets of
'truths' comprising diverse perspectives about the safety of childbirth – one from
new midwifery and one from obstetrics. That these two sciences draw on the same
broad methodological stances (conventional and quantitative) when it comes to
providing evidence of safety, highlights the social and cultural shaping of allegedly
'objective' scientific knowledge (see De Vries and Lemmens, 2006).

In practice settings, the medical profession has been found to dominate midwifery to varying degrees, regulating its work practices and, in some contexts, pro-
hibiting it from legal practice (Bourgeault et al., 2004). However, it is not merely
the dominance of obstetrics that constrains midwives' autonomy. Benoit et al.
(2005) observed definitive variations in the social organization of maternity care
across four high-income countries (namely, the UK, the Netherlands, Finland and
Canada) and argued that the extent to which states were positively disposed both
to women as workers (for example, midwives) and women as recipients of care
(parturient women), often fuelled by consumer support and market principles,
accounted for a good deal of the variation. In the Netherlands, for example,
'woman-friendly' state support for midwifery is high as evidenced in laws and
regulations, the education of midwives, and research into midwifery outcomes. In
contrast, in countries such as Finland, a gender-neutral emphasis and the politics of
playing down the differences between men and women rather than promoting
'woman-friendliness' have served to undermine the professional interests of groups
such as midwives. Benoit et al. (2005) conclude that in terms of maternity care,
biomedical determinism can be undermined in some circumstances.

Compared to nursing, which is inextricably linked to biomedicine because it
deals with actual or potential health problems, midwifery, in claiming exclusive
jurisdiction over healthy women, has the potential to break free of biomedicine
and operate quite independently. While changes in state policies and legislation
in many Western countries have seen expanded roles for nurses that cross over
into medicine's traditional jurisdiction, state support for midwifery in some
contexts has allowed it greater autonomy and independence from medicine. As
the sociological literature on nursing and midwifery increases, the realm of
medical sociology may continue to shift towards health and healthcare sociology
in the future.

See also: *Medical Model; Health Professional Migration; Social Movements and Health*

REFERENCES

Allen, D. (1997) 'The nursing-medical boundary: a negotiated order?' *Sociology of Health & Illness*, 19 (4): 498–520.

Benoit, C., Wrede, S., Bourgeault, I., Sandall, J., De Vries, R. and van Teijlingen, E.R. (2005) 'Understanding the social organisation of maternity care systems: midwifery as touchstone', *Sociology of Health & Illness*, 27 (6): 722–37.

Bourgeault, I., Benoit, C. and Davis-Floyd, R. (eds) (2004) *Reconceiving Midwifery: The New Canadian Model of Care*. Kingston, Montreal: MacGill-Queen's University Press.

Carmel, S. (2006) 'Boundaries obscured and boundaries reinforced: incorporation as a strategy of occupational enhancement for intensive care', *Sociology of Health & Illness*, 28 (2): 154–77.

Davies, C. (1995) *Gender and the Professional Predicament in Nursing*. Buckingham: Open University Press.

De Vries, R. and Lemmens, T. (2006) 'The social and cultural shaping of medical evidence: case studies from pharmaceutical research and obstetric science', *Social Science & Medicine*, 62: 2694–706.

Gamarnikow, E. (1978) 'Sexual divisions of labour: the case of nursing', in A. Kuhn and A.M. Wolpe (eds), *Feminism and Materialism*. London: Routledge and Kegan Paul.

Gamarnikow, E. (1991) 'Nurse or woman? Gender and professionalism in reformed nursing 1860–1923', in P. Holden and J. Littlewood (eds), *Anthropology and Nursing*. London: Routledge.

Hatem, M., Sandall, J., Devane, D., Soltani, H. and Gates, S. (2010) 'Midwife-led versus other models of care for childbearing women', *Cochrane Database of Systematic Reviews*, Issue 4, Art No.: CD004667. DOI: 10.1002/14651858. CD004667.pub2.

Oakley, A. (1980) *Woman Confined*. Oxford: Martin Robertson.

Svensson, R. (1996) 'The interplay between doctors and nurses: a negotiated order perspective', *Sociology of Health & Illness*, 18 (3): 379–98.

Tew, M. (1998) *Safer Childbirth: A Critical History of Maternity Care*, 3rd edn. London: Free Association Books.

Wicks, D. (1998) *Nurses and Doctors at Work: Rethinking Professional Boundaries*. Buckingham: Open University Press.

Witz, A. (1992) *Professions and Patriarchy*. London: Routledge.

Abbey Hyde

Social Divisions in Formal Health Care

Social divisions in formal health care include professional status, power, gender, ethnicity, and socio-economic status. Such divisions represent and perpetuate socio-cultural inequalities, nationally and globally, and can generate inter-professional conflict.

Social class, gender and ethnicity are typically divisive because of differences in the degree of social status and power accorded to them. Social status, usually conferred through birth or profession, is defined by Weber (1995: 155) as 'claims on positive or negative privileges in regard to social prestige' that are gained when such privileges become part of everyday life, and when, through formal education, that way of life becomes assimilated.

Social divisions occur when such privileges are unequally distributed between all groups of people. This generates social stratification between class, gender, and ethnic groups. Unsurprisingly, such divisions are also present within health care, found in the historical origins of the medical, nursing and midwifery professions through to current concerns that 'class differences and gender issues challenge necessary collaborative teamwork' (Hall, 2005: 188). Thus, whilst all the allied health care professions are wholly interdependent, the vast difference in professional status and its accompanying privileges is a source of ongoing conflict and dispute. Such divisiveness is often attributed to the 'professional' status accorded to medicine. Medicine tends to be perceived as having greater autonomy in practice, and dominance in the development and maintenance of health care structures and systems, especially regarding its delivery. In that respect, social divisions are predicated in socio-cultural values and the division of labour. They are at the heart of professional medical supremacy, and have become ingrained contentious relationships that are formalized through the professional boundaries of the various health care professions.

In Western countries, members of the medical profession were historically upper and middle class, the majority White and male. In addition, medicine's systemic and structural dominance in care delivery has been buttressed by a robust and autonomous education system. This supports the medical profession's internal hierarchies and limits access to medicine in a way that both represents and preserves social divisions of class, gender, and ethnicity. These divisions are perpetuated through health care education as professional cultures (accompanying values, beliefs, attitudes, customs and behaviours) that are taught and passed down, thereby reinforcing the inequalities within and between health care professions (Hall, 2005). The privileges enjoyed by the medical profession cause divisions between it and the other allied health care professions. For example, doctors enjoy an education system that enables postgraduate doctors to constantly engage in further study that is fully resourced both materially and, importantly, with time. Nurses and other allied health care professions on the other hand, whilst also expected to undertake further professional development, do not have the same degree of choice in their area of study. Neither do they have access to similar levels of material resources or time. The lack of funding and a reluctance to release staff from work result in many nurses either developing a negative attitude towards continuing professional development, or giving up their own time, money, and often their annual leave in order to achieve postgraduate qualifications (Schweitzer, 2010). Combined with the initial differences in pay between junior doctors and nurses, this inequality means that the former are able to advance more rapidly up the salary and hierarchical scale than their nurse counterparts. Thus, socio-economic divisions persist between nursing, allied health care professions and the medical profession.

In the UK, the state largely dictates both nursing and the allied health care professions' salary scales and professional development. Since Florence Nightingale argued that nurses should be taught and educated, the nursing profession has fought to further its own autonomy and professional status by developing its educational base. During the 1990s this involved pre-registration and postgraduate nurse education moving from nursing colleges to mainstream universities and removing student nurses from the duty roster (introduced under Project 2000) to encourage a more learner student approach to that of contracted worker. However, the aim to produce more highly educated and skilled nurses was undermined by the government's stipulation that the entry gate into nurse education be widened. This widening enabled larger numbers of students to be recruited onto professional programmes. However, the intention that Project 2000's academic curriculum would produce 'knowledgeable doers' was undermined by lower entrance requirements and the recruitment of less academically advanced students. Thus, whilst there was an increase in the numbers recruited from lower socio-economic backgrounds, subsequent opportunities for qualified nurses to advance up the social ladder remained limited as the status of nurse education remained the same – or in fact worsened, as Project 2000 was accused of producing registered nurses who were neither academically competent nor clinically skilled (Ramprogus, 1995). Further social divisions within formal health care also developed with the introduction of more health care assistants (HCAs). HCAs were needed to fill the gap as student nurses under Project 2000 were removed from the duty roster and given supernumerary status. Currently, nurse education has moved from diploma to degree-only pre-registration programmes in an attempt to redress these concerns.

Throughout its broader historical development, nursing in Britain struggled to gain greater professional status. Florence Nightingale aimed to make nursing a more 'respectable' profession, one that was appropriate for upper- and middle-class women of 'good moral standing' (Smith and Mackintosh, 2007: 2215). Now, just as in Nightingale's time when the working classes undertook the majority of 'dirty' work, unqualified HCAs perform these tasks when 'supporting' qualified nurses. Divisions and disadvantage within nursing therefore continue to centre on the issue of basic, hands-on care or 'dirty work' (Allan, 2007). This is now represented within an ideological battle which suggests that if qualified, 'professional' nurses undertake basic hands-on care this will undermine their professional status. Thus, low paid HCAs (who are mainly lower socio-economic income bracket female workers) are now predominantly responsible for the 'dirty work' in nursing care, reinforcing socio-economic social divisions within the profession.

Historically, divisions focused around the dirty and caring nature of nursing were also significantly linked to the gender disparity between the health care professions. Medicine traditionally consisted of predominantly male practitioners, while female workers were largely found in nursing and the allied health professions. However, the gender composition of medicine has radically changed across the UK, the Nordic countries, Russia, Australia and the USA, with a significant increase in the number of women. The increasing share of women in the UK medical profession is well illustrated in a Royal College of Physicians' Report (Elston, 2009). According to that report: 'Compared with the early 1960s, the number of men entering medical schools each year has doubled: but for women the number has increased by a factor of ten' (p. 1). In 2007, 40 per cent of all doctors in the UK were women:

42 per cent of these were GPs and 28 per cent were NHS consultants (Elston, 2009). Such changing demographics have led to the suggestion that the delivery of medical practice will shift in response to the female needs for part-time work and/ or career breaks that are necessary for child rearing (Kilminster et al., 2007).

In addition, it has been claimed that an increase in women has led to medicine becoming feminized, focusing more on the therapeutic, preventative and communication side of medical practice at the expense of scientific, rational process (Philips and Austin, 2009). The feminization of medicine is now widely debated across the West. Feminists argue that medicine's inflexible structural inequalities alienate its female members, thereby protecting male supremacy and prestige, whilst other feminist writers suggest that the impact of medical training actually neutralizes gender differences, thereby inhibiting the positive values and skills that women bring to the profession (Levinson and Lurie, 2004). That this debate even exists highlights the ongoing power of gender division, representing social inequalities within wider society as well as within the health care professions.

The debate around the feminization of medicine is linked to social constructions of 'care' as a 'natural' feminine quality, indicative of women's supposedly 'innate' nurturing ability, and is also linked to emotion, which is perceived as irrational. This is in contrast to science, denoted as masculine and reasoned; the social difference being one of an increased status and prestige for science over care. Because caring is feminized and deemed vocational, the satisfaction in undertaking this kind of work is considered a reward in itself, and therefore constitutes a valid reason for why nursing care, for example, need not be overly financially rewarded (Rafferty, 1996). The nursing profession has worked hard, therefore, to move away from its gendered image in order to raise its professional status (Davies, 1995). However, gender continues to play 'a significant part in reproducing disadvantage among nurses who are generally regarded as underpaid for their work, irrespective of speciality or position' (Smith and Mackintosh, 2007: 2215). For example, in the 1980s only 10 per cent of nurses were men but 50 per cent of these were in management positions. Consequently, when pay for nurse management positions increased in the 1980s, higher salaries became definitively linked to higher status 'male work' as opposed to lower status 'female work'.

These existing socio-economic, gender and status employment divisions within nursing are now being reinforced by the increasing numbers of migrant workers in health care (Smith and Mackintosh, 2007). Since Mary Seacole, a healer and herbalist from Jamaica, was first ostracized when she wanted to nurse in the Crimea alongside Nightingale and her nurses, Black and Asian health care workers have been subjected to racism, exploitation, and unfair treatment. They are more frequently found in lower paid, disadvantaged positions. Like the UK, in many Western countries health care is dependent on migrant nurses. Migrants fill less desirable positions, such as caring for older adults or adults with learning disabilities, as well as undertaking agency work which tends to be lower paid. Currently, significant numbers of nurses, educated in India, the Philippines, South Africa and Sub-Saharan Africa, have been recruited into Western health care systems. This migration of health care workers reflects and reinforces global inequalities. Populations in these nations are left with fewer skilled health care workers, contributing further to poorer health outcomes and the ongoing disparity between a currently rich West and the rest of the world.

Hochschild (2004) has described the transplantation of care workers from the poor South to the rich North as a 'heart transplant'. This is where migrant workers from poor countries leave their own children and elderly relatives to gain employment caring for the children and elderly in families and communities in more affluent nations. In doing so, rather than providing love and care for their own family, they give it (or, rather, sell it) to others. Hochschild, who writes on emotional labour and the commercialization of feeling, asks: 'is an emotion a resource like gold or ivory that can be extracted from one place and taken to another?' (2004: 26). She suggests that the giving of 'love' by immigrants has become an exploited commodity.

In addition to the reproduction of social divisions in health care through global migration, there is significant inequality in the representation of ethnic minorities within health care work. In the USA, a lack of racial representation in medicine, dentistry and public health professions has been linked to disparities in the quality of care received by minority populations. This is because Black patients are more likely to access care from Black health care professionals than their White counterparts. However, in the USA, ethnic minority health care professionals comprise only '5% of dentists, 6% of physicians and 9% of nurses' (Mitchell and Lassiter, 2006: 2094). Social divisions within health care, therefore, significantly reduce the capacity of the professions to draw on the talent of individuals dispersed across all sections of society. This perpetuates and compounds wider social inequalities that directly impact on patient/client need. In the UK, the picture is somewhat different, possibly given the historical legacy of the government's recruitment policies (BMA, 2009). However, while minority ethnic groups tend to be 'over-represented' in medical schools, for instance, disparities remain. Thus, in 2008, for UK applicants to medical schools, Whites had the highest acceptance rate (55 per cent), while Black-African, Black-Other and Asian-Bangladeshi had the lowest rates (24 per cent, 26 per cent, and 30 per cent respectively) (BMA, 2009: 45).

In conclusion, the division of labour amongst health care professionals is an important topic for medical sociology, as well as policy and practice. The complexity of patient need is dependent on the interdependent and integrated provision of care across the professions. Such care necessitates inter-professional collaboration and therefore shared responsibility and accountability. However, matters are complicated by persistent social divisions including socio-economic, gender, and ethnic inequalities. These divisions are also perpetuated within formal health care by socio-cultural norms predicated in the recruitment, education, and organization of service delivery. As discussed above, this is also unfolding on a global stage. All of this begs a question: can a genuine collaboration between and within the professions be achieved, when the global differences of social status and its accompanying privileges generate such persistent social divisions?

See also: *Medical Model; Nursing and Midwifery as Occupations; Health Professional Migration; Informal Care*

REFERENCES

Allan, H. (2007) 'The rhetoric of caring and the recruitment of overseas nurses: the social production of a care gap', *Journal of Clinical Nursing*, 16: 2204–12.

BMA (2009) *Equality and Diversity in UK Medical Schools*. London: British Medical Association.

Davies, C. (1995) *Gender and the Professional Predicament in Nursing*. Buckingham: Open University Press.

Elston, M.A. (2009) *Women and Medicine: The Future*. London: The Royal College of Physicians.

Hall, P. (2005) 'Interprofessional teamwork: professional cultures as barriers', *Journal of Interprofessional Care* (May), Supplement 1: 188–96.

Hochschild, A. (2004) 'The commodity frontier', in J. Alexander, G. Marx and C. Williams (eds), *Self, Social Structure and Beliefs: Essays in Sociology*. Berkeley and Los Angeles: University of California Press.

Kilminster, S., Downes, J., Gough, B., Murdoch-Eaton, D. and Roberts, T. (2007) 'Women in medicine – is there a problem? A literature review of changing gender composition, structures and occupational cultures in medicine', *Medical Education*, 41: 39–49.

Levinson, W. and Lurie, N. (2004) 'When most doctors are women: what lies ahead?', *Annals of Internal Medicine*, 141 (6): 471–4.

Mitchell, D. and Lassiter, S. (2006) 'Addressing healthcare disparities and increasing workforce diversity: the next step for the dental, medical and public health professions', *American Journal of Public Health*, 96 (12): 2093–7.

Philips, S. and Austin, E. (2009) 'The feminization of medicine and population health', *Journal of the American Medical Association*, 301 (8): 863–4.

Rafferty, M.A. (1996) *The Politics of Nursing Knowledge*. Abingdon: Routledge.

Ramprogus, V. (1995) *The Deconstruction of Nursing*. Aldershot: Ashgate.

Schweitzer, D. (2010) 'Deterrents to nurse participation in continuing professional development: an integrative literature review', *Journal of Continuing Education*, 41 (10): 441–7.

Smith, P. and Mackintosh, M. (2007) 'Profession, market and class: nurse migration and the remaking of division and disadvantage', *Journal of Clinical Nursing*, 16: 2213–20.

Weber, M. (1995) 'Basic concepts of stratification', *Sociological Studies*, 5: 155.

Catherine Theodosius

Health Professional Migration

A phenomenon that increasingly raises critical ethical and policy concerns, the migration of health professionals from largely low and middle to high income countries involves a range of issues, from the integration of internationally educated health professionals to the consequences of their migration for health system sustainability.

The migration of health professions is not a new phenomenon, and the role that internationally educated health professionals (IEHPs) play in some Western health systems has always been important. The labour market in health care, however, is becoming increasingly global in scope, in part because labour mobility across national borders is facilitated by many international trade agreements and by neo-liberal globalization policies more generally. The recent shift in the volume and pace of migration, and in particular the movement of much needed health personnel from low and middle to high income countries, has raised a number of ethical and policy concerns (WHO, 2006). The controversy focuses on the consequences of this more rapid migration, particularly in terms of severe staff and skill shortages for the health systems in many 'source' countries. The ethical issues these trends raise are not limited to global health policy circles; they have also permeated foreign policy agendas more broadly (Bach, 2003). More recently, we have also started to witness the increasing migration of health professionals from some developed Western nations, such as Ireland and Greece, following massive government cuts to health services in the wake of the 2008 banking crisis and its deleterious impact on working conditions.

A snapshot of the flow of health professionals into the most saturated immigrant health labour markets of the USA, the UK, Canada and Australia is worth considering. Data gathered from the early 2000s reveal that the USA has the largest number of international medical graduates (IMGs) (208,733), followed by the UK (39,266), Canada (15,701), and Australia (14,346). The percentage of IMGs in each country produces a different demographic reality: the UK has the largest percentage of IMGs in its physician workforce (28.3 per cent), followed by Australia (26.5 per cent), the USA (23.1 per cent), and Canada (23.1 per cent) (Mullan, 2005). In the case of nurses, those trained abroad make up 13 per cent of the workforce in Australia, 10 per cent in the UK, 6–7 per cent in Canada, and roughly 5 per cent in the USA (WHO, 2006). Again, the data reveal that the USA has the largest number (99,456), followed by the UK (65,000), while Canada (19,061) has a significantly lower population of internationally educated nurses (IENs).

Other important trends that have shifted are in terms of the source of IEHPs. A high percentage of IMGs working in the USA, the UK, Canada and Australia originally came from lower-income countries. The IMG workforce of the UK has the highest percentage of IMGs from lower-income countries (75.2 per cent), followed by the USA (60.2 per cent), Canada (43.4 per cent), and Australia (40.0 per cent). Key source countries for physicians include India and South Africa. The Philippines is a primary source of IENs to the USA (50.2 per cent), the UK (46 per cent) and Canada (29.3 per cent), whereas nurses from New Zealand make up the largest demographic group in Australia. In both cases the source countries are linked to destination countries in a way that reveals the legacies of colonialism (Nestel, 2006).

Much of the literature in this area focuses on the factors that *push* health professionals from their country of origin and *pull* them to their destination country. Typical 'push' factors include: low pay, poor working conditions, a lack of resources to work effectively, limited career and educational opportunities, unstable or dangerous work environments, and overall economic instability (see, for example, Aiken et al., 2004). Some have suggested that given that nurses are primarily female, they often emigrate because their opportunities for wages in their usually more gender equitable host country greatly surpass those they could attain in their home country (Brush et al., 2004). Factors that pull IEHPs to typical destination countries include: higher pay, better working conditions, better resourced health systems, career opportunities, the provision of post-basic education, opportunities to travel, and political stability (Aiken et al., 2004). Although migration is often depicted as being individually motivated and economically driven, it is also a cultural and social phenomenon. Choy (2004), for example, argues in her analysis of the migration of nurses from the Philippines to the USA that, 'the desire of Filipino nurses to migrate abroad cannot be reduced to an economic logic, but rather reflects [an] individual and collective desire for a unique form of social, cultural and economic success', which she argues was seen as 'obtainable only outside the national borders of the Philippines' (p. 7).

The migratory flows of IEHPs are also intricately linked to key human health resource policy decisions that have been made both in destination and source countries. Canada, the USA and Australia, for example, all draw upon IMGs to help address shortages in underserviced areas through the use of a range of policy instruments, ranging from visa waivers (in the USA) to temporary licenses and direct recruitment (in Australia and parts of Canada). IENs have become a critical resource in the older adult care sector in the USA, the UK and Canada (Spencer et al., 2010). Most stakeholders in these countries share the position that these are at best temporary solutions. Indeed, it has been argued that governments and employers in destination countries have tended to rely on international recruitment rather than focus on the underlying problems that have resulted in domestic shortages in health workers (Bach, 2003). The broader context in 'source' countries that affects health professional migration can be linked to neoliberal policies, such as Structural Adjustment Programmes, i.e. macroeconomic interventions, also dubbed austerity measures, which amplify social inequalities. These programmes have resulted in severe public sector cutbacks in the health care system, layoffs, and underemployment of health workers who may feel compelled to migrate for employment (Packer et al., 2008).

The literature also reflects a concern with the experiences of IEHPs in workplaces in their destination country. Early research by Joyce and Hunt (1982) found that IENs working in the USA experienced many difficult and unexpected problems, including the prejudice of other workers, assignments to onerous tasks, and distress from family separation. Canadian research has also shown that IENs, particularly those of colour, tend to occupy the lowest echelons of the profession (Calliste, 1996). Similarly, IMGs expressed dissatisfaction with their concentration in less prestigious practice settings, a lack of recognition of their professional backgrounds, and the questioning of their authority by patients (see, for example, Bernstein and Shuval, 1998). These experiences, however, were found to attenuate the longer they were in their destination country (Brown and James, 2000).

The particularly gendered experience of family separation has been conceptualized by Hochschild (2000) in terms of 'global care chains'. This refers to the global transfer of paid and unpaid care labour from women in low and middle to high income countries and the ways that these transfers of care connect children, families and countries across the globe (Yeates, 2004). It also describes the increasing feminization of migration which responds to the care deficits in high-income countries left by women's increased labour force participation. What remains behind is another care deficit that is largely borne by grandmothers, aunts and daughters left at home, but one which is buoyed by the remittances that migrant care workers in high-income countries are able to provide. Although Hochschild discusses domestic workers and nannies, Yeates (2004) has argued that these trends apply equally to the highly-skilled nursing labour sector.

There is limited literature on IEHPs who migrate but cannot find work in their profession – dubbed a 'brain waste' issue. A notable exception is research on the massive emigration of physicians from the (old) Soviet Union to Israel, when it had an open, non-selective migration policy. Bernstein and Shuval (1998) situate the experiences of Soviet physicians in Israel within an implicit professional *social closure* model. Briefly, this approach delineates how the closure strategy of *exclusion* based on credentials limits and controls the supply of entrants to an occupation; in response, those excluded attempt to gain entrance into the profession by employing *inclusionary* strategies. These two strategies are employed to either open or close doors to professional practice, depending on the key market factors of need, supply and distribution. Using this approach, Bernstein and Shuval (1998) describe the mechanisms used by the more dominant Israeli physicians to maintain elitism and control over immigrant physicians in a highly saturated medical labour market.

Brain waste issues have been particularly salient in Canada, especially for IMGs, and in response several policy initiatives have been undertaken to better inform physicians considering moving to Canada of the integration process; to create specific programmes to bridge the competency gap between international and local requirements; and to address associated economic and linguistic barriers to professional integration (Bourgeault, 2007). Making it easier to become integrated, coupled with the practice of international recruitment, gives rise to another ethical dilemma – that of exacerbating the *brain drain* from source countries which in many cases desperately require their locally developed health care professionals.

International migration is commonly viewed as exacerbating shortages in source countries, particularly in Sub-Saharan Africa, where the WHO (2006) has stated that the shortage and migration of health workers threatens the sustainability of their health systems. Among destination countries, the UK has stood out in terms of its explicit policies to address the ethical issues resulting from the active recruitment of health workers from countries in need, perhaps because it was the recipient of the fiercest criticisms for its active recruitment from these countries in the late 1990s. It was the first, for example, to establish an ethical code to guide its recruitment practices within the National Health Service, though many have argued this had little effect, in part because it did not apply to the private care sector (Packer et al., 2008). Ethical issues are also salient in Canada and Australia, but the decentralized and federated nature of their health systems makes coordinated policy difficult. Despite having some of the most vocal critics of the health professional brain drain (Aiken et al., 2004; Mullan, 2005), the USA has done little in terms of putting in place policy to combat it.

Brain drain issues are most salient in source countries for obvious reasons, but are not as simple as mapping out the consequences arising from the emigration of their much needed human resources for health and health care. In some source countries, most notably the Philippines and India, there seems to be a *bifurcation* of interests. On the one hand, there is legitimate concern among some stakeholders about the consequences of the massive migration of their health professionals. Although cited as a model of *managed migration*, basic health indicators in the Philippines have worsened since the enactment of their health labour 'export' policy. Over 4,000 doctors working in the public health sector have retrained as nurses in order to migrate (Packer et al., 2008). On the other hand, the migration of health workers is seen as a 'development' tool because of the remittances that health workers, and nurses in particular, provide to their families back home. Remittances remain largely as a private infusion of funds rather than public funds to sustain the health system.

In conclusion, health professional migration is clearly influenced not only by a wide range of policy decisions within and beyond the health sector in both source and destination countries, but also by the broader context of postcolonial ties and growing global inequity. One must also consider that the situation is more complex than a simple dichotomy because some countries can be both a source and destination; Canada and South Africa, for example, experience an outflow but also benefit from an inflow from other even more disadvantaged nations. So-called 'chain' migration, which involves countries that migrating health professionals transit through, such as in the Middle East, on their way to their ultimate destination, also needs to be more fully taken into consideration in both policy and the literature on health worker migration. Stakeholders and policy makers in all countries – source, destination and transit – will need to at least consider how to address more explicitly ethical concerns in light of the WHO Global Code of Practice for the International Recruitment of Health Personnel which was adopted at the most recent World Health Assembly in May 2010. This code, although not mandatory, seeks to establish and promote *principles* and *practices* for the ethical international recruitment of health personnel as a core component of national, regional and global responses to the challenges of health professional migration and health system strengthening. It remains to be seen how realizable these principles will be, given widening global inequalities and the increasingly transnational nature of health labour flows. In that respect, future research in medical sociology could make a valuable contribution to our knowledge of these processes.

See also: *Neoliberal Globalization and Health Inequalities; Nursing and Midwifery as Occupations; Informal Care*

REFERENCES

Aiken, L.H., Buchan, J., Sochalski, J., Nichols, B. and Powell, M. (2004) 'Trends in international nurse migration', *Health Affairs*, 23 (3): 69–77.

Bach, S. (2003) *International Migration of Health Workers: Labour and Social Issues*. Geneva: International Labour Office Working Paper.

Bernstein, J. and Shuval, J.T. (1998) 'The occupational integration of former Soviet physicians in Israel', *Social Science & Medicine*, 47 (6): 809–19.

Bourgeault, I.L. (2007) 'Brain drain, brain gain and brain waste: programs aimed at integrating and retaining the best and the brightest in health care', Special Issue of *Canadian Issues/Thémes Canadiens*, Spring: 96–9.

Brown, D.E. and James, G.D. (2000) 'Physiological stress responses in Filipino-American immigrant nurses: the effects of residence time, life-style and job strain', *Psychosomatic Medicine*, 62: 394–400.

Brush, B.L., Sochalski, J. and Berger, A.M. (2004) 'Imported care: recruiting foreign nurses to US health care facilities', *Health Affairs*, 23 (3): 78–87.

Calliste, A. (1996) 'Antiracism organizing and resistance in nursing: African Canadian women', *The Canadian Review of Sociology and Anthropology*, 33 (3): 361–90.

Choy, C.C. (2004) *Empire of Care: Nursing and Migration in Filipino American History*. Durham, NC: Duke University Press.

Hochschild, A.R. (2000) 'Global care chains and emotional surplus value', in W. Hutton and A. Giddens (eds), *On The Edge: Living with Global Capitalism*. London: Jonathan Cape.

Joyce, R.E. and Hunt, C.L. (1982) 'Philippine nurses and the brain drain', *Social Science and Medicine*, 16 (12): 1223–33.

Mullan, F. (2005) 'The metrics of the physician brain drain', *New England Journal of Medicine*, 353: 1810–18.

Nestel, S. (2006) *Obstructed Labour: Race and Gender in the Re-Emergence of Midwifery*. Vancouver, BC: University of British Columbia Press.

Packer, C., Labonté, R. and Spitzer, D. (2008) *Globalization and Health Worker Migration*. Globalization Knowledge Network. World Health Organization Commission on the Social Determinants of Health. Online: http://www.globalhealthequity.ca/electronic%20library/Globalization%20and%20Health%20Worker%20Crisis.pdf

Spencer, S., Martin, S., Bourgeault, I.L. and O'Shea, E. (2010) *The Role of Migrant Care Workers in Ageing Societies: Report on Research Findings in the UK, Ireland, the US and Canada*. IOM Migration Research Series No. 41. Online: http://publications.iom.int/bookstore/free/MRS41.pdf

World Health Organization (WHO) (2006) *Working Together for Health: 2006 World Health Report*. Geneva: WHO.

Yeates, N. (2004) 'A dialogue with "global care chain" analysis: nurse migration in the Irish context', *Feminist Review*, 77: 79–95.

Ivy Lynn Bourgeault

Complementary and Alternative Medicine

Complementary and alternative medicine (CAM) refers to a broad set of theories and practices distinct from those of biomedicine and allied therapies.

Complementary and alternative medicine (CAM) is a form of medicine that is commonly juxtaposed with biomedicine. The introduction of the 1858 Medical Registration Act in England defined and regulated the diversity of ideas and practices that formed the basis for scientific medicine. The Act established a General Council of Medical Registration and Education (the GMC), distinguished qualified from unqualified practitioners, and provided the former with legal rights and duties. Mesmerism, spiritualism and other therapeutic approaches, as well as a vast range of 'cures' and patent medicines that competed for the public's attention, were now grouped together and collectively denigrated as 'quackeries'. Long-held beliefs about health and illness and associated treatments were marginalized and depicted as irrational and anti-modern. In effect, only biomedical doctors could now claim to follow scientific methods.

During the nineteenth century an epistemological divide was established between biomedicine and CAM. To put it simply, biomedicine conceptualizes pathology in relation to the individual body and disease as a result of internal or external factors that may be located and understood. In contrast, CAM approaches take a holistic view of the body and illness is considered to emanate from disturbances in some combination of the psychological, spiritual and social environment (Ernst et al., 2008). CAM therapies typically involve utilizing the body's capacity for self-repair and recognizing the need to restore balance, rather than addressing a disease process or preventing particular symptoms from developing. Note that this brief history of CAM is situated within the emergence of biomedicine in the West. Since 1858 there has been a struggle between scientific medicine and CAM to establish the boundaries around medicine and the therapies that are taught, studied and practised in university medical schools, with CAM generally being on the losing side. However, CAM is a culturally-based concept and so it should be remembered that different cultures have differing notions of what is 'conventional' medicine.

There is a degree of ambiguity built into CAM as a category because it covers a wide range of beliefs and practices where the only shared characteristic involves an unfavourable comparison with biomedicine. Indeed, while CAM has become a ubiquitous term it includes two rather different approaches. Complementary medicine generally refers to interventions that may be used in conjunction with biomedical treatments; for example, yoga may be included in a conventional course of treatment provided by a medical practitioner. This has given rise to what is known as 'integrative medicine' whereby selective CAM therapies are incorporated with conventional care. Thus, within Britain's NHS, techniques from acupuncture may be used for pain relief. However, critics would argue that conventional medicine dominates such arrangements and that there is a loss of the essential features of CAM approaches. Those therapeutic approaches that cannot be successfully followed at the same time as medical treatment constitute alternative medicine. Alternative medicine is held by orthodox clinicians to pose a threat to patients' adherence to biomedical treatment. However, CAM users may not report CAM use to their doctor.

Drawing on the sociological literature about professions, the relationship between CAM and biomedicine can be seen as part of an ongoing economic, political and cultural struggle by the medical profession to maintain a legally guaranteed occupational monopoly (Saks, 2003). Evidence-based medicine (EBM) gate-keeps professional legitimacy and this largely excludes CAM practitioners and their holistic approach to health. However, various CAM practitioners have gained a degree of recognition, including professional status and state regulation with the attendant authorized training and statutory bodies. The achievement of professional status is the result of being willing to reorient towards the scientific paradigm and increased specialization that are rejected by some advocates of CAM (Cant and Sharma, 1999). Professional status creates the possibility for therapies to be provided under national health care systems such as the NHS (Report of the House of Lords Select Committee on Science and Technology, 2000). In the UK and USA osteopaths, chiropractors, naturopaths, acupuncturists and homeopaths have a recognized legal status. For example, in the UK the General Osteopathic Council and General Chiropractic Council were established in the 1990s and, as with the General Medical Council, both maintain a register of practitioners and hold disciplinary hearings. However, professionalization strategies with the attendant regulation and standardization of CAM education and practice may restrain the scope of practice for traditional CAM practitioners. Homoeopathy has been part of the NHS since its inception, although the public funding of this therapy has been challenged in recent times due to a lack of clear outcomes from systematic reviews of the EBM research. In particular, it is difficult to separate a homoeopathic intervention from that of a placebo in clinical studies, thereby raising doubts about the effectiveness of the whole approach. The risk for CAM practitioners and their therapeutic approach is that failing to demonstrate the clear benefits and doubts about the veracity of a treatment, from an EBM standpoint, provides the basis for removing public funding and recognition. Yet such challenges are unlikely to diminish the public's enthusiasm for CAM and the diversity of products and practices that promise to maintain health and alleviate symptoms.

Part of the history of medicine includes the spread of biomedicine in colonial times and more recently as a result of the globalizing power of capitalism. The consequent marginalization of local cultures and practices included long-established belief systems about health and illness. Indeed, sociologists and anthropologists will sometimes make a distinction between CAM and traditional or folk medicine. This once again reveals the somewhat ethnocentric nature of the way CAM is defined in that it is conceptualized in relation to Western-based medicine. Such a stance ignores the possibility that CAM is a culturally-based concept and, as stated above, different cultures have differing notions of what is 'conventional'. In some countries, traditional medical practitioners are more accessible for large sections of the population than medical doctors and the attendant apparatus of scientific medicine. Traditional medical systems have been developed over thousands of years and are grounded in culture-bound understandings of what it is to be human, people's relationship with the natural environment and spirituality.

While some traditional approaches have been lost, others, such as the Indian medical Ayurveda and Traditional Chinese Medicine (TCM), are widely used today. TCM is based on the concepts of yin and yang and of Qi energy. Treatment may involve the use of herbal remedies, acupuncture, acupressure and massage. Herbs are credited with qualities such as 'cooling' (yin) or 'stimulating' (yang) and are used, usually in combination, according to the perceived deficiencies or excesses of these qualities in the patient. In China biomedicine is often practised alongside TCM and most public general hospitals have traditional medicine departments. Plant-based medicines, meditation, massage and yoga form part of Ayurveda treatments. Developed in India, Ayurveda is a Sanskrit word that when translated means 'practices of longevity'; it emphasizes a healthy lifestyle and the rejuvenation of the body and mind. In India Ayurvedic practitioners may be trained together with students of Western medicine. This co-existence of differing medical theories and practice has been referred to as 'medical pluralism'. The increased popularity of CAM approaches amongst consumers who have access to biomedical health care has been seen to mark a 'new medical pluralism' (Cant and Sharma, 1999).

Consumer demand for CAM therapies has been increasing in countries where biomedicine dominates the health care system. Many CAM approaches resonate with increased public scepticism about science and the commodification of health that equates healthy bodies and lifestyles with material success and ontological security. Acupuncture, chiropractic, herbalism, homoeopathy, hypnotherapy, spiritual healing and osteopathy are among the most popular CAM therapies used by consumers in the West. Like conventional medicine, more women than men use CAM and they are more likely to come from higher socio-economic groups. Consumers typically seek alleviation from musculo-skeletal symptoms as well as advice about allergy problems, neurological and psychological issues. A desire to maintain a high level of bodily and psychological wellness, as well as addressing problems that are not easy to diagnose conventionally (for example, lack of energy), may result in self-diagnosis and the use of CAM products.

In an era characterized by life planning, risk and reflexivity, the holistic and spiritual nature of CAM approaches may provide many people with an answer to the question, 'how shall I live?' (Giddens, 1991: 14). The self-surveillance and restraint that are part of many CAM therapies are congruent with the contemporary discourse about self-responsibility and self-fulfilment. It is in this context that CAM has been linked to a postmodern turn, comprising an emphasis on authenticity, the consumption of the 'natural', and a willingness to challenge medical expertise (Tovey et al., 2007). At the same time, an investment in CAM therapy is not discordant with putting trust in the doctor–patient relationship and the apparatus of biomedical science (2007).

Indeed, many individuals draw on a plurality of practices in order to foster well-being, maintain health, and address illness. This, in itself, could also be related to postmodern selfhood, defined as a 'pastiche' that borrows from diverse sources and traditions.

CAM continues to be of interest to medical sociologists. Recent work has, for example, examined wellness and CAM use (Sointu, 2006), the relationship between CAM and biomedicine (Hirschkorn, 2006), and how CAM comprises forms of 'body work' (for example, in the context of homeopathy and osteopathy, where bodies are relational, communicative and tactile) (Gale, 2011). In exploring CAM, researchers are drawing on and expanding the heritage of sociological theory and research, including an interest in the power relationship between CAM and biomedical approaches and practitioners and the behaviour of consumers in an era of increasing scepticism about scientific expertise. Future research needs to address the impact of the economic constraints on CAM provision within centrally organized health care systems, the role of CAM within aging populations, the embodiment of CAM in body-oriented societies, and the place of CAM within new diagnostic and treatment regimes such as regenerative medicine and pharmacogenetics.

See also: *Medical Model; Trust in Medicine; Consumerism*

REFERENCES

Cant, S.L. and Sharma, U. (1999) *A New Medical Pluralism? Alternative Medicine, Doctors, Patients and the State*. London: Routledge.

Ernst, E., Pittler, M., Wider, B. and Boddy, K. (2008) *Oxford Handbook of Complementary Medicine*. Oxford: Oxford University Press.

Gale, N.K. (2011) 'From body-talk to body-stories: body work in complementary and alternative medicine', *Sociology of Health & Illness*, 33 (2): 237–51.

Giddens, A. (1991) *Modernity and Self-Identity: Self and Society in the Late Modern Age*. Cambridge: Polity Press.

Hirschkorn, A.H. (2006) 'Exclusive versus everyday forms of professional knowledge: legitimacy claims in conventional and alternative medicine', *Sociology of Health & Illness*, 28 (5): 533–57.

Report of the House of Lords Select Committee on Science and Technology (November 2000) Session 1999–2000: HL paper 123. London: The Stationery Office.

Saks, M. (2003) *Orthodox and Alternative Medicine: Politics, Professionalisation and Health Care*. London: Sage.

Sointu, E. (2006) 'The search for wellbeing in alternative and complementary health practices', *Sociology of Health and Illness*, 28 (3): 330–49.

Tovey, P., Chatwin, J. and Broom, A. (2007) *Traditional, Complementary and Alternative Medicine and Cancer Care*. New York: Routledge.

Michael Hardey

Emotional labour is the induction or suppression of feeling in order to sustain an outward appearance that produces an emotion in others. This kind of labour is controlled by employers and can be seen as a commodity that has an exchange value, even though it draws on a deep sense of self that is integral to the individual.

The concept of emotional labour was first developed by the American sociologist Arlie Russell Hochschild (1983). She was interested in how emotion was used as a commercial commodity to sell products, images and organizations. She drew on the work of Goffman, Dewey, Gerth, C. Wright Mills, Freud and Darwin to create a bio-psycho-social interactionist approach towards emotion and how it was managed. She suggested that in the private sphere individuals learn through socialization how to manage their emotions based on feeling rules. Feeling rules are moral social values that act as internal and external constraints on what emotions should be displayed and exchanged in differing social situations – for example, it is acceptable to laugh at a party and cry at a funeral irrespective of one's actual feelings. Hochschild termed this 'emotion work' (a term she used interchangeably with 'emotion management'), because the management of emotions takes work to achieve.

Socially appropriate emotions are displayed through surface or deep acting. Surface acting is where an individual pretends to feel an emotion they do not really feel – for instance, displaying humour and laughing at a joke they do not actually find funny, for the benefit of the social group. In deep acting, the individual draws on feelings they have learnt through their emotion memory or imagination to generate feelings that they believe they really do feel – for example, by remembering what it felt like when one fell over, it is possible to generate a feeling of sympathy for a friend who has just done the same.

Hochschild argued that private emotion work is exploited in the workplace, where it undergoes transmutation into emotional labour, a saleable commodity that is subject to the supply and demand of market forces. Emotional labour therefore is sold for a wage and has exchange value. Drawing on empirical data on the emotional labour of flight attendants, Hochschild suggested that commercial companies train their workers in what emotions are appropriate to display and what are not. Their emotional labour requires them to 'induce or suppress feeling in order to sustain the outward countenance that produces the proper state of mind in others' (1983: 7). This proper state of mind in others is used to deliver the product the company is selling. In the case of the flight industry this has traditionally been a pleasant, predictable and efficient travel experience that encourages contented customers to re-use an airline. Irrespective of their actual feelings, therefore, flight attendants are not allowed to display anger, frustration or anxiety towards customers, and are instead expected to display geniality and hospitality. The flight attendants' emotional labour is taught and monitored by the company. However, with the arrival of budget airlines and the expansion of the flight industry, 'speed up' has occurred in service delivery. With a massive increase in passenger numbers, the time and consideration spent on emotional labour has been significantly reduced. As a consequence, emotional labour has become less valuable to the company, although flight attendants are still expected to carry it out. This has resulted in them experiencing emotional inauthenticity and ultimately an alienation of the self.

Unsurprisingly, emotional labour has been applied to the health and social care professions, and in particular nursing. Smith (2012) argues that like Hochschild's flight attendants, potential nurse applicants are screened for their nurturing and caring personality, and are then carefully taught the principles of emotional labour as applied to nursing care. This is then monitored as they develop as professional carers. As with Hochschild's flight attendants, therefore, nurses have to display a caring attitude even towards difficult and rude patients. However, the application of emotional labour to the caring professions is not straightforward. Bolton (2000: 584) argues that emotional labour in nursing is in fact emotion work (pertaining to the private sphere) and not labour (which is controlled by employers for commercial gain) because it is offered as a gift: 'the emotion work nurses offer to patients is given with little or no expectation of a return on their investment'. As a gift, emotion work can be given freely or not at all – this suggests that emotion work is not an integral component of nursing care. Arguably, this is to misunderstand the reciprocal exchange of emotion that takes place in the giving of care and receiving of thanks between nurses, patients, and their relatives. Seeing emotion work as a gift also fails to acknowledge that patients need such care because they are sick and vulnerable; they have no choice but to trust those who care for them and effectively have power over them. By acknowledging emotional labour as a component of nursing practice, nurses are rightly made accountable for that care (Theodosius, 2008). Seeing emotion work as a 'gift' also does not take into account that nursing care in the US healthcare system is highly commercialized, with emotional labour being demanded by patients as a commodity to which they have a right (Bone, 2002).

The application of emotional labour to nursing is also important because it challenges the assumption that nurses are naturally predisposed towards caring. As Smith (2012) points out, care and caring are not innate; rather, nurses need to learn how to care, and how to manage both their own and others' emotions. Equally, the application of emotional labour challenges gendered emotion connotations that depict predominantly female nurses as naturally caring and rewarded with satisfying jobs. Instead, the concept of emotional labour suggests that the ability to care is both taught and hard work, and should therefore be recognized as such both financially and professionally (Smith, 2012).

The gendered nature of emotion as the antithesis of reason or science – considered as masculine concepts and therefore desirable – is, however, problematic within a broader division of labour where predominantly female or feminized nursing staff are subordinated to masculine medical practice. Under such conditions, acknowledging emotional labour as central to nursing practice may compromise nurses' professional standing and might be seen to weaken the status of the nursing profession's knowledge base. Unsurprisingly, perhaps, the low status attached to emotional labour is accepted inside the profession just as it has been outside of it. For example, whilst first year student nurses highly valued emotional labour as a component of nursing care, by their third year it was given less status in comparison to clinical nursing skills (Smith, 2012). Emotional labour is primarily linked to basic 'hands on' care, now predominantly the province of health care assistants as a result of the increased 'professionalization' of nursing. Consequently emotional labour has become separated from nursing's medically-based clinical skills, and accorded a lower status value, reinforcing the feminized nature of care in a rationalized field that comprises gendered power relations. Despite acknowledging emotional labour, therefore, it is still reduced to the status of 'women's work' (Guy and Newman, 2004). This renders emotional labour largely invisible or not considered as real work in contrast to 'the heroic work' of curative medicine or the knowledge-based work of professionalized nursing.

It is important to recognize, however, that whilst some may no longer see emotional labour as real work, patients/clients and their relatives still expect nurses to perform it and will often demand it from them as a right. Emotional labour thus becomes visible again when it is not performed (Bone, 2002), because it results in an increased number of complaints from patients and their relatives. Increased complaints are linked to a shift from a paternalistic culture to a consumer one. As in the USA, emotional labour in the UK is becoming subject to the 'culture of the consumer' (Bolton and Boyd, 2003), which gives patients greater power over nurses who are now vulnerable to their complaints. This power has left many nurses who do still value emotional care feeling cautious, and less willing to give freely of themselves in their emotional labour with patients (Theodosius, 2008).

Similarities over the effect of speed-up in the airline industry on Hochschild's flight attendants have also been found in nursing. James (1992: 503) argues that the volume and pace of nursing can compromise the nurse's ability to give emotional labour because it 'takes time and requires considerable knowledge of the patient as a person'. She suggests that emotional labour requires the organizational structure to be flexible. However, with the increase in the pace and volume of work, tensions occur between 'organisational priorities and organising individual patient care' (James, 1992: 495). In fact, nursing care has become increasingly pressured, with too few resources and an increased workload, and an emphasis on ever greater efficiency and physical, clinical-based skills. More worryingly, many nurses prioritize patients' physical care needs over emotional ones to the extent of actively ignoring emotion cues from their patients, in order to accomplish their physical and technical tasks within the given time frame (Brunton, 2005).

Similar to Hochschild's flight attendants, then, emotional labour within nursing is not a neutral process. The combination of a lack of status accorded to emotional labour with increased consumer demand for it, at a time when the pace and workload of nursing care have intensified, has heightened concerns about the vulnerability of health care professionals to inauthenticity of self, alienation, stress and burnout (Mann, 2005). Recently, Erickson (2009) found a direct link between stress and burnout and emotional labour, particularly among younger nurses with less experience in dealing with their own and other people's emotions. Emotional labour has also been linked to job dissatisfaction both in the UK and the USA where it has led to increased retention problems; in the USA, job dissatisfaction among nurses is as high as 40 per cent in comparison to 15 per cent of workers in the general population (Erickson, 2009). Whilst emotional labour remains controversial in terms of its status and benefit to patients, the problem of retention arguably arises as many choose the profession because they are motivated to give emotional care, and then find that such care is devalued during training.

In an attempt to get to the crux of this paradox, Theodosius (2008) argues that emotional labour needs to be taught and practised in such a way that nurses can give freely without fear of exposing their private self, and can respond to changes in the division of labour and the shift towards more consumer-orientated patients without neglecting their patients' physical and clinical needs. To do this, how nurses draw on their sense of personal identity in their emotional labour needs to be facilitated and constantly developed. In addition, the various ways in which nurses carry out emotional labour need to be defined and linked more specifically to their nursing roles. Thus, Theodosius has developed a typology of emotional labour that connects its purpose in nursing practice to the relationships nurses form with their patients and how they draw on their sense of self in the process. She defines *therapeutic emotional labour* as pertaining to the patient's/relatives' emotional and psychological well-being and connected to the nurse's sense of self-worth; *instrumental emotional labour* as pertaining to the patient's physical well-being, and connected to the nurse's self-worth and practical competency; and *collegial emotional labour* as pertaining to emotion interactions between health care professionals for the purpose of carrying out patient/client/relative health care needs, which is related to the nurse's self-worth and their place in the social organization.

Hochschild's notion of emotional labour, therefore, can still be seen to be relevant to health care and particularly to nursing. It highlights typical sociological concerns with power, social stratification (such as gender and the division of labour), and personal and social identity. Research on emotional labour, however, still needs to challenge the 'predominant organisation of health care as an institution governed by a masculine model of professionalism and the medical model of detached care' (Erickson and Grove, 2008: 722). It is, therefore, a dynamic concept, which is still developing in response to significant challenges, findings and needs, yet it is also one that is relevant to nursing within different health systems across the globe.

See also: *Nursing and Midwifery as Occupations; Consumerism; Malpractice*

REFERENCES

Bolton, S. (2000) 'Who cares? Offering emotion work as a "gift" in the nursing labour process', *Journal of Advanced Nursing*, 32 (3): 580–6.

Bolton, S. and Boyd, C. (2003) 'Trolley dolly or skilled emotion manager? Moving on from Hochschild's Managed Heart', *Work, Employment and Society*, 17 (2): 289–308.

Bone, D. (2002) 'Dilemmas of emotion work in nursing under market-driven health care', *International Journal of Public Sector Management*, 15 (2): 140–50.

Brunton, M. (2005) 'Emotion in health care: the cost of caring', *Journal of Health Organisation and Management*, 19: 340–54.

Erickson, R. (2009) 'The emotional demands of nursing', in G. Dickson and L. Flynn (eds), *Nursing Policy Research: Turning Evidenced Based Research into Health Policy*. New York: Springer.

Erickson, R. and Grove, W. (2008) 'Emotional labour and health care', *Sociology Compass*, 2 (2): 704–33.

Guy, M. and Newman, M. (2004) 'Women's jobs, men's jobs: sex segregation and emotional labour', *Public Administration Review*, 64: 289–98.

Hochschild, A. (1983) *The Managed Heart*. Berkeley: University of California Press.

James, N. (1992) 'Care = organisation + physical labour + emotional labour', *Sociology of Health & Illness*, 14 (4): 488–509.

Mann, S. (2005) 'A health-care model of emotional labour', *Journal of Health Organization and Management*, 19: 304–17.

Smith, P. (2012) *The Emotional Labour of Nursing Revisited: Can Nurses Still Care?* Houndsmill: Palgrave Macmillan.

Theodosius, C. (2008) *Emotional Labour in Health Care: The Unmanaged Heart of Nursing*. London: Routledge.

Catherine Theodosius

Informal Care

> *Informal care is given by one person, such as a family member (child or adult), friend or neighbour, on a regular basis to another person without financial payment, though such care does incur (in)visible costs.*

Care is a social relational activity. It is also basic to the preservation of human life, which entails interdependency and vulnerability. The varying capacity of individuals to respond in a caring way towards others, alongside how this work is divided in society, is very much shaped by social and cultural factors. Social constructionist arguments highlight how ideology influences cultural meanings of the value of care and associated need through discourse and social practices; for example, in relation to older or disabled people.

Informal care is distinguished from formal care in that the latter is paid and the former is unpaid. Discussions about informal care evoke a multitude of meanings and practices, explored in a growing body of research. Pertinent themes include the personal qualities of caring *about* someone, physical tasks and duties and the organization of these in the direct engagement of caring *for* someone, modified by the degree of availability and sense of responsibility (Tronto, 1993). As Noddings

(2006) explains, emotional work is important here. It entails empathizing and managing one's own feelings and those of others, alongside changing patterns of demand relating to dependence and independence, as individuals move through the lifecourse, and become ill or disabled. Other contributors flag the political and policy meanings which focus on the role of the state in determining care relations, their gendered character, and the boundaries between the private and public spheres in relation to caring (Daly and Rake, 2003).

As an activity that is inseparable from the privacy of the body, and bodily functions, 'care work' risks being undervalued as 'dirty work' (Fine, 2007). And yet care is also enmeshed with gendered ideologies and configurations of practice, which provide an aura of respectability to caring. The mother/child relationship is typically seen as the blueprint for caring relationships – one that is often idealized but, one might add, also vilified as the cause of personality and behavioural problems in adult life when it does not go well. As an extension of this, women are traditionally/stereotypically seen as being more suited to caring than men (essentialists see caring as part of a woman's natural abilities). This view extends to both the privacy of the family home and more formally and publicly to the paid care sector or the 'caring' professions – exemplified by the nursing profession and the image of the female nurse as a self-sacrificing angel.

Informal care is often socially constructed as a normal and natural activity in the context of family relationships and filial obligations, particularly for women as wives, mothers and daughters. In the West, such thinking has a well-documented history and economic logic. It developed following the Industrial Revolution to avoid interrupting the paid employment of men who found themselves increasingly working outside of the home. The traditional image of a heterosexual marriage within which the woman assumes the duties of care for all family members has since underpinned conservative social policy within Western-style neoliberal capitalist economies. Here the state relies heavily on women to provide the care for dependent members of society, though this division is not absolute. Research and policy in recent years have recognized the increasing significance of men in caring as fathers (see, for example, O'Brien, 2005) and as older spouses looking after their more frail elderly partners (see, for example, Kramer and Thompson, 2002). That said, Hanlon (2009: 197) has reported that masculinities still firmly incorporate breadwinning as the 'dominant referent for men's caregiving'. Hegemonic masculinities thus continue to support the gender inequality in caregiving, reinforcing the moral responsibility for informal care as integrally female and private, and allowing men to legitimately fulfil their care obligations in the workplace based on 'economic achievement, power and public status'.

Informal carers provide the major part of caring in the community and are a significant 'stakeholder' group within the delivery of care. Informal care now has a distinct place in the welfare policy context of most European countries, including the UK where it has received formal legal recognition from the state over the last two decades. Western neoliberal governments in recent years have sought to champion the dedication of informal carers, viewing them as an important resource for the state alongside professionals, and this approach is reflected in policy developments and government literature.

Feminism has significantly shaped debates around informal care. The main critiques of informal care start with feminist writings in the 1960s and 1970s (see, for example, Land, 1978). These writings pinpointed gender as a key determinant in understanding the complex relationship between wider societal expectations, values and domestic family life with its dynamics of servicing and caring. Feminist critiques exposed the unpaid and undervalued care work performed by millions of women in silent support of the male breadwinner as an essential but financially unrewarded component within the organization of capitalism. Much work arising out of the Women's Movement highlighted how women become trapped in positions which require self-sacrifice, often in the long term, along with the many (in)visible costs associated with informal caring. Carers can experience emotional difficulties, financial problems, isolation and social exclusion, physical exhaustion, undervaluing of their efforts, and a disrupted lifestyle with missed life chances and career interruptions. Of course, there are also positive aspects: informal carers may experience satisfaction and fulfilment from the experience of doing something for another person within a caring relationship. Such positive dimensions may assume centre stage in popular representations: in recent times the image of the 'superwoman' has emerged which hails women as heroines who juggle caring and a career, either with or without a partner. Critically, however, such constructions should not be taken at face value. They may further burden women as they struggle to fulfil multiple demands as part of a perceived 'labour of love'.

In the 1980s, the focus of the feminist critique shifted towards an interest in the wider aspects of caring being undertaken by women. Drawing on work which emphasized the exploitative nature of women's unpaid work as carers, feminists mounted a challenge to the emerging community care policies (Finch and Groves, 1980). They took issue with policy makers' 'obvious' reliance on a pool of 'free' labour and instead pointed to the reality of a government reliance on 'family care' as opposed to the rhetoric of 'care in the community'. In line with this critique, they distinguished between biological and social reproduction in order to highlight how women would become 'normalized' into servicing and caring for dependent others within kinship networks. This literature also suggested that these expectations of women's roles were not accidental. Rather, women's roles were viewed by policy makers as a key contribution to keeping down the costs of care in the community. This expectation is reinforced in times of recession. During such times, welfare spending is reduced or threatened alongside women's citizenship rights and limited economic independence (Dalley, 1996).

Gender has not been the only social division that has attracted critical attention. Debates deepened, for example, with the involvement of the Disability Movement. Morris (1997), from both a feminist and a Disability Movement perspective, has contributed to such debates. She took issue with those feminists who, in their struggle to challenge and improve community care services, rigidly split user and carer interests into a false dichotomy. In this dichotomy, carers were distinguished as active contributors and citizens, in contrast to dependent service users who were deemed less valuable in a society that considered personal autonomy as key to its perception of adulthood. Others from the feminist disability lobby argued that mainstream feminists also frequently failed to include the voice of disabled people. Instead they portrayed those cared for as 'burdensome', thereby oppressing disabled people. In short, such portrayals reinforced constructions of disabled people as dependent and as problems for others. The nature of these debates around informal caring has thus become increasingly complex and contested, emphasizing the themes of interdependence and diversity in caring relationships and networks (for example, caring in same-sex relationships, caring within different cultural traditions, the role of young carers, and disabled parents and their caring roles).

Hochschild (2003) picks up on the characterization of care as a 'burden' when she refers to the 'cold', modern ideal of care, which includes collective responsibility for care through the provision of specialist institutions. She rejects the position of some feminist writers in the 1980s and 1990s who continued to champion these institutions as a solution to the restrictions that the conservative welfare policies placed on women carers. Hochschild's alternative vision is her 'warm modern' ideal of care. This vision promotes care as a valued social activity benefitting both the giver and receiver. Accordingly, in this vision care is embedded within the social fabric or structure (i.e. way of life and relationships between people), so as to involve both men and women in an activity that contributes to the well-being of society.

There is further consideration within feminist literature of the sense of social responsibility experienced by women as a result of their socialization into a female identity (a 'caring self' linked to virtue ethics). This critique has resulted in a feminist 'ethic of care' that is applicable to both men and women. Other writers on the ethic of care (see, for example, Tronto, 1993) attempt to bridge the gap between carer and cared for identified by the Disability Movement. Rather than independence as the basis of citizenship, these writers consider *interdependence* as the foundation for a caring relationship. This approach embraces difference, diversity and an awareness of the power relations between caregiver and care-receiver, from which notions of rights and citizenship can then be developed. Work in this area highlights how interdependence and reciprocity are at the root of all human interactions. Noddings (2006) eloquently posits the concept of an ethic of care as a prerequisite for an ethic of justice, in that sensitivity to the needs of others at a one-to-one level can then develop into a wider concern for tackling injustice and inequality.

More recent explorations of caring by social policy commentators have noted new influences on informal caring in families. These influences include changes in the economy and society that have impacted on family structures/relationships, the gendered division of labour alongside demographic factors, i.e. an ageing population with more complex care needs in later years. Economic changes, for instance, have forced more women into full-time employment, and the family unit has diversified from the nuclear family model (to include single-parent families, reconstituted and gay/lesbian partnerships). These changes have not necessarily lessened the demands on women, since those who work full-time still often continue to carry the main caring and domestic responsibilities, unless they can afford to employ usually low-paid female substitute carers from immigrant populations. This moves the discussion into the international arena. It highlights the global issue of poorly paid female migrant workers from developing countries who move to wealthier economies to work in low-paid private domestic, or public care sector, jobs in order to improve the work/life balance of women with disposable income in these countries. These 'global care chains' create care deficits in poor countries as they solve care deficits in wealthy ones (Ehrenreich and Hochschild, 2003).

Informal care work still remains undervalued within welfare systems (Lewis, 2000). The relationship between the public and private worlds of caring in Western welfare regimes continues to be an area of tension. Governments have reluctantly addressed this hidden, private aspect of the economy through policy and legislation on informal care which has become more exposed as a result of economic challenges and demographic changes. Further, it would seem that there is a consistent and enduring gender inequality in that women continue to do the majority of informal (and formal) caregiving (Lynch et al., 2009). This enduring inequality is supported by and reproduced in Western cultural systems that place the primary responsibility for care firmly at the feet of women. Thus informal caring remains a social space which women are generally still expected to fill.

See also: *Gender; Nursing and Midwifery as Occupations; Emotional Labour*

REFERENCES

Daly, M. and Rake K. (2003) *Gender and the Welfare State: Care, Work and Welfare in Europe and the USA*. Cambridge: Polity Press.

Dalley, G. (1996) *Ideologies of Caring: Rethinking Community and Collectivism*, 2nd edn. London: Macmillan.

Ehrenreich, B. and Hochschild, A.R. (eds) (2003) *Global Woman: Nannies, Maids and Sex Workers in the New Economy*. London: Granta.

Finch, J. and Groves, D. (1980) 'Community care and the family: a case for equal opportunities', *Journal of Social Policy*, 9 (4): 487–514.

Fine, M. (2007) *A Caring Society? Care and the Dilemmas of Human Service in the 21st Century*. Basingstoke: Palgrave Macmillan.

Hanlon, I. (2009) 'Caregiving masculinities', in K. Lynch, B. Baker and M. Lyons (eds), *Affective Equality: Love, Care and Injustice*. Houndsmill: Palgrave Macmillan.

Hochschild, A.R. (2003) *The Commercialization of Intimate Life: Notes from Home and Work*. Berkeley: University of California Press.

Kramer, B.J. and Thompson, P.H. (2002) *Men as Caregivers: Theory, Research and Service Implications*. New York: Springer.

Land, H. (1978) 'Who cares for the family?' *Journal of Social Policy*, 7 (3): 357–84.

Lewis, J. (2000) 'Gender and welfare regimes', in G. Lewis, S. Gewirtz and J. Clarke (eds), *Rethinking Social Policy*. London: Sage.

Lynch, K., Baker, B. and Lyons, M. (eds) (2009) *Affective Equality: Love, Care and Injustice*. Houndsmill: Palgrave Macmillan.

Morris, J. (1997) 'Care or empowerment? A disability rights perspective', *Social Policy and Administration*, 31 (1): 54–60.

Noddings, N. (2006) *Starting at Home: Caring and Social Policy*. Berkeley: University of California Press.

O'Brien, M. (2005) *Shared Caring: Bringing Fathers into the Frame*. Working Paper Series No.18. London: Equal Opportunities Commission/UEA.

Tronto, J. (1993) *Moral Boundaries: A Political Argument for an Ethic of Care*. London: Routledge.

Sue Hollinrake

health work and the
division of labour

188

Part 5

Health Care Organization and Policy

Hospitals and Health Care Organizations

> Hospitals and health care organizations refer to institutions that provide professional medical services.

From a socio-historical perspective, the doctor–patient relationship, or medical consultation, has been considered a form of health care organization. In his structural functionalist analyses of medical practice in mid-twentieth century USA, Parsons viewed the medical encounter and the regulation of illness as key to the smooth running of the social system, and within medical sociology the clinical consultation has for a long time represented a major topic. Going beyond consultations, the term 'health care system' signifies the wider organization of health care services for a given population. Such systems differ between nations with regard to organizing and financing and they may share unclear boundaries with other service providers. The organization of health care systems has significant implications for the role, staffing and organization of hospitals and other health care services. Historical observations in Europe are illustrative. In its early medieval version, the hospital was a 'shelter' and caring organization with religious orientations, staffed by nuns and monks. Its history as a formally institutionalized site for professional and scientifically-based medical work is relatively recent and closely connected to the development of sciences within modern universities.

The sociological interest in hospitals started in the 1950s. An early object of interest was the mental hospital. Goffman (1961) conducted a study of a traditional North American state mental hospital and categorized it under the wider concept of 'total institution'. Such institutions had total control of their inmates; control was their primary function and inmates or 'patients' stayed for an indeterminate length of time. To establish and preserve a personal identity or self following their hospital admission, patients engaged in informal and 'self-protecting' activities constituting what Goffman described as 'the underlife' of the total institution. To display a personal identity and resist the mortification of the self, patients sought to resist the full incorporation of the total institution; though this kind of 'deviant behaviour' might be interpreted as a sign of mental illness by the hospital staff. Because of critical studies like this, as well as changing psychiatric ideologies and economic considerations, the organization of psychiatric hospitals started to change during the 1960s in many Western countries.

These changes triggered several micro-sociological studies of psychiatric hospitals as organizations in the process of transformation. Strauss and his colleagues (Strauss et al., 1963) developed the concept of 'the negotiated order' from such studies. The concept refers to social organizations, not as products of formal structures and rules, as might be inferred from a Parsonian functionalist perspective, but as resulting from emergent processes of bargaining and negotiation between organizational members concerning the division of work and the adequacy and functions of institutional roles. Like Strauss et al. (1963), Roth also focused on negotiations in hospital settings, but not in psychiatric hospitals. Roth (1963) described social life in a tuberculosis hospital; he looked upon the organization of time in the hospital and focused on negotiation processes. Tuberculosis hospitals were organizations where patients spent a long and indeterminate amount of time. Patients would typically negotiate with staff members to come to an agreement about the date for discharge.

After the 1960s the sociological interest for hospital organizations gradually disappeared. What took over was an interest in medical work and the health care professions (for example, Strauss et al., 1985). Sharing affinities with Goffman's work, which was stimulated by pragmatism and symbolic interactionism, such studies concentrated on the treatment of chronic illnesses and the diversity of forms of medical work conducted in hospitals. Here researchers employed terms like 'illness trajectory' and 'work trajectory'. Thus, Strong (1979) wrote about 'the ceremonial order of the clinic', which referred to the routinized and ritual form of medical consultations, and the constitutive role formats that organizational members creatively employed. Later studies continued to focus on the ritual forms of medical activities, but also included and developed new theoretical approaches. Hirschauer (1991) emphasized the ceremonial, symbolic and constructive aspects of surgical work in hospitals. Anspach (1988) focused on the ritual characteristics of physicians' talk that secured a professional and institutional adequacy when conducting 'information work' in hospital settings. Similarly, Atkinson (1995) focused on the ritual character of medical talk in hospitals; more specifically he looked at hematologists' development of professional skills and their generation of a professional vision as collaboratively accomplished through talk.

A focus on the medical object as discursively generated and the production of medical knowledge has also been influenced by Foucault (1973), who wrote about the historical development of 'medical perception' as being fundamental for modern medical work. He has inspired sociological studies of medical knowledge and perception, and the social construction of medical problems. Such studies have also been influenced by recent work in the sociology of science and technology and various interactionist approaches. Talk and collaboration in hospital settings have received much attention recently from sociologists and various kinds of discourse analysts, including those from the humanities. The emphasis on medical team talk in the context of the medical problem-solving process has been part of this analysis. These studies are generally restricted to limited parts of the hospital and the activities accomplished there. They include studies of ward meetings (Måseide, 2006) or other specific activities, such as the work of anesthesiologists or surgeons (Hindmarsh and Pilnick, 2007). These ethnographic studies focus on the details of work, the forms of talk and the collaborative nature of medical work, as restricted parts of what Strauss et al. (1985) called 'the work trajectory'.

Taking a perspective from Actor Network Theory (ANT), material semiotics or material theory, Mol (2002) has focused on the nature of medical work in hospitals, the complexity of medical objects or problems, and how this complexity is managed in order to reach a singular medical problem that can be institutionally dealt with. Other studies of medical work in hospitals (see, for example, Berg, 1997) have shown the general need for and use of support systems to generate the routines, efficiency, standardization and institutional control to promote adequate medical work by the various professionals involved in complex problem-solving tasks. The reason why medical sociological studies of hospitals have largely been restricted to limited parts of the arc of medical work may be because of the increasing diversity and distribution of biomedical knowledge and competence, which again has affected the complexity of hospital organizations. In certain countries there is also the difficult issue of getting ethics board approval to do sociological research in hospital settings.

Regarding the issue of diversity and complexity, health care systems have changed considerably in recent years alongside the content and practice of medicine itself (Rose, 2007). Much of the problem-solving work conducted in hospitals requires collaboration between different medical specialists or experts and different professions. The use of sophisticated technological equipment is part of this collaborative process: it produces representations or images, of what might be called 'virtual patients', that replace the actual patient in medical problem solving. Information technology has also become an essential and integrated part of medical work in health care organizations. One area of sociological interest is, for instance, the development and use of electronic patient records and the consequences for clinical work. When studying activities in hospitals and other health care organizations, it is vital for sociological researchers to focus on the content and medical meaning of medical work. This necessitates adopting the actor's point of view and grounding sociological analyses in first-order descriptions. It also demands a minimal understanding of and knowledge about the medical issues and activities in question. A lack of such knowledge and understanding will restrict the sociological understanding of what is occurring.

For medical, economic and technological reasons, the hospital's position and functions within the health care system have changed in many countries: this is a process that Armstrong (1998) has characterized as 'the decline of the hospital'. More medical activities now take place outside the hospital or in out-patient clinics than was the case before. Patients are also discharged earlier from hospitals. In addition to the health care system becoming more complex, then, its functions are more widely distributed than before. This suggests that sociological attention needs to be paid to the relationship and collaboration between its diverse parts amidst changing hierarchical power relations. Hospitals were once sites or organizations characterized by a professional medical dominance. However, this has changed in many countries with the development or introduction of what is termed 'new managerialism'. Studies from various countries indicate that medical doctors do not have the same authority within the health service organization as before. Not only do they have to share power with other health professions, but they are also under the governance of a management system that represents the owners of the health service organization and takes care of those owners' interests. The managers' duty is not only to improve the medical services of the hospital, they are also responsible for the hospital's financial situation. The economy of the hospital may be increasingly constrained under conditions of neoliberalism and associated cuts to public welfare spending by governments in many countries. This means that medical and economic interests may be conflicting. The new managerialism has introduced several systems to guide and control the medical work conducted on hospital wards. An important topic for sociological research will be to study the implementation of managerial control systems and other general 'support systems' by medical practitioners who are involved in the kind of practical medical problem solving that implies their direct contact with the patient. Finally, sociologists in the past decade have focused on patients' role as the consumers of health care services (Henderson and Petersen, 2002) and on the importance of patient empowerment to allow them to regain control of their bodies, health and health problems. This, of course, demands critical research and analysis as part of a sociology *of*, rather than simply *for*, health care and organizations.

See also: *The Sick Role; Managerialism; Consumerism*

REFERENCES

Anspach, R. (1988) 'Notes on the sociology of medical discourse: the language of case presentation', *Journal of Health and Social Behavior*, 29: 357–75.

Armstrong, D. (1998) 'Decline of the hospital: reconstructing institutional dangers', *Sociology of Health & Illness*, 20: 445–57.

Atkinson, P. (1995) *Medical Talk and Medical Work*. London: Sage.

Berg, M. (1997) *Rationalizing Medical Work*. Cambridge, MA: The MIT Press.

Foucault, M. (1973) *The Birth of the Clinic*. London: Tavistock.

Goffman, E. (1961) *Asylums*. Harmondsworth: Penguin.

Henderson, S. and Petersen, A. (2002) *Consuming Health: The Commodification of Health Care*. London: Routledge.

Hindmarsh, J. and Pilnick, A. (2007) 'Knowing bodies at work: embodiment and the ephemeral teamwork in anaesthesia', *Organization Studies*, 28: 1395–416.

Hirschauer, S. (1991) 'The manufacture of bodies in surgery', *Social Studies in Science*, 21: 279–319.

Måseide, P. (2006) 'The deep play of medicine: discursive and collaborative processing of evidence in medical problem solving', *Communication & Medicine*, 3: 43–54.

Mol, A. (2002) *The Body Multiple*. Durham, MD: Duke University Press.

Rose, N. (2007) *The Politics of Life Itself*. Princeton, NJ: Princeton University Press.

Roth, J.A. (1963) *Timetables: Structuring the Passage of Time in Hospital Treatment and Other Careers*. Indianapolis, IN: Bobbs-Merrill.

Strauss, A., Fagerhaugh, S., Suczek, B. and Wiener, C. (1985) *Social Organization of Medical Work*. Chicago: University of Chicago Press.

Strauss, A., Schatzman, L., Ehrlich, D., Bucher, R. and Sabshin, M. (1963) 'The hospital and its negotiated order', in E. Freidson (ed.), *The Hospital in Modern Society*. New York: The Free Press.

Strong, P. (1979) *The Ceremonial Order of the Clinic*. London: Routledge.

Per Måseide

Privatization

> Privatization refers to a set of policies that aim to limit the role of public sector health care, increase the role of the private sector, while improving the performance of the remaining public sector.

The health service in Britain, like those of other developed countries, has long been pluralist in the sense that publicly funded (through taxation) and privately funded (through payment for a service in person or by private health insurance) health care have co-existed. However, health care reforms from the 1980s onwards have shifted the balance profoundly in favour of greater private sector involvement. Below we consider the strategies employed to achieve this and the reasons for doing so, with particular reference to the private acute sector. The consequences of such restructuring for the NHS and the principles on which it was founded will also be considered. As we will see, since political devolution in 1999, the shift in the balance between public and private has been much more marked in England than elsewhere in the UK.

One strategy for shifting the balance between the public and private sector has involved the development of policies to encourage the growth of the private sector. In the 1980s planning controls were relaxed on the development of private hospitals and the power of local authorities to object to such developments was curtailed. In addition, NHS consultants' contracts were revised to enable them to undertake more private practice in addition to their NHS commitments, and tax changes were introduced to encourage higher levels of private health cover. Together these changes created the climate for private hospital development and provided opportunities that were fully exploited by the private sector. Between 1980 and 2001 the number of private hospitals increased by 35 per cent and the number of private beds by 40 per cent. Many of these hospitals were located in the prosperous southeast of England, compounding rather than eliminating geographical inequalities in the distribution of resources. At the same time, the level of private health insurance increased from 5 per cent of the population in 1979 to a peak of 13 per cent in 1989, with company-purchased schemes being particularly popular (Calnan et al., 1993). In 2003 around 11 per cent of the population was covered by private health insurance (Humphrey and Russell, 2001), but numbers have declined further since then, with media reports of a record slump in 2009 as a result of the economic downturn. While Labour were in power between 1997 and 2010, there were no tax deductions for private insurance but this may change with the election of the Coalition government (Harley et al., 2011). Traditionally coverage has been concentrated in London and the south-east of England with policy holders tending to have professional and managerial jobs and to be male, though roughly equal numbers of both sexes are actually covered (Foubister et al., 2006).

A further strategy to shift the balance between the public and private sectors has involved the introduction of reforms that have facilitated greater collaboration between the two sectors. An early attempt was the Conservative government's policy of requiring NHS District Health Authorities to introduce competitive tendering for domestic, catering and laundry services in the 1980s. The intention was to challenge the monopoly of in-house providers of services on the assumption that costs would be reduced and greater 'value for money' would be achieved. In practice the financial benefits proved relatively modest, at least to start with, and the savings achieved were said to be at the expense of quality of service (Mohan, 1995). More recently, the NHS has been encouraged to contract outpatient care to the private sector. These co-operative arrangements were initially undertaken on a voluntary basis by individual Health Authorities (HAs) that did not have in-house alternatives, for example as a result of capacity constraints. Subsequently Conservative and Labour governments have used private hospitals as a way of reducing NHS waiting lists for non-urgent cases and those waiting more than a year. For instance, in 2000 Labour instituted a 'concordat' between the NHS in England and the private sector in order to allow patients to be treated at NHS expense in the private sector when there was no spare room in NHS hospitals. Labour also introduced Independent Treatment Centres as a way to expand private sector involvement in routine NHS work and allowed Primary Care Trusts to award contracts to private companies in addition to GPs. The present Coalition government has built on the latter policy in the Health and Social Care Act (2012) by allowing Clinical Commissioning Groups (in place of Primary Care Trusts) to contract with 'any qualified provider' (AQP), including private and third sector organizations as well as public sector bodies. The decision to introduce contracts to alternative providers is based on the assumption that this diversification of providers will result in improved efficiency through market competition (Pollock and Price, 2011).

Another example of collaboration has been the development of the Private Finance Initiative (PFI). Launched by the Conservatives in the early 1990s and subsequently continued by Labour and now the Coalition government, the aim has been to encourage private capital investment in the NHS, thereby increasing overall resources in the service while avoiding raising taxes or increasing public borrowing. Much of the investment has been used to build new acute hospitals, with 101 of the 135 built in England between 1997 and 2009 being financed under this scheme (Pollock and Price, 2011). Under PFI private companies design, construct, own and operate services over a 25–30-year period in return for an annual fee. While clinical services remain the responsibility of government, PFI is seen as permitting an element of risk to be transferred to the private sector, as building cost overruns are picked up by the private sector. Arguably, it is a win-win situation as the NHS gets improved services while the private sector gains further opportunities to make a profit. Critics would argue, however, that there are serious disadvantages associated with PFI-funded projects, including: reduced bed numbers (substantially in excess of what would be expected from long-term demand trends); the need for a quicker throughput of patients; a significant reduction in spending on clinical staff, especially nurses; higher interest rate charges compared to the cost of government borrowing, thereby putting a severe strain on hospital Trust budgets; and the creation of substantial debt over time (Mohan, 2009).

The third strategy has been to encourage competition between the NHS and the private sector. This is best illustrated by the Conservative government's willingness to encourage the NHS to expand its pay-bed provision, thereby sharpening the competition for private patients and threatening the private providers' profit margins. Originally introduced when the NHS was established in 1948 as a concession to hospital consultants, pay-beds were in decline when the Conservatives came to power in 1979 and they continued to decline subsequently. In the late 1980s, however, the Conservatives decided to revitalize this provision in the face of increasingly severe financial constraints. The policy was also in line with their belief in generating competition between providers in order to enhance consumer choice and maximize efficiency. In 1988 it therefore used the Health and Medicines Act to relax the rules governing pay-bed charges so that hospitals could make a profit instead of simply covering costs. This propelled hospitals to upgrade their private wings or develop dedicated pay-bed units, as well as increasing the number of pay beds on NHS wards. Under Labour there was a strict cap on the number of private patients the NHS could treat. However, under the Coalition government this has been relaxed thus allowing the NHS in England to be a major provider of private health care in the UK.

These three strategies illustrate the shift to a new public/private mix of services, a mixed economy of health care. The policy has been driven in part by ideological considerations, especially those of the New Right with its emphasis on individuals exercising choice in the market. Economic and political considerations have also been important – especially the need to maximize efficiency and get value for money from existing tax revenues and the importance of being seen to act to reduce waiting lists. For Labour these imperatives resulted in the adoption of a pragmatic approach to health policy, in line with 'third way' thinking, and a willingness to embrace those Conservative policies that have been deemed successful, such as PFI. Since coming to power the Coalition government has endorsed the policy and is enthusiastically pursuing this marketization of the health service in England.

Politicians may also have been encouraged to move towards a mixed economy of health care by segments of the medical profession and by some users of health care. Certain members of the medical profession have stood to gain financially from the expansion of the private sector, as a result of an increase in fees for private medical practice, paid out by insurance companies, and from ownership of new private hospitals and private companies providing primary care services. An increase in the 'consumer' demand for private health care could be said to explain the growth in private health insurance in the 1980s although, as noted earlier, this increase was primarily a result of the expansion of company-paid schemes rather than individual-paid schemes. There is also evidence of growing dissatisfaction with the NHS in social attitude surveys, which might have encouraged a greater willingness to use private health care. Historically, however, there has been strong loyalty to the NHS, even amongst those who have private health insurance, and this loyalty has acted as a brake on those politicians who might otherwise have favoured a greater shift towards private health care on ideological grounds.

Whatever the reasons for the development of the public–private mix, it can be argued that the shift towards a greater role for private medicine has undermined the egalitarian principles associated with the founding of the NHS and created a two-tier system. It is certainly the case that those with private health insurance can 'jump the queue' for elective surgery and that these people tend to be better off. However, there is little evidence to suggest that the quality of care provided in the private sector is superior to that offered by the NHS. While private care might be more comfortable and convenient, the levels of medical and technical care are similar. More significant perhaps is the impact of the introduction of commercial imperatives in the NHS and the increasing emphasis on health care as a commodity and patients as consumers. This cultural change is arguably as transformative as any of the other alterations to the public–private mix and supports the claim that the NHS in England is being privatized from within.

See also: *Managerialism; Consumerism*

REFERENCES

Calnan, M., Cant, S. and Gabe, J. (1993) *Going Private: Why People Pay for their Health Care*. Buckingham: Open University Press.

Foubister, T., Thompson, S., Mossialos, E. and McGuire, A. (2006) *Private Medical Insurance in the United Kingdom*. European Observatory on Health Systems and Policies. Online: www.euro.who.int/_data/assets/pdf_file/0007/98422/Private_Medical_Insurance_UK.pdf?

Harley, K., Willis, K., Gabe, J., Short, S., Colyer, F., Natalier, K. and Calnan, M. (2011) 'Constructing health consumers: private health insurance in Australia and the United Kingdom', *Health Sociology Review*, 20: 306–20.

Humphrey, C. and Russell, J. (2001) 'Private medicine', in T. Heller, R. Muston, M. Sidell and C. Lloyd (eds), *Working for Health*. London: Sage.

Mohan, J. (1995) *A National Health Service? The Restructuring of Health Care in Britain since 1979*. Basingstoke: Macmillan.

Mohan, J. (2009) 'Visions of privatisation: New Labour and the reconstruction of the NHS', in J. Gabe and M. Calnan (eds), *The New Sociology of the Health Service*. London: Routledge.

Pollock, A. and Price, D. (2011) 'The final frontier: the UK's new coalition government turns the English National Health Service over to the global health care market', *Health Sociology Review*, 20: 294–305.

Jonathan Gabe

Managerialism

Managerialism refers to an ideology that reframes health care using managerial symbols and language and encourages health care professionals to accept managerialist thinking.

Over the last three decades many countries have recognized that they need to contain health care costs, improve performance and outcomes, and make their services more user-sensitive, and have turned to management as the solution (Numerato et al., 2012). In place of an administrative approach where managers 'oiled the wheels' in consultation with other health care workers, an industrial model of management has been introduced, regardless of its relevance or appropriateness for public services like health care. The emphasis now is on managers taking control, setting performance targets, and imposing budgetary and workload ceilings. This approach has arguably set managers on a collision course with other health care professionals such as doctors because of these professionals' claim to autonomy. In this entry the development of what has been called 'New Public Management' (NPM) in the UK's National Health Service (NHS) is briefly described and the implications for social relations in health care and, in particular, for relations between managers and doctors, are considered. Since political devolution in 1999 it has been claimed that the relationship between management and medicine in Wales, Scotland and Northern Ireland has been less fraught and adversarial than in England and so the impact of NPM since 1999 will be considered only in relation to the latter (Hunter, 2006).

It is possible to see the development of NPM as involving two elements: challenging professionals in the health service and incorporating them (Harrison and Pollitt, 1994). Each will be considered in turn. Challenging health service professionals involves subordinating professional autonomy to managerial will, an approach first adopted in 1983 with the introduction of general managers into the NHS as recommended in the Griffiths Report. Prior to this report NHS managers, or as they were then called, administrators, acted as diplomats, helping to organize the facilities and resources for professionals to get on with their work and reacting to problems as they arose. Decisions were made consensually by multidisciplinary teams that included doctors and nurses as well as administrators. The Griffiths Report recommended altering the organizational culture of the service by introducing features from business management, along the lines suggested particularly by US management theorists. General managers were to be appointed at each level of the service, in place of consensus teams, to take responsibility for shaping the NHS and control its direction. These new managers would take responsibility for developing management plans, ensure quality of care, achieve cost improvements, and monitor and reward staff. At the same time managers would be paid by performance as a spur to good management, as happened in the private sector.

These proposals, which were accepted wholesale by the Conservative government of the time, were designed to alter the balance of power in favour of managers at the expense of other professionals, and especially doctors (Hunter, 2006). Before the Griffiths Report, doctors' clinical freedom to make decisions about patients regardless of cost had been seen as a major determinant of the level of expenditure. In the new system doctors were to be more accountable to managers, who had strict control over professional and labour costs through a system of management budgets that related workload objectives to the resources available. In practice, general managers were unable to challenge the medical domain, let alone make significant inroads into it. While they now found it easier to close hospital beds and make other changes to the service without long periods of consultation, in every other respect they were no more able to control doctors than their predecessors (Harrison and Pollitt, 1994). Consequently, doctors continued to exercise considerable autonomy and managers continued to lack real control over medical work.

In 1990 the Conservative government enacted the NHS and Community Care Act, which attempted, among other things, to shift the balance of power more forcefully in the direction of managers. Following the Act managers became more involved in the specification and policing of consultants' contracts, discussing consultants' job description with them on a yearly basis and helping to determine the merit awards which are presented to some consultants to supplement their salaries. At the same time a plethora of new techniques of managerial evaluation were developed. Quality assurance and performance indicators, made possible by advances in information technology, increased opportunities for the managerial determination of work content, productivity, resource use, and quality standards (Flynn, 1992).

Under the Labour government from 1997, managers were given further powers to challenge doctors' autonomy through the introduction of 'clinical governance'. Chief Executives of hospitals now became responsible for clinical as well as financial performance and from 1999 were expected to make sure that their clinicians restricted themselves to treatments recommended on grounds of clinical and cost-effectiveness by the National Institute for Clinical Evidence (since 2005 renamed as the National Institute for Health and Clinical Excellence) (NICE). They were also expected to see that clinicians complied with the service guidelines for specified conditions under the National Service Frameworks (NSF). Furthermore, managers were required to provide evidence to demonstrate that doctors in their Trusts were complying with these guidelines for the rolling programme of inspections to be conducted by the Commission for Health Improvement (Harrison and Ahmad, 2000) and its successor (the Care Quality Commission). This focus on measuring service quality via metrics has been described as a shift from government to governance, because of the wider range of agencies and stakeholders involved in health service delivery (Dopson, 2009). From a Foucauldian perspective the logic of management discourse has been internalized by physicians to become part of their identity. Managerialism has thus resulted in physicians developing a new mentality of self-monitoring 'at a distance' (Numerato et al., 2012).

These developments, at least in England, would seem to have given managers the opportunity to constrain doctors as never before, along the lines identified by the proletarianization/corporatization thesis. Advocates of this position argue that doctors are being deskilled, are losing their economic independence, and are being required to work in bureaucratically organized institutions under the instruction of managers, in accordance with the requirements of advanced capitalism (McKinlay and Marceau, 2002). However, as Freidson (1989) indicates, the widespread adoption of new techniques for monitoring the efficiency of performance and resource allocation does not, on its own, illustrate reduced professional autonomy. What really matters is whose criteria for evaluation and appraisal are adopted and who controls which actions are taken. More recent work, undertaken in a range of countries within and outside of Europe (for example, Sweden and Australia), illustrates how doctors often retain clinical autonomy by intervening in the process of creating rules and protocols or actively influencing their implementation (Numerato et al., 2012).

The more oblique approach to the management control of professionals involves the incorporation of professionals into management activity on managers' terms. In England this approach pre-dated the 1990 NHS and Community Care Act, but was significantly enhanced by it. For example, under the Griffiths Report doctors were encouraged to become general managers and a few experiments were set up involving the delegation of budgetary responsibility to doctors. At the same time most were reluctant to become managers and continued to exercise considerable autonomy. Following the 1990 Act, however, doctors were required to be involved in management at every level. They were forced to become part-time managers, integrated into the management structure, and could no longer ignore it. Thus doctors became part-time clinical directors who, while retaining their professional identity, became subordinate to managers and were expected to 'manage', using their position to control their medical colleagues. Although sometimes reluctant to take the role initially, they generally came to see it subsequently as a way of retaining control over the service. Having learnt the language of management, their bilingual skills enabled them to reinterpret and reframe problems, and to adopt a clinical perspective on managerial issues and a managerial perspective on clinical matters (Thorne, 2002). Through clinical directors the medical profession thus retained a central position in shaping services and work organization.

In contrast to arguments about proletarianization/corporatization, mentioned earlier, attempts to incorporate the medical profession by turning them into managers have arguably been used by doctors to enable them to re-professionalize. Creating new forms of expertise by assimilating management skills has enabled clinical directors to extend their jurisdiction and domain. The resulting differentiation between these clinical directors and other doctors may, however, lead to greater internal stratification and hence the fragmentation of the medical profession (Thorne, 2002). Others have pointed out that such internal stratification does not exclusively result in growing inequalities within the medical profession. It can also provide new opportunities for lower segments of the profession such as GPs, facilitating their re-positioning (Numerato et al., 2012).

Whatever its impact on the medical profession, the growth of managers has been enhanced by a series of government policies, initiated first by the Conservatives and subsequently modified by New Labour. The introduction of an internal market in the 1990 NHS and Community Care Act, with the division of the NHS into providers and purchasers, has given managers a pivotal role. Likewise, the introduction of the Patient's Charter in 1991, involving the setting of the rights and service standards that consumers could expect, and its modification by the Labour government on coming to power in 1997, has helped to enhance the power of managers who have been responsible for monitoring and enforcing these service standards. The passing of the Health and Social Care Act by the present

Coalition government (of Conservatives and Liberal Democrats) in 2012, which re-enforced the market for health care in England, has given further power to managers in the drawing up of contracts for suppliers and producers of services and in monitoring clinical performance through clinical and patient outcome data.

At the same time there are countervailing forces at work which may restrain the advance of management (Harrison and Pollitt, 1994). We have already seen that doctors (and nurses) have taken up management posts, bringing a different set of priorities and values with them. In addition to this 'colonization of management' by health care professionals, managerial power and authority may be curtailed by the fragmentation of management itself. Thus, those working for Hospital Trusts providing services may have different interests from those involved in purchasing these services. And top management, who are concerned with controlling the overall system, may prioritize things in a different way from middle managers who are more interested in maximizing service provision. Furthermore, managers may be constrained by consumer power, by having to take heed of surveys of consumer opinion that they are then expected to act upon. Information about such preferences can be used by professionals seeking to defend their specialty as well as by middle managers seeking to convince top management that they need more resources.

The march of NPM may therefore be constrained but its impact on professionalism will still be significant. While some have argued that doctors have been proletarianized or corporatized, others have suggested that they have responded by employing management skills to extend their jurisdiction and thus re-professionalize. Either way the development of NPM has arguably transformed what used to be a high-trust relationship between managers and other health care workers, with all the parties observing a diffuse pattern of mutual obligation, into a low-trust relationship with mutual suspicion replacing the mutual honouring of trust. The longer-term impact of such a transformation is yet to be seen.

See also: *Medical Autonomy, Dominance and Decline; Trust in Medicine; Consumerism*

REFERENCES

Dopson, S. (2009) 'Changing forms of managerialism in the NHS: hierarchies, markets and networks', in J. Gabe and M. Calnan (eds), *The New Sociology of the Health Service*. London: Routledge.

Flynn, R. (1992) *Structures of Control in Health Management*. London: Routledge.

Freidson, E. (1989) *Medical Work in America: Essays in Healthcare*. New Haven, CT: Yale University Press.

Harrison, S. and Ahmad, W. (2000) 'Medical autonomy and the UK state', *Sociology*, 34 (1): 129–46.

Harrison, S. and Pollitt, C. (1994) *Controlling Health Professionals: The Future of Work and Organization in the NHS*. Buckingham: Open University Press.

Hunter, D.J. (2006) 'From tribalism to corporatism: the continuing managerial challenge to medical dominance', in D. Kelleher, J. Gabe and G. Williams (eds), *Challenging Medicine*, 2nd edn. London: Routledge.

McKinlay, J. and Marceau, L. (2002) 'The end of the golden age of doctoring', *International Journal of Health Services*, 32: 379–416.

Numerato, D., Salvatore, D. and Fattore, G. (2012) 'The impact of management on medical professionalism: a review', *Sociology of Health & Illness*, 34: 626–44.

Thorne, M. (2002) 'Colonizing the new world of NHS management: the shifting power of professionals', *Health Services Management Research*, 15: 14–26.

Jonathan Gabe

Consumerism

> Consumerism, when applied to health care, suggests that the users of health services should and do play an active role in making informed choices about health.

The term 'consumer' has its origins in the world of private business and reflects recognition that producers should take account of the preferences of the purchasers of their goods in order to maximize their profits. Its use blossomed first in North America where market researchers were employed by manufacturers after the Second World War to establish consumer demand for their products and customer relations departments were set up to provide a service to customers and seek to meet their needs. In the UK context the rights of the consumer were recognized with the founding of the Consumers' Association in 1957. This organization aimed to provide readers of its magazine with information about the quality of high-street products in order that they could make an 'informed choice' when making purchasing decisions (Seale, 1993).

The language of consumerism is now commonplace in health care policies in many Western countries (Harris et al., 2010). It was first applied to users of UK public-sector services like health care in the late 1970s and early 1980s. It was initially criticized on the grounds that the consumption of medical care was different from, say, the consumption of supermarket goods. For example, in the UK people do not pay directly for medical care provided by the National Health Service (NHS), but do so through taxation. And they can exercise more choice when buying from a shop, compared with deciding which doctor to see and which treatment to have. Furthermore, consumers of health care are at the same time producers of good health in that they are involved in the prevention of illness through health maintenance practices in contexts of everyday life, such as the home. From this standpoint the distinction between consumption and production is artificial (Stacey, 1976). Despite these concerns consumerism has become a leitmotif of health policy and practice over the last forty years in the UK, as will be seen below.

The influence of consumerist principles can be seen, first and foremost, in a range of policies introduced by Conservative governments during the 1980s and 1990s. An early example was the decision by the Thatcher administration in 1983 to follow the advice of the Griffiths Report and introduce managerialism into the NHS. In line with New Right thinking, with its emphasis on individuals exercising choice through the market, Griffiths stated that managers should give pride of place to the preferences of 'patients', or as they were renamed 'consumers', when making health care decisions. He argued that managers should try to establish how well the service for which they were responsible was being delivered by employing a range of market research techniques to find out the views of their customers. While the use of these techniques may have legitimated managers' knowledge claims about their customers and what they wanted, the kind of information collected seemed to be of limited use to patients, as the focus was on their views of hotel aspects of care (for example, cleanliness and food) rather than their assessment of clinical effectiveness (Calnan and Gabe, 2001).

The 1990s witnessed further policy initiatives intended to enhance 'consumer choice'. The 1990 NHS and Community Care Act turned the NHS into an internal market, with purchasers and providers of health care, while reaffirming the principle of health care being free at the point of use. To make the market work, supply-side providers such as large hospitals were given the opportunity to become self-governing trusts, with the promise of increased financial freedom and greater autonomy. On the demand side, general practitioners (GPs) were permitted to become fundholders, who could then place contracts for non-emergency care on behalf of their patients. A justification for the development of this market for health care was that it would shift the culture of the NHS from one determined by the preferences and decisions of professionals to one shaped by the views and wishes of users. GPs were however purchasing services on their patients' behalf, and were thus acting as proxy or surrogate consumers, with patients having no purchasing rights of their own. It was assumed that these fundholders had the incentive to fulfil this role effectively as otherwise their patients would simply switch to a competing practice. However, as patients lacked the necessary knowledge or inclination to shop around in the medical marketplace and often did not have much choice of alternative GPs with which to register, critics argued that there was little evidence that this aspect of the reforms markedly increased consumer choice (Calnan and Gabe, 2001).

Consumerism was also promoted by the introduction of the Patients' Charter in 1992, one of a number planned by the Conservatives to transform the management of the public services. The Charter was designed to make the health service more responsive to consumers and raise quality overall at nil cost, by setting the rights and service standards that consumers could expect. New rights were established such as the right for detailed information about quality standards and waiting lists and having any complaint investigated and dealt with promptly. Its critics agued that while it may have increased individual users' right to information, it was premised on the dubious assumption that making such information available to the public would of itself change clinicians' and managers' practices. As such, the different health care occupations' vested interests in the maintenance of the status quo were ignored (Crinson, 1998).

When Labour regained power in 1997, the emphasis shifted from one of competition to that of partnership and co-operation, with Primary Care Trusts (PCTs) replacing fund holding. Central to these organizational arrangements was the requirement that users and local people were involved in decision making. In the NHS Plan, published in 2000, it became a statutory duty for Strategic Health Authorities (responsible for the oversight of trusts), PCTs and NHS Trusts in England to involve users and the public in the planning and operation of services. The Plan, and subsequent policy developments discussed below, did not apply to Wales, Scotland and Northern Ireland, as these countries have followed an increasingly divergent path since administrative devolution in 1999. At a national level lay participation in policy making in England was increased, with lay people invited to sit on bodies set up to enhance the governance of the NHS (for example, the National Institute for Health and Clinical Excellence, or NICE, which was responsible for providing guidance on the cost-effectiveness of treatments). In addition, citizens' juries were used to gauge views on issues such as the out of hours service provided by GPs. While these forms of collective involvement were welcomed, especially by health consumer groups, it was generally felt that the Department of Health in England was still setting the agenda and rules of engagement. Moreover, there was a danger that decision makers and service providers would respond first and foremost to more articulate groups at the expense of those that were hidden or less well organized (Forster and Gabe, 2008).

Alongside this concern with public participation at the collective level, the Labour government also continued to talk about the individual consumer. Indeed, in the latter stages of their time in power this individual-level approach came to dominate, as it had with their predecessors. Initially it revised the Conservative government's Patients' Charter, making it a contract between the NHS and its clients, and turning those clients into responsible consumers who had both rights (old Left) and responsibilities (New Right). As such it reflected Labour's preference for the 'third way', pragmatically drawing on values from both sides of the policy spectrum. At the same time Labour focused on ways to make patients more informed and more actively involved in their health care by introducing the 'Choose and Book' computer system to give them more choice about how, when, and where to receive elective care. They also introduced the NHS Choices website to provide comparative information about a range of services provided by hospitals and GPs and their performance against quality indicators. These developments assumed that patients wanted to exercise choice about where they were treated, even though much of the evidence suggested the opposite (Forster and Gabe, 2008). Indeed it may well have increased inequalities amongst those who lacked sufficient 'health literacy' to interpret the information on the website or travel to what were perceived to be the highest quality providers (Farrington-Douglas and Allen, 2005).

While the language of choice became more popular, the longer Labour remained in power, they continued to stress the notion of partnership at the micro level of the doctor–patient interaction. Doctors were encouraged to share information and decision making with their patients and patients were talked about as 'experts' in their own care. However, it was unclear to what extent users wanted to be involved in the decision making about their care (Coulter, 2005). Nor was it clear that doctors would necessarily be willing to share information with patients as the basis for joint decision making. In some cases they might have preferred to limit the nature of the information they imparted to patients, thereby maintaining their professional dominance.

Since the Coalition government of Conservatives and Liberal Democrats came to power in 2010, consumer choice has remained a dominant discourse in English health care policy, with it being assumed that a 'more decisive market orientation will bring about more patient choice [and hence] improved quality and increased efficiency' (Asthana, 2011: 817). As a further initiative to develop choice, patients are now to be given the right to choose to register with any GP practice, without any restriction in terms of where they live, effectively giving patients the right to choose their own commissioner of services.

Given the above, how is the popularity of consumerism and partnership in policy circles to be explained? One explanation is that the different government initiatives have been driven by ideology. Certainly the policies of the Conservatives (and now the Coalition) seem to have been heavily influenced by a neo-liberal ideology based on a belief in the value of self-reliance, individual responsibility and the rule of the market, with sovereign consumers expressing demand on the basis of knowledge about the choices available. Yet the Conservatives have not followed this ideology to the letter, as the service remains free at the point of use. The last Labour government also seemed to accept elements of neoliberalism (increasing individual choice, and maximizing personal responsibility for health care), but combined this with a more collectivist approach, thus reflecting a preference for pragmatism.

An alternative explanation is that the emphasis on consumerism reflects more general socio-economic changes, encapsulated in the phrase 'post-Fordism' (Bury, 2010). From this standpoint the health service reforms described above parallel a shift from Fordist principles (mass production, universalization of welfare, mass consumption) to those of post-Fordism (flexible production techniques designed to take account of rapid changes in consumer demand and fragmented market tastes). In a post-Fordist society it is the consumers rather than the producers who call the tune. While this approach has some value in placing the health policy changes mentioned above in a broader context, it fails to distinguish between surface changes in appearance and underlying social relations. While the rhetoric has been about enhanced consumer power or partnership, producers in the form of the medical profession and health service managers arguably continue to hold the upper hand over the users of services.

See also: *Practitioner–Client Relationships; Managerialism; Citizenship and Health*

REFERENCES

Asthana, S. (2011) 'Liberating the NHS? A commentary on the Lansley White Paper, "Equity and Excellence"', *Social Science & Medicine*, 72: 815–20.

Bury, M. (2010) 'The British health care system', in W.C. Cockerham (ed.), *The New Blackwell Companion to Medical Sociology*. Oxford: Wiley-Blackwell.

Calnan, M. and Gabe, J. (2001) 'From consumerism to partnership? Britain's National Health Service at the turn of the century', *International Journal of Health Services*, 31: 119–31.

Coulter, A. (2005) 'Shared decision making: the debate continues', *Health Expectations*, 8: 95–6.

Crinson, I. (1998) 'Putting patients first: the continuity of the consumerist discourse in health policy: from radical right to New Labour', *Critical Social Policy*, 18: 227–39.

Farrington-Douglas, J. and Allen, J. (2005) *Equitable Choices for Health*. London: Institute for Public Policy Research.

Forster, R. and Gabe, J. (2008) 'Voice or choice? Patient and public involvement in the National Health Service in England under New Labour', *International Journal of Health Services*, 38 (2): 333–56.

Harris. R., Wathen, N. and Wyatt, S. (eds) (2010) *Configuring Health Consumers: Health Work and the Imperative of Personal Responsibility*. Basingstoke: Palgrave Macmillan.

Seale, C. (1993) 'The consumer voice', in B. Davey and J. Popay (eds), *Dilemmas in Health Care*. Buckingham: Open University Press.

Stacey, M. (1976) 'The health service consumer: a sociological misconception', in M. Stacey (ed.), *The Sociology of the National Health Service*. Sociological Review Monograph No 22. Keele: University of Keele.

Jonathan Gabe

Citizenship and Health

'Citizenship and health' refers to those aspects of health affected by the changing nature of the state, and the relationships between the state, health care organizations and the people they serve, under varying social and economic conditions.

The concept of 'citizenship' has a long history and a complex set of connections to 'democracy', 'rights' and modern concepts such as 'welfare', 'consumerism' and 'community participation'. During the course of the twentieth century, health services, and latterly health itself, became the focus for arguments about the proper relationship between the modern state and its citizens. In the twenty-first century, widening inequalities, nationally and globally, new biomedical and information technologies, and concerns over the sustainability of funding for health and social care systems in societies with ageing populations are creating new politicized questions about citizenship and entitlement to societal resources.

'Equality among citizens', along with liberty and respect for law and justice, was one of the building blocks of classical democracy in Athens and other Greek city-states from the sixth century BC onwards, and became a central, evolving motif in Western traditions of political theory from the seventeenth century AD. The idea of the 'citizen' – for the French philosopher Rousseau, the highest role to which an individual could aspire – has been at the heart of the struggles of workers, women and oppressed and disenfranchised people throughout the modern world. However, there is nothing intrinsically left or centre-left about the concept of citizenship. In the UK, Conservatives have employed it as a way of emphasizing the need for community vigilance about crime, disorder and other signs of moral degeneration and decay (Marquand, 1997); and, more recently, their controversial idea of the 'Big Society' claims to be directed at devolving power to the lowest possible level and thus enhancing citizenship.

Citizenship is an evolving concept. In the post-war period the debate can be traced back to T.H. Marshall's celebrated essay on the relationship between citizenship and social class (Marshall, 1950). Marshall argued that citizenship had three elements: (1) *civil*, emphasizing freedom of speech, thought and belief; (2) *political*, stressing the right to participate in the exercise of political power through voting and representation; and (3) *social*, by which he meant the right to welfare, social security and a general share in the benefits of economic and cultural development. In Marshall's work these three elements were placed within a developmental theory moving from civil through political to fully social citizenship. Although his theory has been criticized for oversimplifying the developmental process, and understating the importance of gender, it remains a useful conceptual starting point (Walby, 1994).

During the twentieth century health became an increasingly important signifier of citizenship, and universal access to health care also became one of the great expectations of modern electorates. In the UK, in a series of bold political moves, Lloyd George, William Beveridge and Aneurin Bevan manoeuvred health services progressively to the centre of the political stage, alongside housing, social security and education. When the National Health Service (NHS) came into existence on 5 July 1948, it had been designed, as Bevan put it, 'to universalise the best', and was the first health system to offer free care at the point of use to the entire population. Similar developments with different funding mechanisms emerged in other European countries in subsequent decades. These arrangements for health care in times of sickness were an important part of an enduring social compact between the state and the people, which provided the foundations for the 'welfare state', as it came to be called from the 1940s, where basic provision and security 'from the cradle to the grave' were assured for the entire population.

These developments are now viewed as being the defining mark of a political consensus that emerged in response to the catastrophes of the twentieth century: the horrors and deprivations of war, economic slumps, fascism, and the anxiety created in the ruling elites by the enduring threat of a disenchanted and radicalized working class (Hobsbawm, 1994). There was a strong belief that progress in science, politics and society was possible, and that reconstruction was necessary. Although it was undoubtedly a political compromise, the NHS in the UK came to embody the hopes and values of post-war Britain. It was built on the belief that the whole population should have access to health care and that this care would be built on the best available scientific expertise and professional organization.

The inter- and post-war discussions about health care and welfare provided a context in which social scientists and others working in social medicine and social administration could make a contribution to political thinking and policy development. During this time there was nothing that might be characterized as a critical perspective on medicine or health care. In terms of policy analysis, Fabianism was the dominant approach to intellectual engagement, and within this framework health services were simply the vehicle through which medicine and care could be more effectively delivered to the whole population. The approach was implicitly if not explicitly rooted in a Parsonian sociology of the sick role: illness was dysfunctional and medical care and health services represented the knowledge and social organization available to deal with illness and re-stabilize the individual and their social relationships.

Modern health care systems were the beneficiaries of what are now seen as the 'Golden Years' of twentieth-century Western capitalism, stretching from the start of the 1950s to the OPEC oil crisis and economic turbulence of 1973 and after. Increasingly the only certainty in health care was that it was going to cost more. Much of the sociological analysis that emerged during the 1970s represented the beginnings of an extended examination of the relationship between citizens and professionally controlled health services in the light of growing evidence of the limited effectiveness of much modern medicine, persisting health inequalities in an era of neoliberal globalization, the perception that patients are disenfranchised in the organization and delivery of health care systems and, latterly, the unfolding consequences of new genetic knowledge and medical technologies.

From the 1980s onward, the issue of the relationship between citizens and their health became increasingly sharp as the UK and other Western societies engaged in severe economic 'restructuring', moving away from the corporatist social contract between Labour and the trade unions on which they had hitherto been based towards market-style expectations and relationships. Management systems and budgets were introduced to control health professionals' expenditure, and quasi-markets were employed to stimulate competition between providers and, so it was argued, expand consumer choice. Health services, along with the rest of the welfare state, were increasingly framed in terms of value for money, and 'cradle to the grave' security was seen as a vice rather than a virtuous safety net for the casualties of economic dislocation. At the same time, evidence accumulated of widening inequalities in health status that were closely related to the growing disparities in income and wealth.

In spite of, or perhaps because of, the severe squeeze on public services that took place during the late 1980s and early 1990s, the debate about the roles and rights of patients, consumers, users and citizens in the planning and delivery of health services became much more high profile (Calnan and Gabe, 2001). Knowledgeable and informed consumers making rational choices about treatment became the leitmotif of reform across Europe and North America. Developments during the 1990s such as the Patients' Charter in the UK – a list of rights (not legally binding) to certain standards of care – were designed to make services more responsive to 'consumers' and thereby improve quality at no extra cost, though such improvements have been hard to detect in the evidence available (Calnan and Gabe, 2001). However, during this period, there was growing evidence that some groups, such as mental patients, were having a range of citizenship rights threatened by systems that were under strain (Rogers and Pilgrim, 1989); and recent revelations about the care of older people in both NHS facilities and in care homes have indicated that even the basic needs of older people are not being met.

During a period when health services came under increasing pressure from neo-liberalizing governments enthusiastic about free markets, space was created for debates about the place of consumers within professionally dominated health care systems. Within this space critics were able to argue for the limitations of a consumer model of patient or community involvement in health services, and the need for a more radical citizenship approach to involving the public in decisions affecting their health. However, there has been little sign subsequently of a movement of power away from professionals to their patients or clients.

In the UK the Labour government elected in 1997 modified the emphasis on markets and toned down the language of consumerism. However, in their first term of office the government tied itself to the previous Conservative government's spending plans in an attempt to display the kind fiscal prudence which would please business and the middle-class vote. As a consequence, the Labour government spent most of its first term battling against a growing sense of crisis and disappointment, pricked by the rising tide of waiting lists, waiting times and high-profile cases of medical malpractice. In this context increasing patient, citizen and community involvement, hinted at in a series of documents, was unlikely to be prioritized. Nonetheless, health service analysts argued that many of the changes taking place under New Labour would '… bring patients and citizens into decision-making at every level of service' (Lewis and Gillam, 2001: 113). In a detailed and comprehensive analysis of patient and public involvement under New Labour in England between 1997 and 2006, Forster and Gabe (2008: 348) concluded that: '… there has been a significant extension of opportunities for individual patients and the public to communicate their views in more ways and on different levels'. The current UK Coalition government's claim to want to put patients in England 'at the heart of everything we do … Patients will be in charge of making decisions about their care' (Department of Health, 2010: 1), suggests a continuation of this emphasis on a strengthened role for patients. However, the extent to which this is more than a rhetorical flourish is something we will have to await with sceptical anticipation.

Potentially more significant for healthy citizenship than greater patient involvement in health services, is the growing attention given to the determinants of health, and the need for partnership between agencies and communities in fighting the root causes of ill health in the populations of which they are a part (Popay and Williams, 2009). With the tendency for 'lifestyle drift' to emerge as governments move from analysing the problem to deciding what needs to be done (Hunter et al., 2010), there is always the likelihood that these policies will be little more than yet another opportunity to hit 'health deviants' over the head or, in the more subtle language of 'libertarian paternalism', 'nudge' them into better behaviour while letting the producers of tobacco, alcohol and unhealthy foods off the hook. Nonetheless, in the context of devolution, there are signs that other parts of the UK are not working with quite such a relentless focus on the behaviour of individuals, framing the issues more strongly in terms of 'fairer health outcomes for all' (Welsh Assembly Government, 2010), with an idea of citizens rather than consumers at the centre.

Arguments developed during the 1980s for a less professionally-dominated health care system, and the concomitant demand for greater lay (consumer, community or citizen) representation may have signalled a distorted rediscovery of the political element in Marshall's theory of citizenship in discussions about welfare. Whether this will survive the abolition of Primary Care Trusts in England and what, as I write, is a stuttering move toward GP commissioning (but not in Wales or Scotland) remains to be seen. The increasingly urgent emphasis on the social determinants of health, the implications of pharmaco-genetics and the pharmaceuticalization of society (Williams et al., 2011), the global uncertainties for health created by environmental change, and the continuing dominance of post-recessional neoliberalism have each widened the scope of the debate on health and citizenship. The debate now embraces not only simple consumer demands for better quality health services but also more fundamental aspects of the relationships between health and social, economic and political conditions.

See also: *Neoliberal Globalization and Health Inequalities; Geneticization; Managerialism*

REFERENCES

Calnan, M. and Gabe, J. (2001) 'From consumerism to partnership? Britain's National Health Service at the turn of the century', *International Journal of Health Services*, 31 (1): 119–31.

Department of Health (2010) *Equity and Excellence: Liberating the NHS* (White Paper). London: Department of Health.

Forster, R. and Gabe, J (2008) 'Voice or choice? Patient and public involvement in the National Health Service in England under New Labour', *International Journal of Health Services*, 38: 333–56.

Hobsbawm, E. (1994) *Age of Extremes: The Short Twentieth Century, 1914–1991*. London: Michael Joseph.

Hunter, D., Popay J., Tannahill, C. and Whitehead, M. (2010) 'Getting to grips with health inequalities at last?', *British Medical Journal*, 340: c684.

Lewis, R. and Gillam, S. (2001) 'The National Health Service Plan: further reform of British health care', *International Journal of Health Services*, 31 (1): 111–18.

Marquand, D. (1997) *The New Reckoning: Capitalism, States and Citizens*. Cambridge: Polity Press.

Marshall, T.H. (1950) *Citizenship and Social Class and other Essays*. Cambridge: Cambridge University Press.

Popay, J. and Williams, G.H. (2009) 'Equalizing the people's health', in J. Gabe and M. Calnan (eds), *The New Sociology of the Health Service*. London: Routledge.

Rogers, A. and Pilgrim, D. (1989) 'Mental health and citizenship', *Critical Social Policy*, 9: 44–55.

Walby, S. (1994) 'Is citizenship gendered? ', *Sociology*, 28 (2): 379–95.

Welsh Assembly Government (2010) *Fairer Health Outcomes for All: Reducing Inequities in Health – Strategic Action Plan*. Cardiff: Welsh Assembly Government.

Williams, S., Martin, P. and Gabe, J. (2011) 'The pharmaceuticalisation of society? A framework for analysis', *Sociology of Health & Illness*, 33 (5): 710–25.

Gareth H. Williams

Social Movements and Health

> *Social movements, including health movements, are'(1) Informal networks, based on (2) shared beliefs and solidarity, which mobilise around (3) conflictual issues, through (4) the frequent use of various forms of protest' (Della Porta and Diani, 1999: 16).*

The concept 'social movements' is used widely and in varying ways both within and outside of social science, not least by activists within social movements themselves. This variation in use makes it impossible to arrive at criteria which are both sufficiently inclusive and sufficiently exclusive to give a precise definition that is suited to all cases. Like 'games', as defined by Wittgenstein (1953), 'social movements' share 'family resemblances' and are clearly identifiable as such but also very difficult to pin down (Crossley, 2002). However, the above definition, by Della Porta and Diani (1999), captures many properties of movements deemed important by contemporary analysts.

Examples of movements include the environmental movement, feminist movements, and the global justice and anti-war movements, whose mobilizations enjoyed a high profile in the first decade of the twenty-first century, and a variety of movements mobilized around conflicts concerning health and medicine. I shall return to these health conflicts and movements shortly. First, however, we must unpick 'social movements' in more detail.

The informal networks to which Della Porta and Diani (1999) refer might be networks of individual activists but they might equally be networks of 'social movement organizations' (SMOs). They are most often networks of both. SMOs, in turn, might include anything from a formal organization with paid workers, strong income streams, membership lists, etc., to a very loose cluster of activists or an affinity group with no official structure and little to demarcate it except the collective actions of its participants. It might also refer to loose groups experimenting with social practices salient to the conflictual issues underlying the movement, for example, a feminist commune or an alternative therapeutic community. Likewise, addressing Della Porta and Diani's second criterion, the extent to which beliefs are shared and solidarity is achieved, can be highly variable not only between movements but also across time and context. Factional infighting is by no means uncommon. Finally, the forms of protest that Della Porta and Diani refer to are highly variable as well, including everything from petitions and marches, through various forms of obstruction, to the political violence of al-Qaida and related groups. Generally, however, 'social movements' operate outside of the mainstream, institutionalized channels of government, putting pressure upon government, insofar as government is the target of their actions (it might not be), by means of either a symbolic challenge to its legitimacy or by coercion. This distinguishes them from political parties, who seek to effect political change by becoming elected within government, and from lobby and pressure groups, who tend to work through the official channels of the political system.

Contemporary ways of analysing social movements draw from two, once distinct but now merged schools, the American and the European, each of which is itself widely recognized to be the culmination of a history of paradigmatic shifts. Both traditions draw from Marxism to varying degrees but the key European writers, such as Habermas (1987) and Touraine (1981), follow Marx more directly in seeking to identify where the key fault-lines of society lie and which movement will emerge from the conflicts surfacing around that fault-line, constituting itself as the agent of change for its epoch. They reject Marx's own answers to these questions, which identify class relations as the fault-line of (capitalist) society and the working class as the agents of historical change, arguing that capitalism has moved on and that the working class have been incorporated within it. But they remain focused on the question, suggesting that the contradictions of society have been displaced rather than resolved and also suggesting that the 'new social movements' which took to the political stage in the late 1960s have replaced the working class as society's key agents of change.

This argument is pertinent to health movements because both Touraine and Habermas recognize health-related movements amongst the new social movements and Habermas, in particular, theorizes their emergence as resistance to a 'colonization of the lifeworld' by both the state and economy; a colonization whose form includes the birth and growth of the welfare state in the latter half of the twentieth century, with its implications in terms of surveillance and regulation of conduct. Movements such as the anti-psychiatry movement of the 1960s, which sought to resist the power of psychiatrists (as agents of the state) to define normality and deny the liberty of those deemed 'mentally ill', might be one example of this. 'Fat' activists, who challenge obesity discourse and related attempts to 'enforce' an ideal of slimness, would be another.

However, the distinction posited in these accounts between 'new' and 'old' movements has been hotly contested (Edwards, 2004) and 'health' was a focus of social movement activism long before the 1960s. Indeed, the establishment of welfare states and related forms of public health care provision in the West was in many cases and many ways influenced by the campaigns of working-class and women's movements in the late nineteenth and early twentieth centuries, and the campaigns of bourgeois reform movements before them. The latter included, for example, the 'lunacy reformers' who campaigned for reform of the private market in 'madhouses' during the early nineteenth century (Crossley, 2006). Furthermore, many of the issues apparently associated with the 'old' social movements, including issues relating to health, have resurfaced in the context of a 'global justice movement', whose high-profile international protests (at meetings of the G8, IMF and World Bank, amongst others) in the early years of the twenty-first century have reshaped the face of social movement politics once again (Crossley, 2003). These protests have focused upon economic inequalities at the global level, highlighting, amongst other things, their deleterious effects upon the health of the poor.

In contrast to the European focus on 'the' agent of change in any given historical juncture, the American school tended to recognize that a plurality of movements was in play at any time and was more concerned to identify the mechanisms which would explain, for example, how movements form and recruit, their effects and efficacy. This 'school' too must be approached through its history. It underwent a paradigm shift in the 1970s when a new generation of scholars launched a fierce attack upon their predecessors, who, they claimed, had characterized protest as an irrational 'crowd' response to 'structural strain' on behalf of previously atomized individuals (Crossley, 2002). In contrast, the new generation deemed activists rational (often in a 'rational choice' sense), claimed that they were usually well-embedded in social networks, and focused upon the impact of the availability of resources and 'political opportunities' on mobilization.

This paradigm was itself subject to attack in the 1990s, however, when a successive generation criticized its rational choice assumptions and neglect of such issues as culture and emotion (2002). Protest and campaigning were not mere irrational outbursts, the new generation agreed, but neither were they an outcome of pure economic rationality. It is important to understand the role of different emotions, identities and cultural practices both within movements and within their wider environments. This move has also involved a merging of the European and American schools with most movement scholars now borrowing insights from both.

New developments within the field have also included a more sustained focus upon health movements of various kinds. There is a growing literature in this area comprising both focused case study monographs on specific movements (see, for example, Epstein, 1996; Crossley, 2006) and broader reflections upon health and medical movements as a sub-type of movement in general (see, for example, Brown and Zavestoski, 2005; Landzelius and Dumit, 2006). This undoubtedly reflects the proliferation of health movements of various kinds in recent years. As noted above, mobilization around health issues, whether by bourgeois reform, working-class or women's movements, is by no means new and has played a key role in shaping health provision at various points in its history. However, the enormous expansion of health care provision in Western societies over the last fifty years, with the related extension of the remit of health professionals and the sheer growth of what is technically possible, has fuelled a proliferation of new movements.

In some part conflicts centre upon the allocation of resources. Medical capability outstrips what the medical profession and the wider society which funds it can afford to provide, prompting an inevitable competition over the available resources by both 'disease-specific' movements and groups and movements representing wider constituencies (for example, women, children, older people, specific ethnic groups). Where this is simply a matter of lobbying for funds, it is not technically social movement activism. As noted above, social movement activism utilizes extra-government means to achieve its ends. Many routine resource-related health campaigns do use such means, however, and some take on an additional aspect when they address such issues as the practices of major pharmaceutical companies. These are social movements.

Beyond resource issues, the 'medicalization' of conditions has also proved a major issue of contention, especially in relation to disability and 'mental illness'. In the case of mental illness, for example, a succession of movements involving both medical professionals and 'patients' have sought to challenge medical categories, authority and language, arguing that the difficulties experienced by those labelled 'mentally ill' are not symptoms of an illness and should not be treated as such (Crossley, 2006). In this case, furthermore, where 'survivors' (as radical-ized 'patients' have re-labelled themselves) can be incarcerated and 'treated' against their own will with electro-convulsive therapy (controlled electric shocks) and mind-altering drugs, both of which can have deeply debilitating side-effects, issues of personal liberty have been predominant as well. As often happens, however, these movements have provoked counter-movements who would argue that the more libertarian position called for by the critics of medicalization leads to the neglect of both vulnerable individuals and the family members who seek to support them, and thus a great deal of personal misery (2006). As a result, conflicting movements and SMOs compete, generating a 'field of contention' around psychiatric practice.

Where disability activists and psychiatric survivors challenge medicine for, in their view, wrongly identifying their difficulties as illnesses, other movements, like the counter-movements in mental health, attack medicine for failing to recognize illness where, they claim, it does exist. Recent important examples include mobilizations around both chronic fatigue and gulf war syndrome. What both share in common, however, and share also with a range of other health-related movements, including most famously the movement mobilized around HIV/AIDS (Epstein, 1996), is a championing of lay knowledge and the patient perspective relative to medical knowledge. Activists have argued that the experience of the 'patient' is, or rather should be, a legitimate source of knowledge with respect to both definitions of illness and measurement of the efficacy and value of treatments. They have challenged the monopoly and authority which the medical profession enjoys in relation to these matters.

In some cases this challenge coincides with the shift towards a consumerist ethos within health provision, introduced by neoliberal policy makers. And some campaigners would recognize – often with ambivalent feelings – that neoliberal health reforms have opened certain doors to them in their quest to break medical monopolies and promote the view of those on the receiving end (Crossley, 2006). Their critique is generally more fundamental than that of the consumer-focused agenda of neoliberalism, however, and the language of consumerism is in many cases alien to them.

As the capacities of medicine expand, we should expect that these and other health-political issues will enjoy a greater profile in the public sphere, along with the movements that champion them. Health never has been and never will be a matter of politically/morally neutral knowledge and intervention. It is a central facet of our well-being and thus of our political life.

See also: *Medicalization; Disability; Lay Knowledge; Consumerism*

REFERENCES

Brown, P. and Zavestoski, S. (2005) *Social Movements in Health*. Oxford: Blackwell.
Crossley, N. (2002) *Making Sense of Social Movements*. Buckinghamshire: Open University Press.
Crossley, N. (2003) 'Even newer social movements?', *Organisation*, 10 (2): 287–305.
Crossley, N. (2006) *Contesting Psychiatry*. London: Routledge.
Della Porta, D. and Diani, M. (1999) *Social Movements*. Oxford: Blackwell.
Edwards, G. (2004) 'Habermas and social movements: what's new?', in N. Crossley and J.M. Roberts (eds), *After Habermas*. Oxford: Blackwell.
Epstein, S. (1996) *Impure Science: AIDS, Activism and the Politics of Knowledge*. Berkeley: University of California Press.
Habermas, J. (1987) *The Theory of Communicative Action, Vol II*. Cambridge: Polity Press.
Landzelius, K. and Dumit, J. (eds) (2006) *Social Science & Medicine*, Special Issue on Patient Organisation Movements, 62 (3): 529–792.
Touraine, A. (1981) *The Voice and the Eye*. New York: Cambridge University Press.
Wittgenstein, L. (1953) *Philosophical Investigations*. Oxford: Blackwell.

Nick Crossley

Medicines Regulation

> Medicines regulation refers to the role of the state in regulating the safety and efficacy of medicines.

In recent years medical sociology has paid growing attention to medicines and their production by the pharmaceutical industry and how the state controls which medicines are available for consumption. Informed by political sociology and the political economy of medicines, the focus has been on the way in which the interests of the state and pharmaceutical industry may play out to the disadvantage of consumers. Particular attention is being given to the possibility of 'regulatory capture', where the government agency responsible for regulating the pharmaceutical industry comes to represent that industry rather than the 'public interest' (Abraham, 1995). The extent to which the relationship between government regulators and drug companies can be characterized in terms of 'corporatism' and 'corporate bias' is also receiving attention. Corporatism refers to whether drug companies have been granted semi-official status, giving them 'internal representation' in executive decision-making structures, thereby enabling them to assist government to implement policies that directly affect them (Wiktorowicz et al., 2012). Corporate bias is demonstrated by the industry having privileged access to and influence over the state that are not afforded to any other interest group (Abraham, 2009).

In order to explore these issues, a brief history of medicines regulation in the UK and the USA will be provided. This account will illustrate differences in the degree of corporatism, corporate bias and regulatory capture in the two countries and the possible reasons for these. Reference will also be made to the Europeanization of medicine's regulation and the extent to which the agency established to harmonize standards of regulatory evaluation across Europe has adopted the UK approach to regulation with its attendant consequences.

In the UK, before the 1960s, the safety and efficacy of medicines were, for the most part, not regulated by the state. Pharmaceutical companies could sell drugs as remedies, as long as they were unadulterated, at prices that the market could bear. Regulation was thus by the market, with drugs usually only falling out of favour if it became clear that they were toxic or ineffective. The government trusted the pharmaceutical industry to test their products for safety and efficacy before bringing them to market. In the early 1960s this trust was breached when reports started to be published about the disastrous side-effects of the sedative Thalidomide. It seemed that drugs could destroy lives as well as save them (Abraham and Lewis, 2002). To restore public confidence in medicines, the UK government introduced regulatory mechanisms to check that new medicines were safe and effective before they were introduced. From the start, however, the government agreed that information submitted by the manufacturers would be treated as confidential, thereby sealing off the regulators from public scrutiny. It was also accepted that the review process should be rapid, so as not to delay the introduction of possibly valuable drugs (Abraham, 2009). Producers' interests thus remained dominant, with citizens' right to security in healthy medications being circumscribed.

In 1968 the Medicines Act was passed which provides the basis for contemporary British medicines regulation. This Act, which came into force in 1971, required the Department of Health, advised by a new Committee on Safety of Medicines (CSM), to become legally responsible for assessing drug safety and efficacy. Members of the CSM were permitted to hold consultancies and shares in pharmaceutical companies, allowing a low level of differentiation between the regulators and these companies (Abraham, 2009). Under the Act, pharmaceutical companies were required for the first time to obtain approval from the government for the marketing of new medicines. As before, however, it was agreed that all information about new drug applications should be treated as confidential. Moreover, information on adverse drug reactions was withheld from citizens, including lawyers and journalists, on the grounds that they lacked the medical expertise to interpret such information. Citizens' right to health thus remained limited in the face of producer interests and medical power.

Since the 1970s the pharmaceutical industry has attempted to maintain its influence over the regulatory authorities through close consultation about regulations on the data requirements for product licences. It has also complained regularly about the length of time taken to obtain decisions from regulators. In the 1980s, these concerns were heeded by a Conservative government that was keen to reduce state intervention in the economy, in line with its neoliberal agenda. In 1981 it reduced the amount of toxicological data drug companies were required to submit to the regulators before gaining the necessary approval to conduct clinical trials; and in 1989 it set up the Medicines Control Agency (MCA) in response to industry claims that regulators were inefficient and reluctant to approve drugs quickly. The MCA was to be funded by the industry through the licence fee charged and run as a business, selling its regulatory services to the industry and promoting itself as the fastest licensing authority in the world (Abraham, 2009). In effect, then, the British government had decided to reform the regulatory authorities as a new neoliberal, corporatist partnership between industry and regulators. Consumers continued to be excluded despite attempts over the period to extend their rights through legal action against certain pharmaceutical companies, in the face of drug disasters such as Opren (prescribed for arthritis sufferers) and Ativan (for anxiety) (Medawar, 1992).

This corporatist partnership between industry and regulators has also shaped the process surrounding the Europeanization of medicines regulation. This process dates back to 1965 when the European Community, now the European Union (EU), made provision for regulating medicines within the Community. It acquired greater urgency in the 1990s when European governments and industrialists realized that an integrated EU-wide pharmaceutical market was needed if European drug companies were to be competitive on the world stage (Abraham, 1997). Common technical standards were agreed and a committee of European experts – the Committee for Proprietary Medicinal Products (CPMP) – was established, with representatives from each of the national regulatory bodies. Under this system pharmaceutical companies were encouraged to seek simultaneous approval for their products in more than one Member State. Once a drug had been approved by a single Member State, other Member States were encouraged to accept this decision. This body was incorporated into the European Medicines Agency (EMA) in 1995, as one of its core scientific advisory committees. The EMA is funded by the EU and the pharmaceutical industry. From 1995 its recommendations have become binding on Member States. The EU also agreed, under pressure from the drug companies, to introduce strict timescales for coming to approval decisions. National regulatory agencies now compete for licensing fees from the industry by presenting themselves as the fastest in approving drugs. Acting primarily on the basis of this economic imperative increases the chances that scientific checks, needed to provide adequate levels of drug safety, are undermined (Abraham and Lewis, 2002). Under this neoliberal model the regulatory science on which decisions are based remains secret, despite challenges from transnational consumer organizations for greater openness. As in the UK the same arguments are used about the need for secrecy in order to protect valuable intellectual property from commercial competitors. Thus it can be argued that the corporate bias towards the drugs industry at the national level has been reproduced supra-nationally.

Such corporate bias is also apparent in the post-marketing surveillance of adverse drug reactions (ADRs) to long-term use of medicines. Such surveillance is based on pharmacovigilance: 'the science of collecting, monitoring, researching and evaluating information on ADRs to identify and prevent harm' (Wiktorowicz et al., 2012: 165). In the EU and the UK, drug companies have been allowed to negotiate the basis of evidence used in pharmacovigilance. This is because the EMA and the UK MCA, and its successor (since 2003 the Medicines and Health-care-products Regulatory Agency (MHRA)), lack the resources to undertake independent research. European regulators are reliant on drug companies to establish their own pharmacovigilance systems to monitor their products, thereby allowing the industry to influence regulatory decisions (Wiktorowicz et al., 2012).

Medicines regulation is rather different in the USA, mainly as a result of a different political environment. Regulation started much earlier than in Britain and the rest of Europe. Since 1938 drug manufacturers have been required to obtain permission to market a new drug from the American drug regulatory authority, the Food and Drug Administration (FDA). In the late 1950s the industry was exposed to embarrassing criticism during Congressional hearings conducted by Senator Kefauver. The result was the 1962 Kefauver-Harris Amendment to the 1938 Act. From then on manufacturers had to provide substantial evidence of effectiveness as well as safety and the FDA was required to withdraw approval already granted for a drug if it lacked evidence of its efficacy (Light, 2010). The FDA was thus specifically required by Congress to protect the public from ineffective as well as unsafe drugs. In addition, as a result of the passing of the 1967 US Freedom of Information Act, members of the public now had the right to access information about the FDA's grounds for approving a new drug and records of its meetings with particular drug companies. Drug regulators in the USA therefore operate in a political climate in which consumers have much greater opportunity to examine the extent to which regulators are protecting their interests instead of operating primarily in the interests of the drug industry. Moreover, the litigious nature of US society means that the relationship between the regulators, the drug industry and consumers is much more adversarial than is the case in the UK (Abraham, 1997).

Opportunities for regulatory capture still exist, however, as was recognized by Congress in the 1970s. It acknowledged that the FDA, during the Nixon administration, had become more 'industry-friendly' and had sought to neutralize medical scientists within the organization who were felt to be adversarial towards the pharmaceutical industry. In response, it prohibited FDA scientists from joining the industry for two years after leaving the Administration. In the 1980s, in the face of the neoliberal political agenda of the Reagan and Bush administrations, the FDA was pressurized to limit its regulatory activities in order to avoid harming the drug industry's competitiveness. However, Congressional Committees reminded the FDA that it could be called to account and required to demonstrate that it was acting in the 'public interest' by subsequently investigating some of its regulatory decisions. These procedural checks, combined with the ability of consumer groups to use the Freedom of Information Act to examine the basis for regulatory decisions, generally made the FDA much more cautious about embracing the values of the drugs industry than has been the case in Britain.

However, pressure from the Reagan and Bush Senior administrations in the late 1980s and 1990s for the FDA to reduce its regulatory burden and adapt a 'lighter touch' regulatory approach like that of the UK resulted in the FDA being less cautious. This was illustrated through its adoption of accelerated approval of drugs intended to treat serious or life-threatening conditions in response to industry concerns – a policy which was subsequently followed in the EU. Davis and Abraham (2011) have interpreted this policy change as reflecting a 'tentacled corporate bias', with the industry extending its influence by seeking a range of strategic partnerships with various elements of the state. However, they also acknowledge the role of patient groups and the medical profession in successfully demanding accelerated drug approvals. This suggests that a tentacled theory of corporate bias needs to be modified to take account of demands from such interest groups, as they helped to cement a smooth partnership between industry and the state.

While the case of accelerated drug approval suggests a convergence in regulatory-state relations between the USA, the UK and the EU, the case of pharmacovigilance highlights some continuing differences. As noted above, UK and EU policy in this area demonstrates the role of corporatism. In the USA, however, a more pluralist approach is apparent, with industry as just one research partner. The FDA has the funds to commission independent epidemiological research on adverse drug reactions to specific drugs which allows it managerial discretion. It is also subject to Congressional oversight.

In sum, it seems that there is some movement in the direction of corporate bias in the USA as well as the UK although important differences still remain. In the USA regulators still operate in a more adversarial climate and the political checks and balances reduce opportunities for regulatory capture and corporatism. In the UK and other EU countries, a culture of secrecy continues to prevail and corporatism and industrial capture are more apparent. There is, however, increasing pressure from consumer organizations and patient groups in Europe which may eventually threaten the stability of the relationship between the regulators and the pharmaceutical industry. Time will tell how successful this more active citizenship is in making regulators in Europe more accountable.

See also: *Consumerism; Citizenship and Health*

REFERENCES

Abraham, J. (1995) *Science, Politics and the Pharmaceutical Industry*. London: UCL Press.

Abraham, J. (1997) 'The science and politics of medicines regulation', in M. Elston (ed.), *The Sociology of Medical Science and Technology*. Oxford: Blackwell.

Abraham, J. (2009) 'The pharmaceutical industry, the state and the NHS', in J. Gabe and M. Calnan (eds), *The New Sociology of the Health Service*. London: Routledge.

Abraham, J. and Lewis, G. (2002) 'Citizenship, medical expertise and the capitalist regulatory state in Europe', *Sociology*, 36 (1): 67–88.

Davis, C. and Abraham, J. (2011) 'Desperately seeking cancer drugs: explaining the emergence and outcomes of accelerated pharmaceutical regulation', *Sociology of Health & Illness*, 33: 731–47.

Light, D. (2010) 'The Food and Drug Administration: inadequate protection from serious risks', in D. Light (ed.), *The Risks of Prescription Drugs*. New York: Columbia University Press.

Medawar, P. (1992) *Power and Dependence: Social Audit on the Safety of Medicines*. London: Social Audit.

Wiktorowicz, M., Lexchin, J. and Moscou, K. (2012) 'Pharmacovigilance in Europe and North America: divergent approaches', *Social Science & Medicine*, 75: 165–70.

Jonathan Gabe

Evaluation

Evaluation refers to the use of social research methods to assess the extent to which a policy, programme or service is implemented and achieves its goals.

Evaluation in the health field involves assessing, in a structured and rigorous way, whether public health programmes and health care achieve their intended goals, including improving health and quality of life, and at what cost. Evaluation is a generic term that can equally be applied to assess the value of any area of public policy such as education, welfare benefits, and transport or penal systems. However, the high costs and high public profile of modern health and health care systems have made evaluation an increasingly important feature of developed countries' health policies. Those paying for health interventions, such as businesses funding health insurance for their workers and governments providing publicly financed health care or health promotion (for example, measures to restrict smoking), are typically interested in assessing the value of their expenditure. Clinicians too have increasingly espoused the concept of 'evidence-based health care' (Gray, 1997), which includes undertaking randomized clinical trials to assess the effectiveness of drugs and procedures (see below), while resisting external attempts by managers to assess the quality and efficiency of their services.

Since the Second World War, evaluation research has evolved in a number of ways, most notably via:

1 The development of methods of economic evaluation that attempt to quantify the costs and benefits of programmes and policies;
2 The development of methods for the synthesis of findings from individual evaluations, such as meta-analysis of randomized controlled trials of the effectiveness of treatments; and
3 A gradual shift away from an exclusively positivist and experimental approach to programme evaluation towards a wider range of more sociologically informed, interpretive approaches, including more participatory approaches designed to stimulate democratic dialogue and empower stakeholders, and even post-modern, relativist perspectives.

Though evaluation is a form of social research, its typical product is primarily instrumental knowledge that is produced to meet the needs of policy makers, in that it focuses on assessing the value or worth of policies, programmes and services. Sometimes, value is inferred from the description and quantification of a range of costs and benefits expressed in 'naturally occurring units' (for example, the number of hospital bed days averted by a hospital-at-home scheme); at other times, formal economic methods are used to estimate either the monetary value (as in cost-benefit analysis) or the 'utility' (as in cost-utility analysis) of a particular pattern of effects (Weimer and Vining, 2010). The most high profile form of cost-utility analysis is cost per quality-adjusted life year (QALY) analysis. This attempts to calculate the non-monetary value of the health gains generated by different treatments for the same condition, or different treatments for different conditions, in order to guide priority setting and subsequent resource allocation (Drummond et al., 2005).

Contemporary policy and programme evaluations often use a range of research methods, both qualitative and quantitative. Typically health evaluation draws on methods and insights from psychology, sociology, economics, statistics, epidemiology, anthropology, policy science and the basic clinical sciences. The nature, range and combination of methods reflect wider trends in the social sciences towards more integrative approaches, and the increasing use of 'mixed' methods in which qualitative and quantitative data are triangulated as well as contrasted.

Evaluation can, in principle, contribute to policy decisions throughout the policy process. For example, it can be used prospectively at the design stage to help model the likely impacts of different approaches to achieving a policy goal. It can also be used during the implementation stage to identify the conditions for successful implementation (known as 'process' or 'formative' evaluation), and later on to measure the impact of the programme or policy (known as 'summative' or outcome evaluation). If an intervention is novel, the evaluation process may well start with a formative evaluation looking at the feasibility and acceptability of the programme, followed by an efficacy evaluation looking at its impact under optimal conditions and then a (cost) effectiveness evaluation examining its impact under ordinary conditions.

Donabedian (1966) developed a valuable framework for the evaluation of health services. He distinguished between structures, processes and outcomes. An evaluation of *structures* typically focuses on the adequacy of the facilities, equipment, staffing, funding and organization of health services. A simple example would be examining the number of general practitioners available per capita. Such evidence might help to assess the extent of geographical equity in the availability of doctors between different parts of a country. However, it would not be possible to determine what the optimal distribution of doctors should be without next asking questions about the range of services general practitioners provide. This leads to Donabedian's second type of evaluation: the examination of *processes*. Processes are the activities of history taking, examination, diagnosis, treatment, follow-up and coordination that constitute care, including the quality of the relations between patients and clinicians. The final dimension of Donabedian's framework focuses on *outcomes*. Outcomes are the effects in terms of health change that result from the structures and processes of health services. Outcomes of health care have frequently been assessed in terms of survival rates. However, outcome measures more appropriate to the role performed by contemporary health services in relation to chronic conditions need to include an assessment of the impact of services upon pain, disability, health-related quality of life, reassurance and patients' ability to cope with health problems; all of these are outcomes that are more complex to measure.

The method that has proved most reliable in evaluating the effectiveness of health care is the randomized controlled trial. With their informed consent, patients are randomly allocated to receive either the novel treatment, or a placebo, or the best available alternative treatment. The purpose of randomization is to minimize the possible influence on outcomes of factors other than the treatments under study, such as severity of illness between patient groups. Randomization makes it very likely that such factors are equally present in the groups of patients receiving alternative treatments.

The randomized controlled trial has proved to be the most successful form of evaluation in relation to drugs. A particularly valuable feature of many drug trials is that both patient and doctor are unaware of which treatment the patient is receiving. This so-called 'double-blind' trial substantially reduces the risks of biased results. However, many of the interventions in health services that need to be evaluated cannot be subject to the double-blind trial. For example, it may be desirable to evaluate the advantages of the nurse prescribing drugs instead of the general practitioner, compare hospital with home-based rehabilitation after a surgical procedure, or compare self-help groups with health professionals in their ability to provide counselling, support and advice for people with long-term conditions. In these situations, the options being compared are not like drugs. Drugs are now delivered in formats that completely standardize the active ingredient for each dose. By contrast, the 'active ingredients' that make a nurse practitioner, hospital-at-home scheme or self-help group effective in improving health outcomes may be multi-faceted and may also vary enormously from one setting to another.

Considerable attention has thus been devoted to developing methods for evaluating these so-called 'complex' interventions and programmes. The UK Medical

Research Council's guidance on the evaluation of complex interventions defines them as 'interventions that contain several interacting components', plus features such as the number and difficulty of behaviours or changes required by those delivering or receiving the intervention and a degree of flexibility in the way the intervention can be delivered (Craig et al., 2008). As a result, the active elements are subject to more variation than in, say, drug or even surgical trials. Though more challenging to evaluate, such studies may not require fundamentally different methods from simpler evaluations, particularly if the analyst is not too concerned to discover how a programme has its effect (i.e. the intervention can sometimes be treated largely as a 'black box' receiving inputs and then generating outputs and outcomes).

Where there is more interest in the precise operation of a programme, with a view to optimizing its delivery, evaluation designs such as randomized controlled trials need to be adapted and/or supplemented by other, qualitative research methods that can explain how and why interventions improve outcomes (Campbell et al., 2000). Only when 'the active ingredients' (for example, specific skills or ways of organizing services) of a new way of providing care are uncovered by more detailed ethnographic study is it possible to reproduce such effects outside the original evaluative study.

Sociology, until recently, has neglected the experimental approach to the evaluation of wider behavioural, social and population-based ways of improving health. This neglect is unfortunate because 'experimentation' is potentially powerful (Oakley, 1998). Despite some sceptics who would argue that randomized trials are simply infeasible for assessing social policies and community-based interventions, there are grounds for claiming that randomized trials of social and public health policies are not only feasible but also an ethical imperative. This is because such programmes cannot be assumed to be benign and some will have unexpected negative consequences that are contrary to common sense. For example, school-based driver education programmes that are provided before young people start to learn to drive have been shown in RCTs to lead to increased crash and injury rates. This is because participants in these programmes typically pass their driving tests at younger ages than non-participants, and younger age is strongly related to higher accident rates (Roberts and Kwan, 2008).

As a result, pragmatic trials of more complicated whole programmes of care, or public health interventions that compare real-life alternatives, are increasingly being undertaken. Such evaluations typically collect data on a range of effects or outcomes over a considerable period of time, but can also include data on the process of implementation (feasibility) and the acceptability of programmes to individuals and communities. They may also include non-health effects at a societal level, including spillover impacts in other sectors such as the economy (Smith and Petticrew, 2010).

There has been considerable interest in the 'realist' approach to evaluation developed by Pawson and Tilley (1997), as another sociologically informed response to the challenges inherent in evaluating more complex behavioural and social programmes. Realist evaluations aim to answer the question: 'what works for whom in what circumstances, in what respects and how?' The approach is based on three fundamental insights: social programmes are 'theories' in the sense that they are built on implicit or explicit causal propositions about how to produce change; similar programmes have variable effects when implemented across different settings; and the local context of each setting influences the ability of the mechanisms underlying programmes to produce the outcomes desired (i.e. programmes are socially embedded). Realist evaluations attempt to develop and test empirically the range of 'context-mechanism-outcome' configurations relevant to understanding the impact of a particular programme or policy.

However sophisticated its design, methods and theoretical underpinning, the fate of evaluation as applied social science is largely dependent on the institutions and political imperatives faced by decision makers (Taylor and Balloch, 2005). Health policies are rarely initiated with evaluation in the forefront of either planning or implementation. Programmes are often not articulated with sufficiently clear objectives for straightforward evaluation and are frequently rolled out before their effects can be definitively assessed. As a result, evaluations often have to focus on inputs, outputs, user experience and professional views, rather than being able directly to attribute 'final' outcomes (for example, health improvements) to specific policies.

It is also important to recognize that while much of health care evaluation practice is premised on the modernist Enlightenment assumption that health care can be studied and then adapted on the basis of a single rational, objective evaluation to improve its effectiveness and efficiency (for example, particularly health economic evaluation in the service of practices of the New Public Management), this assumption is contested. Post-modernist approaches posit multiple competing rationalities and forms of knowledge reflecting the interests of particular groups (Fox, 1991). Under this approach, not only is knowledge seen as contingent and far from universal, but evaluation practice is also seen to require the participation of a far wider range of players in order to democratize the process and attempt to ensure that a wide range of 'voices' is heard. In this world, the role of the evaluator is to negotiate between different versions of truth and value rather than produce a summative account.

See also: *Quality of Life; Lay Knowledge; Managerialism*

REFERENCES

Campbell, M., Fitzpatrick, R., Haines, A., Kinmonth, A., Sandercock, P., Spiegelhalter, D. and Tyrer, P. (2000) 'Framework for design and evaluation of complex interventions to improve health', *British Medical Journal*, 321: 694–6.

Craig, P., Dieppe, P., Macintyre, S., Michie, S., Nazareth, I. and Petticrew, M. (2008) 'Developing and evaluating complex interventions: the new Medical Research Council guidance', *British Medical Journal*, 337: a1655.

Donabedian, A. (1966) 'Evaluating the quality of medical care', *Milbank Memorial Fund Quarterly*, 44: 169–79.

Drummond, M., Sculpher, M.J., Torrance, G.W., O'Brien, B.J. and Stoddart, G.L. (2005) *Economic Evaluation of Health Care*, 3rd edn. Oxford: Oxford University Press.

Fox, N.J. (1991) 'Postmodernism, rationality and the evaluation of health care', *Sociological Review*, 39: 709–44.

Gray, J.A.M. (1997) *Evidence Based Health Care*. London: Churchill-Livingstone.

Oakley, A. (1998) 'Experimentation and social interventions: a forgotten but important history', *British Medical Journal*, 317: 1239–42.

Pawson, R. and Tilley, N. (1997) *Realistic Evaluation*. London: Sage.

Roberts, I.G. and Kwan, I. (2008) 'School-based driver education for the prevention of traffic crashes', *Cochrane Database of Systematic Reviews*, Issue 4.

Smith, R.D. and Petticrew, M. (2010) 'Public health evaluation in the twenty-first century: time to see the wood as well as the trees', *Journal of Public Health*, 32: 2–7.

Taylor, D. and Balloch, S. (eds) (2005) *The Politics of Evaluation: Participation and Policy Implementation*. Bristol: The Policy Press.

Weimer, D. and Vining, A. (2010) *Policy Analysis: Concepts and Practice*, 5th edn. Upper Saddle River, NJ: Prentice-Hall.

Nicholas Mays

Malpractice

> *Malpractice refers to the improper treatment or culpable neglect of a patient by a health service professional.*

Malpractice is often discussed in the context of regulating doctors' behaviour and, in particular, the ways in which they are held accountable for their mistakes or errors. There are various types of regulatory control. These range from self-regulation through the General Medical Council (which is responsible for adjudicating on allegations of professional misconduct and revalidating a doctor's licence to practice) and medical audit (the continuous peer review of practice) to regulation as a result of individual patients making complaints or seeking legal redress through the courts. The focus here will be on the last form of regulation – malpractice litigation.

Malpractice litigation is based on common law, particularly torts of negligence. The term 'tort' is derived from Norman French and means a wrong or wrongdoing. Tort law is based on the view that people owe a duty of care to others and should avoid harming or injuring those they come into contact with. In the case of medicine, this means that a doctor has caused harm to a patient as a result of failing to act in accordance with their profession's customary standards (Dingwall and Hobson-West, 2006). In bringing a case of malpractice, a plaintiff needs to prove that there was negligence and that this negligence caused or contributed to damage or injury.

Medical negligence claims have grown considerably in Britain in recent years. There was a sharp increase in claims in the 1980s and 1990s with a 72 per cent increase between 1990 and 1998. The cost of settlement grew from £50 million in 1990 to £294 million in 2000–1. These costs have continued to rise since the millennium, reaching £769 million in 2008-9 and £787 million in 2009–10 (Feinmann, 2011). In 2011–12, the situation looked even worse with the NHS paying out a record £1.28 billion in damages and legal charges, a rise of more than 45 per cent on the previous year's total of £863 million. This was said to reflect a 30 per cent rise in the number of claims in 2010–11 (Dyer, 2012).

Most negligence claims are for small sums of up to £10,000, with amounts in excess of £150,000 being claimed by a small number of plaintiffs. The hospital specialties most likely to be claimed against are Obstetrics and Gynaecology, Orthopaedics, and Accident and Emergency. Doctors working in these specialties tend to be sued for negligence as the result of a misdiagnosis, often leading to a delay in treatment or inappropriate treatment. The other main cause of negligence relates to technical or surgical mistakes made before, during, or after an operation (National Audit Office, 2001). Doctors working in Obstetrics and Gynaecology are particularly prone to large claims because damage at birth (for example, brain damage) carries with it lifetime costs in terms of health care. A single claim in this area can now run into millions of pounds.

In the past, hospital doctors in Britain subscribed to a medical defence organization (MDO) to cover their possible liability for damages. As membership fees escalated in the 1980s, Health Authorities found themselves subsidizing their staff. In 1990, the British government responded by requiring Health Authorities and Trusts to meet the full cost of negligence actions. Since 1995 the NHS Litigation Authority (NHSLA) has taken responsibility for claims against Trusts. To begin with, Trusts could identify an excess figure and accept responsibility for meeting the cost of claims below this figure. Since 2002, however, the NHSLA has taken full responsibility for dealing with claims against the NHS. Such arrangements however only apply to the NHS in England. Since political devolution in 1999 NHS bodies in Scotland and Wales have put in place their own fault-based schemes (Stephen et al., 2012).

It has been suggested that the medical profession has responded to this state of affairs by being more defensive in their medical practice. This defensive medicine has involved hospital doctors ordering treatments, tests and procedures (or on occasion withholding them) primarily to protect themselves from criticism or potential litigation. Fears about being sued are also said to have encouraged GPs to make practice changes such as deciding not to treat certain conditions, increasing diagnostic testing, engaging in more detailed note taking, and giving patients more detailed explanations (Summerton, 1995). In the USA there is also evidence of physicians attempting to recognize 'suit-prone' patients in the consultation, in order to reduce the likelihood of litigation. Patients who appear to be 'dependent', 'demanding', 'self-styled experts' or 'subservient' are all seen as potentially malpractice-prone. However, there is an inconsistency in such perceptions. Patients who are deferential and those who are consumerist and want to take responsibility for decisions about their health seem to be perceived as equally problematic. This apparent ambivalence among physicians actually reveals a reluctance to accept a reduction in authority, standing and control. Consequently, exhortations for doctors to provide more information and share decisions with patients in order to minimize the threat of litigation may fall on deaf ears (Annandale, 1989).

The rapid increase in medical negligence claims in recent decades has led many commentators to talk about a medical litigation 'crisis'. Reference is regularly made to the USA where the total cost of malpractice claims has risen faster than inflation. Doctors in Britain and the USA tend to blame the growth of consumerism for encouraging patients to complain and take legal action if they feel their rights and expectations have not been met. Reference is also made to the greed of lawyers who have benefited financially from the rapid increase in claims. Such lawyers are said to have sought out patients and touted for business. Certainly there is evidence of lawyers in Britain advertising in NHS hospitals on the basis of 'no win, no fee' in the hope of finding clients who might claim for road- or work-related injuries. In the USA, physicians also criticize lawyers for their ignorance of medicine and the application of a confrontational, argumentative approach to solve what they perceive as medical disputes (Hupert et al., 1996).

In so far as there is a crisis, it is necessary to ask 'a crisis for whom'? For doctors the crisis is one of increasing negligence claims, proactive lawyers and assertive patients. For patients, however, the crisis may be one of a loss of confidence in the medical profession and a lack of sufficient resources to take negligent doctors to court. Certainly there is evidence that when patients (and their relatives) do take legal action, intense emotions are aroused that continue to be felt long after the original injury. For these patients the decision to seek legal redress is determined not just by the original injury but also by a desire to hold doctors to account and to make sure that lessons are learnt so that others do not experience similar incidents in future (Vincent et al., 1994).

Some commentators have nonetheless questioned the extent to which increased medical negligence represents a crisis. Dingwall and Hobson-West (2006) have argued that we should not take the claims of doctors that they are facing a crisis at face value. Instead they suggest that the increase in malpractice claims should be seen as part of a wider cultural shift which is affecting the professions in general and not just medicine. Accountants, architects, engineers and veterinary surgeons have all seen their liability claims increase in frequency and severity in recent times. The medical profession's response is therefore best seen as a moral panic and a symbolic expression of discontent with wider social and cultural changes that are affecting all professions.

Regardless of whether other professions are facing increased litigation, it can nonetheless be argued that the increase in medical negligence claims does represent a challenge to medical authority that has real consequences for the doctor–patient relationship. While malpractice as a regulatory tool may empower some patients and lead some doctors to make more considered decisions, it may also have the unintended consequence of encouraging doctors to undertake unnecessary tests and of undermining the trust necessary for the shared decision making and patient partnership advocated by policy makers. Despite this, medical negligence action does have a role as a regulatory tool in that it encourages at least some public discussion of standards. Any changes to the tort system, such as the partial no-fault compensation scheme (where the emphasis is on proof of causation rather than proof of fault), introduced in England after the NHS Redress Act of 2006 and yet to be fully implemented, will need to demonstrate that they make doctors more accountable as well as being less costly (in terms of legal fees) and providing quicker redress.

See also: *Medical Autonomy, Dominance and Decline; Consumerism*

REFERENCES

Annandale, E. (1989) 'The malpractice crisis and the doctor–patient relationship', *Sociology of Health & Illness*, 11 (1): 1–23.

Dingwall, R. and Hobson-West, P. (2006) 'Litigation and the threat to medicine', in D. Kelleher, J. Gabe and G. Williams (eds), *Challenging Medicine*, 2nd edn. London: Routledge.

Dyer, C. (2012) 'NHS bill for compensation exceeds £1bn for the first time', *British Medical Journal*, 345: e4638.

Feinmann, J. (2011) 'Why sorry doesn't need to be the hardest word', *British Medical Journal*, 342: d3258 (doi: 10.1136/bmj.d3258).

Hupert, N., Lawthers, A.G., Brennan, T.A. and Peterson, L.M. (1996) 'Processing the tort deterrent signal: a qualitative study', *Social Science & Medicine*, 43 (1): 1–11.

National Audit Office (2001) *Handling Clinical Negligence Claims in England*. London: The Stationery Office.

Stephen, F., Melville, A. and Krauser, T. (2012) *A Study of Medical Negligence Claims in Scotland*. Edinburgh: Scottish Government.

Summerton, N. (1995) 'Positive and negative factors in defensive medicine: a questionnaire study of general practitioners', *British Medical Journal*, 310: 27–9.

Vincent, C., Young, M. and Phillips, A. (1994) 'Why do people sue doctors? A study of patients and relatives taking legal action', *The Lancet*, 343: 1609–13.

Jonathan Gabe

malpractice

Such caveats concerning the medical model suggest that its role is at one and the same time more powerful and more limited than critics have recognized. These complexities need to be addressed in future work on the medical model.

See also: *Practitioner–Client Relationships; Social Constructionism; Geneticization*

REFERENCES

Atkinson, P., Glasner, P. and Lock, M. (eds) (2009) *The Handbook of Genetics and Society*. London: Routledge

Foucault, M. (1976) *The Birth of the Clinic*. London: Tavistock.

Freidson, E. (1970) *The Profession of Medicine: A Study of the Sociology of Applied Knowledge*. Chicago: University of Chicago Press.

Jewson, N. (1976) 'The disappearance of the sick man from medical cosmology 1770–1870', *Sociology*, 10: 225–44.

Lawrence, C. (1994) *Medicine in the Making of Modern Britain 1700–1920*. London: Routledge.

McKeown, T. (1976) *The Role of Medicine: Dream, Mirage or Nemesis?* Oxford: Blackwell.

Parsons, T. (1951) *The Social System*. New York: The Free Press.

Porter, R. (1997) *The Greatest Benefit to Mankind: A Medical History of Humanity from Antiquity to the Present*. London: HarperCollins.

Rose, N. (2009) 'Normality and pathology in a biomedical age', *Sociological Review*, 57 (s2): 66–83.

Mike Bury

Social Constructionism

> *The basic premise of social constructionism is that reality is a product of definitional practices and the task of sociology is to explain the social processes involved in the production of knowledge pertaining to, or which constitutes, this reality.*

In their book *The Social Construction of Reality* (1967), Berger and Luckmann attempt to bring together the two key strands of classical sociology: the first, which emphasizes the objective structures of society and their influence in shaping human action (constraining individual action), and the second, which emphasizes the role of human agency in constructing the social world through (inter)subjective meanings. Berger and Luckmann are concerned with everyday knowledge, as distinct from expert knowledge; that is, the social stock of knowledge that constitutes the background cultural assumptions orientating our everyday social actions. This knowledge becomes coextensive with, although not reducible to, what is knowable, in the sense of how social actors come to perceive a fit between their subjective reality and what they know to be the objective world. This is why the world appears to societal members as an objective reality. Berger and Luckmann 'define "reality" as a quality appertaining to phenomena that we recognize as having a being independent of our own volition (we cannot "wish them away")' (1967: 1). Since sociology cannot decide in any unequivocal way the ontological status of what people believe to be real, relativity is intrinsic to the sociological enterprise. In medical sociology these ideas are taken up by Freidson (1970) when discussing the social construction of illness. The question for Freidson is not about whether illness has an independent reality as a disease entity existing in nature, but concerning the social conventions established in particular spheres of relevance in which illness acquires meaning.

There is nothing problematic for sociologists in the proposition that knowledge is socially constructed. However, in the context of a postmodernist current in social theory, which rejects the synthesis of structure/agency discussed above, constructionism has become mired in a theoretical division between relativism and realism. This is because postmodernist theories conflate questions concerning ontology (what exists as external realities in the social and natural worlds) and epistemology (what we can know about these realities). This stance is known as radical constructionism: it rejects the notion that the foundation of knowledge is based on an external reality and denies that there is any rational basis for deciding between alternative conceptualizations of reality. However, just as there are a variety of constructionist views of knowledge, there are a variety of realist positions. As we will see below, different versions of social constructionism are compatible with different realist epistemologies. The following does not offer a survey of the variety of constructionist approaches, which is beyond the limits of what can be achieved here; instead it focuses on one current of constructionist thought as applied to medical knowledge – namely, the sociology of scientific knowledge (SSK).

Sociology seeks explanations for scientific knowledge by exploring science as an institution. In paying attention to the social organization of knowledge, sociologists focus on the social structures that impinge upon the production of knowledge. Such accounts can be both structuralist and constructionist. In the former, the focus of analysis is on the broader structures of power that influence scientific knowledge and its applications. A structuralist approach also addresses the structural reproduction and transformations that knowledge brings about. For example, new knowledge can reproduce or alter cultural norms, institutional structures and the structure of political discourse in terms of how social problems are understood. In the case of a constructionist approach to knowledge, the focus is on the 'doing' of science. Constructionism emphasizes the culturally constructed character of knowledge and how this is influenced by local contingencies such as professional turf wars, dominant cognitive frameworks, professional credibility strategies, and the alignment of vested interests.

There are tensions, however, between structuralist and constructionist approaches to knowledge. The starting point for SSK lies in its fundamental challenge to the classical view of scientific knowledge, which is based on a realist philosophy of science known as positivism. Positivists make the strong ontological claim that

Mechanical Engineering Craft Studies Part 3

A. Greer C Eng, MRAeS
Senior Lecturer in Mechanical Engineering
Gloucester City College of Technology

Edward Arnold
A division of Hodder & Stoughton
LONDON MELBOURNE AUCKLAND

© 1973, 1977

First published in Great Britain 1973
Second edition 1977
Reprinted 1978, 1979, 1982, 1984, 1989

ISBN 0 7131 3390 2

Typeset by Photoprint Plates Ltd, Rayleigh, Essex.
Printed and bound in Great Britain for Edward Arnold, the
educational, academic and medical publishing division of
Hodder and Stoughton Limited, 41 Bedford Square, London
WC1B 3DQ by J. W. Arrowsmith Ltd, Bristol